Capitalist Democracy on Trial

Capitalist democracy has been on trial in the West for over two hundred years. The American Revolution and its aftermath dominated intellectual controversy during the nineteenth century. The Soviet experiment has challenged western ideology and practice during the twentieth. Economic growth has become the principal test of success. Now established assumptions face new threats – from the rise of Japan, the impact of *glasnost* and *perestroika*, and the gathering ecological crisis.

This text explores the long transatlantic debate on capitalist democracy. It examines the conflicting verdicts of writers and politicians in the USA and Europe. The first section focuses on democracy and the rise of big business. It discusses the views of Tocqueville, Mill, Carnegie, Chamberlain, Bryce, Ostrogorski, Veblen, and Hobson. The second section covers capitalism and the rise of big government. The writers represented are Laski, Lasswell, Hayek, Schumpeter, Galbraith, Friedman, Miliband, Brittan, Piven, and Cloward.

Using a historical and comparative framework, Dennis Smith argues that the transatlantic debate on capitalist democracy has passed through three phases. By the outbreak of the First World War the early nineteenth-century ideology of 'participation' had been replaced by a conception of capitalist democracy as 'manipulation'. Between the wars this was superseded by an ideology of 'regulation'. More recently the drift has been towards the need for 'conservation'. His systematic approach demonstrates the dynamics of an unfolding debate and combines theoretical insight with clarity of exposition. The book will be an invaluable text for students of political science, sociology, social theory, and the history of political economy.

The Author

Dennis Smith is Senior Lecturer in Sociology at Aston University, Birmingham. His previous books include *Conflict and Compromise: Class Formation in English Society 1830–1914* (1982), *Barrington Moore, Violence, Morality and Political Change* (1983), and *The Chicago School: A Liberal Critique of Capitalism* (1988).

Capitalist Democracy on Trial

The transatlantic debate
from Tocqueville
to the present

Dennis Smith

Routledge
London and New York

First published 1990
by Routledge
11 New Fetter Lane, London EC4P 4EE

Simultaneously published in the USA and Canada
by Routledge
a division of Routledge, Chapman and Hall, Inc.
29 West 35th Street, New York, NY 10001

© 1990 Dennis Smith

Phototypeset in 10pt Times by
Mews Photosetting, Beckenham, Kent
Printed in Great Britain

British Library Cataloguing in Publication Data
Smith, Dennis, *1945–*
  Capitalist democracy on trial: the transatlantic
  debate from Tocqueville to the present.
  1. Capitalism. Theories
  I. Title
  330.12'2

Library of Congress Cataloging in Publication Data
Smith, Dennis, 1945–
    Capitalist democracy on trial : the transatlantic debate from
  Tocqueville to the present / Dennis Smith.
      p.   cm.
    Bibliography: p.
    Includes index.
    1. Capitalism – United States – History. 2. Capitalism – Great
  Britain – History. 3. Democracy – History. I. Title.
  HB501.S636   1989
  330.12'2 – dc19   89-5960
                                                              CIP

ISBN 0-415-04044-2
ISBN 0-415-04188-0 (pbk)

Contents

Acknowledgements   x

1   **Introduction**   1
    The end of an era?   1
    Letting the good times roll   3
    The Jeffersonian vision   5
    The eastern and western roads   6
    Three challenges   8
    The logic of ideological development   10
    Big business and big government   11

Part one: Democracy and the Rise of Big Business

2   **Tocqueville and Mill**   17
    Democracy versus capitalism   17
    A brief friendship   17
    Tocqueville in America and England   19
    Aristocracy versus democracy   21
    Despotism or liberty?   23
    Threats to liberty   25
    Mill on Tocqueville   27
    Life as a well-run seminar   30
    Principles of political economy   30
    The well-tempered bureaucrat   32
    Conclusion   35

3   **Carnegie and Chamberlain**   37
    The problem or the solution?   37
    Two businessmen   37
    Inherited problems   38
    Herbert Spencer   40
    Triumphant democracy   42
    The gospel of wealth   45
    Homestead   47

Contents

	Between property and the people	48
	A paradox	50
	The civic gospel	51
	The importance of performance	53
	The national stage	54
	Conclusion	56
4	**Ostrogorski and Bryce**	58
	Law, politics, and democracy	58
	Getting the facts	59
	Emancipation of the individual	61
	The caucus in England	64
	The caucus in America	65
	Private affluence, public apathy	66
	A possible cure	67
	The professional optimist	68
	The American commonwealth	70
	Modern democracies	72
	Conclusion	75
5	**Veblen and Hobson**	77
	Two economic heretics	77
	Reconstructing economic man	80
	The theory of the leisure class	83
	The theory of business enterprise	85
	The need for a new liberalism	89
	Imperialism	90
	Welfare and the market	93
	A new democracy	94
	Conclusion	96
6	**Who rules?**	98
	Replacing the nobility	98
	Models of capitalist democracy	100

Part two: Capitalism and the Rise of Big Government

7	**Laski and Lasswell**	107
	A new world	107
	The politics of experience	108
	The good life	111
	The grammar of politics	112
	Democracy in crisis	115
	Promise and performance in America	119

Subjectivity and the state		120
Tension and fantasy		122
Elites and the mass		125
Personality and power		126
Conclusion		128
8 Schumpeter and Hayek		131
The challenge from Vienna		131
Innovation and the entrepreneur		134
The aristocracy and bourgeois society		135
Marxian theory and socialist politics		138
Can capitalism survive?		139
Can socialism work?		141
The road to serfdom		144
The constitution of liberty		148
Conclusion		150
9 Galbraith and Crosland		151
Demystifying conventional wisdom		151
The affluent society		153
The new industrial state		155
Economics and the public purpose		159
Left of centre		162
The future of socialism		163
Going for growth		167
Conclusion		168
10 Friedman, Brittan, Miliband, Piven, and Cloward		169
Capitalism versus democracy		169
Free to choose		169
New Deal and after		171
Economic consequences of democracy		173
New rules		174
The new class war		177
The people strike back		178
Capitalist democracy in Britain		180
Hegemony and force		181
Conclusion		183
11 Who benefits?		185
Two concepts of property		185
Nostalgia and idealism		187
From manipulation to regulation		188
Vice becomes virtue		189

Contents

12 **Three phases of capitalist democracy**   191
    Ten types of capitalist democracy   191
    Three sequences of ideological development   193
    National culture re-examined   197
    Post-modernism and its antecedents   199
    The conservatory model   200

    Bibliography   204

    Name index   218

    Subject index   222

Acknowledgements

Many thanks to Tanya, Pen, Sue, Ed, Freda, and Cleo for putting up with the midnight whisper of the word processor. Ian, Val, and Harriet Riddell were a great help. Once more, Val Riddell read through everything, gave me her expert opinion and stopped me following false trails.

Chapter one

Introduction

The end of an era?

Capitalist democracy has been on trial in the West for over two centuries. Global changes – economic, political and ecological – in the late twentieth century are about to present yet another series of challenges. It is a good time to look back and place current crises in a historical context.

A sense of perspective is urgently needed. During the 1980s capitalist democracy in the West presented a confusing pattern of optimism and pessimism. The optimism came, by and large, from the right, which looked forward to the benefits which would flow from a return to the original wisdom of Adam Smith (e.g., Friedman and Friedman 1980) and drew confidence from the Thatcher–Reagan years. Pessimism came from all points of the political compass. The strong feeling that an era was coming to an end was conveyed by titles such as *The Rise and Decline of Nations* (Olson 1982), *The Rise and Decline of Western Liberalism* (Arblaster 1984), *The Rise and Fall of the Great Powers* (Kennedy 1987), *The End of Organized Capitalism* (Lash and Urry 1987), and *The Closing of the American Mind* (Bloom 1987).

It is fashionable to predict the decline of the West, or the end of the American empire, but there are some obvious difficulties with this argument. For example, which society is going to shoulder, willingly, the immense international burdens taken up by the United States during the Second World War? (Thorne 1978; Thorne 1986). Japan's tremendous economic success has been due, at least partly, to the very low level of military spending made possible by American protection (Kitamura *et al.* 1985; Olsen 1985). The leaders of China have their hands full with the tasks of internal development, and the case of Russia shows how difficult it is to combine these tasks with an active global strategy.

This book offers a more modest thesis: simply, that capitalist democracy in the West is currently facing a series of new challenges – especially the resurgence of South-East Asia, the impact of *glasnost*

1

and *perestroika* upon our perceptions of Russia, and, not least, the gathering ecological crisis. These challenges cast doubt upon basic assumptions built into recent manifestations of capitalist democratic ideology. They also raise questions about how those assumptions came about in the first place. How did the historical experience of the United States and Britain get woven into the debate about the nature of capitalist democracy? What part did the development of the Soviet Union play in the shaping of western ideology? How did economic growth become so central to capitalist democracy?

This enquiry will focus upon Britain and the United States from the 1830s to the present. What is the connection between the American Republic described by Alexis de Tocqueville in the 1830s, and the United States as seen through the eyes of Milton Friedman? Or between British society as perceived by John Stuart Mill in the early and mid nineteenth century and the Britain observed by Ralph Miliband in the 1970s and 1980s?

This book contributes to the debate by examining the content and, to a limited extent, the context of several American and British analyses of capitalist democracy. These analyses stem from successive points in the historical past and near present: from Tocqueville to Friedman; and from Mill to Miliband. The historical and structural logic of successive elaborations, transformations and re-evaluations of capitalist democracy will be examined.

It is argued that at least ten models of capitalist democracy have been generated during the 150-year period with which the book is concerned. It is not claimed that these were the only models to have been produced in that period. However, these models were not only highly influential but also express an unfolding logic working its way through three phases.

The first phase began with a model of *participatory* capitalist democracy, and took the form of a spiralling process of delegitimisation from the 1830s to the First World War. This phase culminated in a model of *manipulatory* capitalist democracy.

The second phase ran from the 1920s to the 1940s. It consisted of two interlocking processes of transformation, elaboration and relegitimisation, whose eventual outcome was a model of *regulatory* capitalist democracy.

A third phase is under way whose main outlines are clear, and it is predicted that it will lead into a renewed downward spiral of delegitimisation. A possible terminus for this third phase is *conservatory* capitalist democracy, which may achieve dominance towards the end of the century.

However, it is worth beginning by reviewing some of the complexities of the current situation.

Letting the good times roll

What you see partly depends upon where you stand. As far as the British were concerned, during the 1980s the influence of the United States was not declining but increasing. Ronald Reagan, the most powerful man in the world, missed no opportunity to bolster the image of Margaret Thatcher. When she visited Washington in November 1988 to bid the President a fond farewell at the end of his final term, their mutual congratulations were delivered with a blaze of publicity in true Hollywood style.

During the greater part of the 1980s the Western public scene was dominated by the policies of Reagan and Thatcher. Patterns of conservative thought in Britain and America became more closely aligned. Conservatives both sides of the Atlantic were heavily influenced by the ideas of Friedrich A. Hayek and Milton Friedman.

Most of the movement towards convergence occurred from the British side – British politicians became more Americanised. The advertising skills of corporate business were brought into the presentation of politics. Traditional figures disappeared or fell into the background. Trade union barons went out of fashion. So did country squires. In the words of one Tory of the old school, the Conservatives turned from a party of estate owners into a party of estate agents (or realtors).

Americanisation of British life penetrated the styles of cultural production also. Some of its effects were catalogued by Christopher Huhne as follows:

> British films inject an American into the cast to improve their sale-ability in the United States. In *A Fish Called Wanda*, John Cleese has an affair with Jamie Lee Curtis; in *A Touch of Class* . . . it was Glenda Jackson with George Segal. As with films, so it will be with books: British books will increasingly become books which will also sell in the United States, a little bit of gold or silver shimmering on the cover to attract the passing Peoria purchaser. Specifically British concerns will be less prized than trans-Atlantic ones.
>
> (*Guardian*, 28 December 1988)

Martin Amis's recent novel *Money* (1984) followed the rules. It had silver on the cover and a transatlantic 'hero', half-English, half-American. However, it carried a subversive message. The central character, Self, a monument to self-pollution and self-abuse, is deceived and ripped off on a grand scale by smart operators in the entertainment business. Amis provided an ironic commentary on the central theme promoted by Reagan and Thatcher.

Both leaders argued that the fundamental spirit of freedom, individualism and enterprise had been reawakened. British society, claimed the Thatcherites, had moved away from the dependency culture and returned to the world of 'Victorian values' (Skidelsky 1988). Meanwhile, the ethos of the pioneer had been rediscovered in the United States. It was, to use a Reagan line, 'morning again in America'. The President, a graduate from the school of 'cinepatriotism' (Gould 1928), was a master of 'storytelling techniques' (Miller 1984: 68) with an unparalleled ability to manipulate 'the national psyche' (Yankelovich 1982: 5).

It was not all greasepaint and razzmatazz, though. The 1980s, especially the middle and late 1980s, were indeed prosperous years for most Americans and Britons. This was not, in the main, the result of industrial restructuring, although a certain amount took place. The effects of that continuing process will take much longer to come through. More relevant were tax cuts and, in Britain's case, revenue from North Sea oil and sales of public assets.

A major factor putting purchasing power into the hands of British and American voters was the growth of credit. Prosperity was based upon borrowing. In the United States the key mechanism was the budget deficit. This permitted a regime of low taxes. In Britain restrictions upon lending were greatly reduced within the domestic economy. The good times of the 1980s were not due to a surge in enterprise by home producers so much as an expansion of consumer credit which sucked in foreign imports. Much of this credit also originated overseas. Names such as Nomura, Daiwa, Nikko and Yamaicha were prominent among the suppliers. Japan became the world's greatest creditor nation. Seven of the world's ten largest commercial banks – measured by asset value – were Japanese.

The Economist recently noted that in California, America's most highly populated and influential state, the Japanese were the largest foreign employers. Only Canada had a larger stake of foreign capital than Japan. The rest of the United States was likely to go the way of California.

Confronting the possibility that 'perhaps America will have to choose between the Pacific and the Atlantic', the writer took comfort in the power of capitalist democratic ideology. Americans were defined by

> their eager adherence to ideas based on the notion that everybody has the right to 'life, liberty and the pursuit of happiness'. These are not the ideas of Confucius or Buddha; they are the ideas of eighteenth century Britain and France. However much Americans and Europeans have since diverged in their experience and practice, that still matters.
>
> (*The Economist*, 24 December 1988: 41, 44)

This present book is concerned with the long transatlantic debate on capitalist democracy which lies hidden behind that assertion.

The Jeffersonian vision

In his *Common Sense*, a tract on the American Revolution published in 1776, Tom Paine proclaimed that 'no natural or religious reason can be assigned . . . [for] the distinction of man into KING and SUBJECTS' (Paine 1976: 72). In America, where all were equal, 'THE LAW IS KING' (98). Paine went even further than this in his assertion of the rights of man (Paine 1969). Indeed, he was a little too advanced for many of the propertied and highly respectable leaders of the American Revolution (see, for example, Hartz 1955; Arblaster 1984).

In *The Wealth of Nations*, published the same year as *Common Sense*, Adam Smith observed that

> commerce and manufacture gradually introduced order and good government, and with them, the liberty and security of individuals, among the inhabitants of the country, who had before lived almost in a continual state of war with their neighbours, and of servile dependency upon their superiors.
>
> (Smith 1979: 508)

To summarise: free and equal citizens would dispense with despots. Civilised urban traders would bring peace and enlightenment to the feudal countryside. The economic interests of human beings would tame their passions (see Hirschman 1977; Pocock 1975).

Capitalists and democrats were much clearer about the kind of society they wished to see destroyed than the kind of society they wanted to see evolve. It was widely assumed that once absolutist and feudal institutions were disposed of, enlightened Christian men of property would settle things pragmatically among themselves in a world still largely rural and human-sized. This was Thomas Jefferson's hope, at least (Peterson 1977).

Implicit in the writings of late eighteenth-century liberal intellectuals was a vision of property-owning citizens sharing public responsibilities. This very soon became quite unrealistic. It did not apply to Manchester in the 1830s, as Alexis de Tocqueville readily saw. Nor was it applicable to the Chicago explored by Thorstein Veblen in the 1890s.

Capitalism and democratisation were dynamic. Allied to urbanisation and industrialisation they were dynamite. In the name of capitalist democracy and progress, control was torn out of the hands of enlightened Christian merchants and commercial farmers. Power was seized by plutocratic businessmen whose base was the large manufacturing city. They, in turn, faced challenges from government bureaucrats, a host of professionals and experts and, not least, organised labour. That was the American pattern during the nineteenth and twentieth centuries. In the case of Britain, despite some important similarities, the picture was complicated by the long, slow decline of the aristocracy, the stronger state tradition and the delayed advent of universal suffrage.

If the South had won the American Civil War, or if the United States had disintegrated politically during the 1850s and 1860s, the career of capitalist democracy in the West would probably have been a relatively short one. After all, Britain, the most industrialised and urbanised society in the world during the nineteenth century, and possessor of unprecedented imperial power, had one of the narrowest parliamentary franchises in Europe in 1914 (Matthew 1976: 724–5; Moorhouse 1973: 352). Apart from America, Britain's biggest rival was Germany, a centralised and authoritarian society in which social support for liberal freedoms was relatively slight (Blackbourn and Eley 1984).

In the event, the material dynamism and unprecedented growth of the United States provided abundant practical evidence that capitalism and democracy 'worked'. The eclipse of the Jeffersonian vision of a freeholder future left a large gap in capitalist democratic ideology. However, this potential liability was converted into an asset by stressing the unfixedness of American society, its lack of boundaries, its openness, its experimental character. In America, it was said, all things were possible. The ideological gap became an ideological virtue, especially when presented by enthusiasts for 'triumphant democracy' such as Andrew Carnegie (Carnegie 1886).

The eastern and western roads

By the First World War this message was wearing thin. The skyscrapers of Chicago and New York symbolised the belittling of human beings by social constructs. The magnificent victories of Man over Nature on the frontier gave way to the hegemony of Institutions over men and women in the city (see Smith 1988). How much progress towards individual freedom had really been made since the days of despots and feudal overlords? Subversive questions of this kind were stilled, or at least shouted down, by exploiting the new ideological opportunity provided by the Russian Revolution of 1917.

Attention was focused upon the contrast between the 'servility' and 'despotism' of the Soviet system and the 'freedom' and 'individualism' of the West. Urban commuters harrassed by the boss, locked into daily traffic jams and befuddled by pressures to work and consume in ways convenient to a bureaucratic system ought not to feel trapped. They should see how much worse off the Russians were. Freedom was the absence of socialism.

During the nineteenth century, capitalist democracy had been presented, in effect, as a huge signpost pointing west to a frontier of promise and opportunity. Following the First World War it was complemented by another signpost pointing east and carrying the warning: 'that way lies a threatening and dismal place'. During the 1980s the key text of capitalist democracy in its dominant ideological form was Friedrich A. Hayek's *The Road to Serfdom* (1976a), originally published in 1944. Its power derived from the existence of societies whose servile nature seemed obvious: especially Hitler's Germany and Stalinist Russia, both regarded as variants of the same oppressive type.

The westward trek to the frontier and the eastern road to serfdom have provided two powerful images, one positive and the other negative. They have buttressed dominant economic and political interests in the western capitalist democracies, especially the United States. Each image has been hammered home by a mighty propaganda machine. Both are becoming increasingly implausible.

The negative 'eastern' image came increasingly into play as the positive 'western' image lost its grounding in experienced reality. The latter acquired an icon-like status, providing a focus for nostalgia rather than a guide for everyday life or public affairs. For a while the pursuit of opportunity through industrial growth provided a substitute for the freedom of the open frontier. Unfortunately, by the 1970s and 1980s it was becoming clear that untrammelled growth produced congestion, pollution and dissatisfaction. Speculation focused upon possible futures which might avert these consequences (e.g., Hirsch 1977; Bell 1973; Kumar 1978; Gershuny 1978; Schumacher 1974; Roszak 1979; Brown 1981).

The empirical basis of the 'eastern' image has now also been fundamentally weakened. Whatever the fate of Mikhail Gorbachev's attempt to introduce *perestroika* and *glasnost* in the USSR, it will no longer be possible to present Russia as a mighty and diabolical monolith dedicated to conquest of the West. Instead, during the 1980s we have seen an overstretched and conflict-ridden bureaucracy trying to modernise a thoroughly disunited and rebellious empire. Modernisation has meant, in part, westernisation. The Russian leadership in the 1980s even began to talk about competitive elections and the profit motive. Information began to flow more freely through the mass media.

As Russia has become more western, the eastern threat has transferred to Asia, and has become economic rather than military. According to Japan's Economic Planning Agency, before 2000 the Japanese will be the richest people in the world in terms of purchasing power (*The Economist*, 24 December 1988). The American response has been to search energetically for 'the Japanese formula' in order to apply it to their own industrial management (e.g., Vogel 1979; Pascale and Athos 1982; Ouchi 1981).

Deep confusion has followed from the discovery that central aspects of the Japanese approach – such as an overriding commitment to the work community and a willingness to sacrifice short-run individual rewards for long-term collective success – are directly opposed to the

American cult of the fast buck and looking after number one. The lack of individualism in the work place might win grudging applause from Americans as a fine show of team spirit, but not so the rigid conformity and strict hierarchy found in the wider society, within as well as outside the home. Basic assumptions are under threat.

Double confusion has occurred in Britain. Its leaders are trying to Americanise and 'Japanise' its industry at the same time. Ronald Dore summed up the British situation as follows:

> In the dimension, or bundle of dimensions, which I have, following convention, called 'individualism–collectivism' or 'individualism-groupism', the United States and Japan stand at opposite ends, with Britain somewhere in the middle. It is not unknown for British politicians, looking at growth rates and unemployment levels, to urge us in one breath and a single sentence, to take a leaf out of the book 'of the Japanese and the Americans'. But *they are very different books*.
>
> (Dore 1987a: 245; original emphasis)

Three challenges

Three challenges confront capitalist democracy in the West as we consider the prospects for civilised survival into the twenty-first century. These challenges derive from, respectively, the political, economic and ecological spheres.

The first challenge stems from the increase in critical attention to which western capitalist democracy has been subject as the Cold War begins to thaw in earnest. The Soviet Union appears less and less threatening in military terms. The costs of aggression are too high and the benefits too low for a fragile empire in the throes of internal modernisation. Criticism is losing some of the taint of 'treachery' it has had in the past. This will remove a massive obstacle to self-analysis in the West.

The process of inquiry is already under way. The nature and interplay of capitalism and democracy are firmly on the agenda (e.g., Alford and Friedland 1985; Andrain 1984; Berger 1987; Bobbio 1987; Bowles and Gintis 1987; Carnoy and Shearer 1980; Crozier 1987; Dahl 1985; Dunn 1979; Ellis and Kumar 1983; Faher and Heller 1983; Goodell 1985; Held 1987; Hoffman 1988; Jessop 1982; Keane 1984; Macpherson 1980; Przeworski 1986; Reddy 1987; Roper 1989 – to name only a few).

Approaches based upon Marxism and critical theory (e.g., Jessop 1978; Miliband 1977; O'Connor 1973; Offe 1984; Offe 1985; Habermas 1976) are being complemented by a more serious and sympathetic examination of the liberal tradition (e.g., Gray 1986; Hall 1988; Lustig 1982; Paul *et al.* 1986; Seidman 1983; Smith 1988). New interest is being taken in the work of T.H. Marshall on citizenship and social class (e.g., Dore 1987b; Mann 1987; Marshall *et al.* 1985; Marshall *et al.* 1987; Turner 1986).

Second, the industrial challenge from Japan raises the question of the relationship between the legal forms of capitalism and democracy on the one hand and, on the other, the histories, social structures and cultural identities of specific capitalist–democratic nations. There are clearly different ways of being capitalist and democratic, and some of them are better adapted than others for international competition in the late twentieth century. This second challenge also directs attention inward to our own economic institutions, political values, social habits and cultural assumptions.

The huge academic industry devoted to the examination of the Japanese is matched by a continuing concern to understand the 'peculiarities' of western societies, building on the sound basis established by the work of, for example, Barrington Moore (Moore 1969; Smith 1983), Seymour Martin Lipset (Lipset 1964; Lipset 1981), Daniel Bell (Bell 1975) and E.P. Thompson (Thompson 1965). The debate on American exceptionalism (e.g., in recent years, Foner 1984; Oestreicher 1988) has been greatly enlivened by the contributions of Ira Katznelson on class, ethnicity, race and locality (e.g., Katznelson 1981; Katznelson 1986) and Theda Skocpol on the welfare state (e.g., Skocpol and Finegold 1982; Skocpol and Ikenberry 1983; Orloff and Skocpol 1984; see also Klass 1985).

Our understanding of the Anglo–American comparison has been recently advanced by work on topics as diverse as factory politics (e.g., Burawoy 1985; Haydl 1985), ethnic residential segregation (e.g., Massey 1985), urban development (e.g., Cannadine 1980), the interplay of growth, equality and efficiency (e.g., Lindert and Williamson 1985), political culture (e.g., Hart 1978) and the religious dimension of world hegemony (e.g., P. Smith 1986). However, apart from a few recent examples (e.g., Roper 1989) historical and comparative analysis of the development of capitalist democratic ideology in different national societies is relatively underdeveloped.

A third issue, only mentioned briefly so far, stems from the environmental effects of industrial development. At worst, to put it crudely, the physical consequences of uncontrolled growth are killing the planet. Facing this latter issue squarely will put the political ideology of the West under immense strain. Environmental issues threaten to drive a wedge between capitalism and democracy. When standards of health, safety, decency and comfort directly oppose the overriding drive for profit, the latter usually wins. However, acid rain, water pollution, infected food and other evils are affecting a very large proportion of the population. It is becoming clear that disgust, dirt and disease from such sources are

9

no longer the prerogative of the poor. On this issue democracy is liable to strike back.

If capitalist democracy is not primarily about economic growth, what *is* it about? We may eventually have to ask that question as a matter of practical politics. It directs attention to the moral basis of the social order. Apart from recent enquiries into the condition of Britain (e.g., Dahrendorf 1982) and the United States (e.g., Bellah *et al*. 1988), a lively debate is under way about the possible bases of a viable liberal democracy. Classic contributions have, of course, been made by John Rawls, Alisdair MacIntyre and Robert Nozick (Rawls 1973; MacIntyre 1982; Nozick 1974; see also Riley 1985; Walzer 1983; Walzer 1984; Mulhall 1987; Sandel 1982).

The logic of ideological development

There is no intention of pursuing in detail all these lines of enquiry. This text provides neither a philosophical treatise nor a social history. Instead it tries to explore some of the ground lying between the two forms. Its subject is the logic of ideological development as this was shaped by historical circumstance.

The framework of the argument is historical and comparative. Readers will not need to be reminded of the central part played in American historical development by such factors as the differing traditions associated with the slave-owning South, the industrialising North-East, and the western frontier; the devastating experience of the Civil War during the 1860s; the enormous surge of capitalist development which occurred during the late nineteenth century; the waves of foreign immigration which flowed in until the early twentieth century; the Great Depression of the 1930s and the New Deal which sought to alleviate some of its worst effects; the steady growth of government, especially at the federal level, during this century; and the increased involvement of America in world affairs after the Second World War.

Britain and the United States have obviously followed very different patterns of change since the 1830s. For example, Britain was an urbanised industrial capitalist society with a legally recognised trade union movement many decades before the people achieved universal suffrage in 1918. By contrast, the United States became a full political democracy (though with slower progress for Blacks and women) while it was still a commercialised rural–agrarian society. Industrial capitalism took shape within a society where most white males already had the vote, although federal backing for trade union organisation was delayed until the New Deal.

Finally, although the United States dwarfs Britain in terms of population and territory in the late twentieth century, this certainly was not the case when Tocqueville paid his visit to the American Republic in the mid 1830s. In 1830 the population of the United States was under 13 million, mainly living east of Chicago (then little more than a village) and north of Washington. The population of the United Kingdom in 1831 was almost twice this: over 24 million. British territory included India, Australia, New Zealand, Canada, and a galaxy of other possessions within an empire upon which the sun never set. During the subsequent century and a half, the relative positions of the two nations reversed decisively.

Big business and big government

The presentation takes the form of a number of paired comparisons. Two writers from the middle third of the nineteenth century – Alexis de Tocqueville and John Stuart Mill – are examined first. Second to be considered are Andrew Carnegie and Joseph Chamberlain, two men of the later nineteenth century, both strongly connected to industry and politics. Third, the works of Moisei Ostrogorski and James Bryce around the turn of the century will be compared. The fourth pair consists of Thorstein Veblen and John Hobson, both of whom became well known in the early decades of the twentieth century. These four chapters make up the first part of the book – 'Democracy and the rise of big business' – which is principally concerned with contemporary discussions of the implications of industrialisation for developing a civilised capitalist democracy.

The second part of the book – 'Capitalism and the rise of big government' – deals mainly with the period after the First World War. It is principally concerned with contemporary discussions of the implications of increases in state power for the goal of developing a civilised capitalist democracy. Once more in a series of comparative chapters, attention is paid to Harold Laski and Harold Lasswell (mainly 1920s to 1940s), Friedrich A. Hayek and Joseph A. Schumpeter (mainly 1940s), John Kenneth Galbraith and Anthony Crosland (mainly 1950s to 1970s) and, finally, a series of writers who consider the origins and implications of the inflationary crises of corporate capitalist democracy in the 1970s. These include Milton Friedman, Samuel Brittan, Ralph Miliband (who studied under Laski) and the co-authors Frances Fox Piven and Richard A. Cloward. The reasons why these particular people were chosen for discussion will be considered shortly.

In the period before the First World War, considerable attention was given to exploring the conditions under which the rise of industrial capitalism could be made compatible with urban democracy. The debates were very influenced by evidence flowing from the 'American experiment' inaugurated by the revolution of 1776. The example of the American Republic provided a powerful challenge to the conventional arguments justifying the privileges of the landed establishment in Britain, as Andrew Carnegie, for one, was very ready to point out. In the period after the First World War, the focus of attention switched from the American experiment to the 'Russian experiment' begun in 1917. The character of the debate also altered, becoming more concerned with the conditions under which the rise of a more powerful state apparatus could be made compatible with industrial capitalism.

Four issues run through the contributions to be examined. They can be expressed as four questions. Who should rule? What should be the rewards and responsibilities of participating in a capitalist democracy and on what basis should they be distributed? How should property and the people be related? And how should the public and private spheres intersect?

As far as possible, the individuals chosen for discussion are people whose ideas had a widespread influence in their day. Mill became compulsory reading in the mechanics' institutes and people's colleges. Veblen was the rage in radical American circles by the end of the First World War. Hobson popularised a theory of underconsumption which influenced both Lenin and Keynes. Galbraith introduced the term 'affluent society' to the English language. Crosland's work defined a major position in debates within the Labour party, at a time when it was much closer to government than it has since become. And so on. Although the principal societies discussed are Britain and the United States, the commentators include a Frenchman, a Russian, a Czech (who became American) and an Austrian (who became British).

Many of the people discussed were politically active and drew upon practical experience when formulating their ideas. Mill, Tocqueville, Chamberlain, Bryce, Ostrogorski, Schumpeter and Crosland were all parliamentarians. Five of them (all but Mill and Ostrogorski) had been government ministers. Galbraith and Bryce both served as ambassadors. Laski was a town councillor. Friedman worked in the US government service and provided advice for foreign governments. Samuel Brittan acted as an adviser to the Treasury. Carnegie was the regular correspondent of kings and prime ministers. When his book *Triumphant Democracy* appeared, it was reviewed by William Gladstone in *Nineteenth Century*.

Despite the past influence of many of the people concerned, on occasion this project took on the nature of an archaeological dig. It is, for example, quite rare to find modern discussions of Harold Laski or James Bryce on capitalist democracy or, indeed, anything else. Yet Bryce was widely considered to be the success of his generation and Laski was, for a while, every British right-winger's favourite demon. In the midst of the Hayekian renaissance, Crosland and Galbraith have fallen out of fashion. After long years of neglect, Hobson is making a welcome comeback. Tocqueville and Mill never quite go out of style, but are in perpetual danger of being referred to rather than read. The same is true of Lasswell who invented the well-known definition of politics as 'who gets what, when and how'.

The phrase 'transatlantic debate' in the title is not unjustified. Tocqueville and Mill were, for a while, friends, though their analyses differed. Carnegie regarded Chamberlain as the rising hope of English liberalism, though Chamberlain's liberalism was quite different from Carnegie's. Bryce provided a (dissenting) introduction to Ostrogorski's best-known work. Hobson wrote a book about Veblen. Laski and Lasswell diverged from a common base in American pragmatism, the former towards Marx, the latter towards Freud. Hayek and Schumpeter provided two contrasting 'Viennese' perspectives on the rise of big business and big government. Crosland once declared himself a 'Galbraith man', but had very serious reservations.

A recurring sub-theme in some early chapters is the response of a number of the people concerned to radical and liberal political movements in Birmingham (UK). Tocqueville, Carnegie, Ostrogorski and, of course, Chamberlain all have something to say on the matter. In some of the later chapters Chicago provides a similar element of counterpoint. In terms of population size, Birmingham and Chicago were the second cities of England and America during much of the period covered; in the late nineteenth century, leading citizens of each claimed that their city was in the advance guard of capitalist democracy. This is a book about ideas rather than about cities, but the two cases are more relevant than most.

Part one

Democracy and the Rise of Big Business

Chapter two

Tocqueville and Mill

Democracy versus capitalism

Tocqueville's *Democracy in America* and Mill's essay 'On Liberty' are standard references. They are convenient citations for people asserting the excellence of democracy or the importance of the individual. However, Tocqueville's study of America must be seen in the context of his views on England and France. Mill's 'On Liberty' should be set alongside his writing on representative democracy and political economy. It is also revealing to compare the two men with each other.

The work of both men is a response to a feeling of political and social danger. However, they perceived different threats. Tocqueville judged that the democratic revolution was an irresistible tide, and saw the need for democracy to become civilised. He could not envisage such a prospect occurring unless industrial capitalism was held in check. By contrast, Mill accepted with relative equanimity that industrial capitalism was here to stay. However, he wanted to prevent the bourgeois world of commerce from monopolising public opinion and investing the working class with its values. His plan was to civilise capitalism. This strategy entailed placing very strict limits upon urban democracy. To oversimplify, Tocqueville thought that democracy could be civilised only if industrial capitalism did not become a major force within society. Mill believed that industrial capitalism could be civilised only if democracy was restricted.

A brief friendship

Alexis de Tocqueville was an offspring of the Norman aristocracy, John Stuart Mill the grandson of a Scottish shoemaker. For a short while they became friends. It was an unlikely relationship, cutting across boundaries of class and nationality. In the opinion of Harriet Taylor, Mill's companion and (eventually) wife, Tocqueville was 'a notable specimen of the . . . gentility class – weak in moral, narrow in intellect, timid, infinitely conceited, and gossiping' (quoted in Packe 1954: 93). Mill rose above this middle-class prejudice. On 11 May 1840 he wrote to Tocqueville:

> you have changed the face of political philosophy, you have carried on the discussions respecting the tendencies of modern society, the causes of those tendencies, and the influences of particular forms of polity and social order, into a region both of height and of depth, which no one before you had entered, and all previous argumentation and speculation in such matters appears but child's play now.
> (Mayer 1954: 328–9)

Harriet's dislike of Tocqueville was probably one of the reasons why, following a regular exchange of letters during the late 1830s and early 1840s, the two scholars stopped corresponding. Only in the late 1850s was the correspondence, briefly, resumed (see Pappe 1964: 221–2).

In fact, Tocqueville and Mill had quite a lot in common, not least an admiration for France and an active interest in politics. Tocqueville served in the Chamber of Deputies at the time of Louis Philippe. Under the Second Republic he was minister of foreign affairs for a short while. Mill became a Liberal Member of Parliament in 1865, and during his brief period of service spoke on matters such as Ireland, land reform and colonial affairs.

The two men belonged to the same generation: Tocqueville was born in 1805, Mill the following year. Most important of all, both were deeply concerned with the role of the individual within democracy and the potential of democracy for sustaining civilised life. Their analyses were original, crucially dissimilar, and deeply influential.

Mill and Tocqueville were odd men out. Neither was representative of his class – each broke away from the social group which nurtured him. Tocqueville's family had been strongly royalist during the French Revolution. His grandfather and aunt both went to the guillotine, and his parents only just escaped with their lives. However, at the age of twenty-five and having a public career in mind, Alexis confronted a personal crisis. Following the 'July days' of 1830 he turned his back on the Bourbon cause and, in his capacity as a magistrate, swore allegiance to the new bourgeois monarchy of Louis Philippe. For Tocqueville, this difficult decision was a victory of reason over emotion. His judgement was that the new regime might establish an acceptable constitution. This fact overcame the pull of family loyalty. Tocqueville also set aside the antipathy he felt, as an aristocrat, for the commercialism and mediocrity of Louis Philippe's followers.

By contrast, Mill's father James felt contempt for the aristocratic ruling order. He forced his way into public life through journalism, authorship and, eventually, a post at the East India Company in London.

James Mill personally provided his son with an intensive intellectual training: Greek at three years old, Latin at eight, logic soon after. He gave him the chance of a job in India House; John subsequently worked there as a bureaucrat for thirty-five years. Through his father, John gained access to the radical wing of the metropolitan intelligentsia, including David Ricardo and Jeremy Bentham. As a young man, he was an active spokesman for the utilitarian cause.

Like Tocqueville, John experienced a crisis in his twenties. Tocqueville had used reason to subvert the claims of emotion. By contrast, Mill experienced a deep emotional reaction against the intellectual regime he had been subjected to since the cradle. During the winter of 1826–7 he felt very dejected and miserable. What else could be expected from a work regime which at about that time included the year-long task of editing five volumes of Bentham's *Rationale of Judicial Evidence*? When a passage in a book of memoirs he was reading moved him to tears, he began to recover his spirits. He was delighted to find that he still had emotions. After this experience, Mill became dissatisfied with Bentham's crude pleasure/pain calculus which regarded poetry as a useless amusement. He began to read Wordsworth. In 1829 he resigned from his debating society, publicly renouncing Benthamite utilitarianism.

In these different ways, two men with highly cultivated minds were able to cut themselves free from some of the mental confines imposed by their upbringing. Each produced a new paradigm which helped to define for future generations 'the problem of democracy' within the western liberal tradition. As will be seen, capitalism was part of this problem.

Tocqueville in America and England

In his late teens, Tocqueville wrote to a friend about 'a plan of the utmost extravagance' to visit England with a borrowed passport: 'We might well get ourselves arrested, and that is where the extravagance lies. But one must surely risk something' (Tocqueville to Louis de Kergorlay, 1824; Tocqueville 1985: 31). The same spirit took him, seven years later, across the Atlantic with his companion, Gustave de Beaumont. After a short stay in New York, he plunged straight into the frontier wilderness 'full of memories of M. de Chateaubriand and of Cooper' (Tocqueville 1959: 329). The trip to the American Republic was undertaken with the official purpose of studying penal institutions in the United States. In this case there was no need for fraudulent documents: Tocqueville and Beaumont went as government commissioners on behalf of the new regime in France. As Tocqueville later wrote: 'The penitentiary system was a pretext: I used it as a passport . . .' (Tocqueville to Kergorlay, 1835; Furet 1984: 227).

According to Sainte-Beuve, Tocqueville 'started to think before having learned anything' (quoted in Lerner 1968: *xliii*). However, America – as an idea or a country – had apparently not been very much on Tocqueville's mind before 1831. The subject of the American trip only surfaced in his correspondence with Beaumont two weeks before they departed. Serious reading on the subject of America did not begin until the trip was over (Furet 1984).

The intellectual object which preoccupied Tocqueville in 1831, as it had done for some years, was not America as such but the nature of democracy as a social order. Not democracy merely as a set of slogans or principles with which to oppose an absolutist regime, but democracy as a functioning society.

Europe provided no examples. Contemporary liberals perceived that France in 1789 and England in 1688 had overturned existing or would-be absolutist regimes. However, neither society offered an example of 'pure' democracy. In the former case, the institutional expressions of democratic principle were closely intertwined with the consequences of revolutionary violence upon the social order. In the latter case, democratic and aristocratic tendencies were mixed together, as Montesquieu had pointed out.

America entered Tocqueville's frame of reference as a case study which might help to solve a problem facing European liberalism. The United States represented democracy without aristocracy, democracy unmarked by the depths of violence experienced in France. It provided a way of thinking about possible futures – not necessarily pleasant – for European societies. As Tocqueville wrote to Mill in 1836, 'America was only my framework, Democracy the subject' (Tocqueville to Mill, 1836; Tocqueville 1954: 315).

Tocqueville arrived at New York in May 1831 during the presidency of Andrew Jackson. The war for independence was still in living memory. A populist spirit had developed which was opposed by some of the older well-off families, as Tocqueville found when he dined with men and women from the leading circles of Boston and Baltimore. His primary concern was to discover the character of this new movement.

During a period of nine months he first made his way into the North West frontier and over the border into Canada. Then he journeyed back down to New England, travelled as far south as New Orleans, and trekked westwards into Ohio. He made notes on interviews with a small army of lawyers, diplomats, clergy and politicians as well as a scattering of people drawn from the worlds of banking, education, literature, the plantation, prison administration and the frontier wilderness.

Tocqueville returned to Europe in February 1832. He had much of the raw material for *Democracy in America* (1968), the first volume of which appeared in 1835, the second in 1840. Before the first volume was completed he paid a short visit to England. He was very friendly with an Englishwoman, who was later to become his wife. However, Tocqueville also had intellectual motives for his trip.

As he had noted towards the end of his journey to the United States,

America gives the most perfect picture, for good and for ill, of the special character of the English race. The American is the Englishman left to himself . . . . Spirit coldly burning, serious, tenacious, selfish, cold, frozen imagination, having respect for money, industrious, proud and rationalist.

(Tocqueville 1959: 177)

By 'left to himself', Tocqueville meant not subject to aristocratic influence. There were indeed aspects that were 'brilliant, generous, splendid, and magnificent in the British character'. However, he commented: 'all that is aristocratic and not English' (ibid.). It is relevant that Tocqueville's ancestral home was very close to the harbour from which William set out in 1066 with a Norman army to conquer England and impose a feudal ruling class. The aristocratic virtues were, originally, French.

During a five-week stay in mid 1833, Tocqueville observed English politics in the wake of the Reform Bill of the previous year. He heard the Duke of Wellington speak poorly in the House of Lords, saw a working man brilliantly address a meeting in support of Polish freedom, observed a parliamentary election in the City of London, visited Oxford University, sat in on a magistrate's court in Salisbury, and met a number of activists for reform.

Two years later, Tocqueville made a longer visit (May to September 1835). This time industrial towns such as Birmingham, Manchester and Liverpool were on his itinerary. His notes of this second English journey include a conversation with John Stuart Mill on the nature and extent of political centralisation. Tocqueville, now well known, moved widely in London political circles. He even gave evidence to a House of Commons select committee on bribery at elections.

Tocqueville's observations in America and England contributed to his views on two issues: the global shift from aristocracy to democracy, and possible paths along which democratic societies might travel in the future.

Aristocracy versus democracy

According to Tocqueville, in an aristocratic society, the hereditary ruling class conceived 'a high idea of itself and man'. The aristocracy imagined 'glorious delights', set 'ambitious targets' and generally raised the tone. Scientists in such societies acquired a 'sublime, almost a divine love of truth' (Tocqueville 1968: 592–3). An aristocracy in government was 'master of itself . . . [and] not subject to transitory impulses; it has far-sighted plans and knows how to let them mature until the favourable opportunity offers'. In fact, almost all the nations which have power-fully influenced the destiny of the world from the Romans down to the English were controlled by an aristocracy – and Tocqueville added, with just a hint of self-congratulation, 'how can one be surprised by that?' In his view, an aristocracy was like 'a firm and enlightened man who never dies' (283–4).

Unfortunately, the legal and economic privileges which sustained these qualities could not survive the 'great democratic revolution . . . taking place in our midst' (5). If the keynotes of aristocracy had been inequality, stability and high ideals, those of democracy were to be equality, individualism, restlessness and mediocrity.

The principle of equality had implications in almost every sphere: in relations between social classes, men and women, parents and children, masters and servants, and so on. Democracy meant that every person was as good as another. An individualistic spirit developed, carrying with it the possibility of psychological isolation. The self-centred, self-reliant individual faced the danger of being 'shut up in the solitude of his own heart' (654). He regarded everyone else as his equal but would only accept a few people as his friends and guests.

Restlessness was another product of equality. People no longer had or knew their 'proper place'. Desires had no limit. The individual engaged in a 'futile pursuit of that complete felicity which always escapes him' (693). Happiness in a democracy consisted in satisfying a multitude of 'little wants', leading to 'a kind of decent materialism . . . which will not corrupt souls but soften and imperceptibly loosen the springs of action' (688). Instead of 'great and public emotions' (836), inhabitants of democratic societies experienced the nagging excitement of private frustration.

The general level of education among ordinary people was higher in a democracy than in an aristocratic society, but thought was less lofty. Alertness and practicality were much admired. Useful innovations were frequent but fundamental intellectual revolutions rare. Formulae were valued, while underlying theory was neglected. Instead of great art, there was inventive craftsmanship. The English language was used with less precision and less style: 'vacillating thoughts' needed 'language loose enough to leave them play' (619).

Political affairs within a democracy were plagued by inexperience, faulty judgement and limited foresight. Fortunately, American democracy could afford to make mistakes and learn from them. Especially since, in Tocqueville's view, the particular interests of politicians were not, in the end, fundamentally hostile to the general interest.

In Tocqueville's eyes, England was a mixture of aristocratic and democratic principles. He wrote:

> The English have left the poor but two rights: that of obeying the same laws as the rich, and that of standing on an equality with them if they can obtain real wealth. But those two rights are more apparent than real, since it is the rich who make the laws and who create for their own or their children's profit, the chief means of getting wealth.
>
> (Tocqueville 1958: 911)

Tocqueville was amazed and impressed by English social arrangements, comparing them to a trembling rope bridge 'suspended more than a hundred feet above the ocean' (74).

Experience, skill and luck were needed to make this system viable. The English aristocracy was – unlike its French equivalent before 1789 – politically active and relatively open, being based upon wealth, not birth. It lacked clear boundaries and thus did not provide a clear target. Although privilege was under legislative attack, the aristocracy was protected by the profound effect it exercised upon social attitudes and behaviour at all levels.

The nearest equivalent to an equal and democratic social order was found in Birmingham, a city of many small industrialists and few large industries. As in the United States, local patriotism and restless mobility were in tension. The visitor was told that in Birmingham, 'Everybody works to make a fortune. The fortune made, everybody goes somewhere else to enjoy it'. Tocqueville noted in his diary: 'The folk never have a minute to themselves. They work as if they must get rich by evening and die the next day. They are generally very intelligent people, but intelligent in the American way' (Tocqueville 1958: 94). His travelling companion, Gustave de Beaumont, commented: '*It's absolutely America*' (Drescher 1964a: 64; italics in original). Birmingham must have been reminiscent of Ohio, on the frontier of America. Four years earlier, Tocqueville had written: 'In Ohio everyone has come to make money. No one has been born there; no one wants to stay there . . . . The whole society is an industry' (Tocqueville 1959: 262).

Despotism or liberty?

In contrast to England, democracy had triumphed in a very big way in the United States. This latter case allowed Tocqueville to explore possible futures for democratic society. One possibility was a kind of schoolmasterly or benevolent despotism, which would relieve citizens of 'the trouble of thinking and all the cares of living' (Tocqueville 1968: 898). Men and women would be equal but unfree.

The other possibility led not to despotism but to liberty. This was a necessary adjunct to equality if the worst propensities of democracy were to be avoided. The European manner of establishing liberty was to attack the monarchy, nobility and other privileged vested interests. This carried the danger of anarchy and, eventually, despotism. However, there was another way of 'diminishing the influence of authority'.

By 'dividing the use of its powers among several hands' (Tocqueville 1968: 86), the repressive capacity of the central state and ruling class could be undermined without endangering the socially useful functions of public authority. That was the American approach. Indeed, the President of Harvard University told Tocqueville in 1831: 'The state of Massachusetts is a union of little republics. . . . We have put the people's name in place of that of the king. For the rest one finds nothing changed among us' (Tocqueville 1959: 51).

The New England township was a good example of the way 'The Americans have used liberty to combat the individualism born of equality' (Tocqueville 1968: 658). The affairs of the local community were administered by public officials elected from among the citizenry. County and state government followed similar principles. This system worked because everyone had a stake in society as an actual, or potential, property owner: 'there are no proletarians in America' (294). Public business was a pleasant extension of an American's private affairs. In fact, 'He always speaks to you as if addressing a meeting' (300).

Two main institutions moulded and expressed the people's will. One was the press. It made political life circulate in every corner of that vast land. 'Its eyes are never shut'. Public figures were forced to appear before 'the tribunal of opinion'. This opinion could be shaped by the press in some cases. When several newspapers took the same line, 'public opinion, continually struck in the same spot, ends by giving way under the blows' (229). The other institution was the political association. In Europe, such associations tended to be conspiratorial armies. In America they were, in general, peaceful organisations interested in winning support by petition and argument.

Local patriotism meant that 'Political passions, instead of spreading like a sheet of fire instantaneously over the whole land, break up in conflict with individual passions of each state' (200). This effect was strengthened by the federal constitution. Elections were frequent and politicians often second rate. Public administration was unmethodical, expensive and liable to corruption. Government provided no opportunity for corporate learning, due to the high rate of turnover in personnel. In spite of all this, the political advantages brought by popular involvement compensated for its costs in terms of efficiency and enlightenment.

Politics reflected the typical American mix of agitation and orderliness. Americans were constantly moving: changing their occupations, their residence, their opinions, their tastes. At the same time, a strong spirit of religion upheld a remarkably strict moral code enjoining trustworthiness, self-reliance, neighbourliness. Enlightened self-interest preached the same message.

The American balance of equality and liberty was rooted in colonial history. The early settlers brought to the wilderness not only their religion, but also 'a middle-class and democratic freedom' (Tocqueville 1968: 37). The pioneer was not a peasant but 'a civilised man . . . plunging into the wildernesses of the New World with his Bible, axe and newspapers' (375). The local political order was established before the national framework developed. The land was, in general, not sufficiently fertile to support idle landlords. A society of smallholders developed in many areas. Although a class of rich landowners existed for a while, providing 'the best leaders of the American Revolution' (59), the aftermath of revolution undermined it. The inheritance laws were altered and the vast domains broken up.

Threats to liberty

Apart from the specific threat of racial violence, the United States illustrated a further danger likely to occur in all modern democracies. Americans assumed that the majority was always right: 'It is the theory of equality applied to brains' (305). The results were disastrous for the imagination: 'the majority has enclosed thought within a formidable fence' (315). The people had to be flattered like any European monarch. At worst, the omnipotence of the majority might lead to tyranny and injustice.

Fortunately, argued Tocqueville, a counterbalancing force existed in the pervasive influence of the legal profession within American life. The lawyers were conservative, formalistic, secretly hostile to democracy: 'It is at the bar or the bench that the American aristocracy is found' (331). The judiciary's influence was exercised most notably through the institution of the jury, which was effective both in establishing the people's rule and teaching them how to exercise this function.

Tocqueville became more sensitive to the danger inherent in democracy during the five years between the appearance of the first and second volumes of *Democracy in America*. There are at least three differences in tone and content between the two volumes (see Drescher 1964b).

First, in the initial volume the people were characterised as restless, sociable and dynamic. In the sequel, following Tocqueville's experience of French politics during the late 1830s, they appeared as atomised, apathetic and inward-looking. Second, the benign pattern of decentralised and amateurish government in American democracy, as depicted in the first volume, was supplanted in the second by a picture of remorseless

25

centralising power, inspired once again by the French case. This latter theme was to emerge very strongly in his later work, *The Old Regime and the Revolution* (1955). Third, it became evident to Tocqueville that, in some respects, and in some places, social change was producing not less but more inequality. The culprit was industrialisation.

American democracy as described by Tocqueville could not survive if the sights he saw in the shock city of Manchester in England ever became normal:

> Thirty or forty factories rise on top of the hills. . . . Their six stories tower up; their huge enclosures give notice from afar of the centralisation of industry. The wretched dwellings of the poor are scattered haphazard around them. Round them stretches land uncultivated but without the charm of rustic nature, and still without the amenities of a town . . . the land is given over to industry's use. . . . The roads . . . show, like the rest, every sign of hurried and unfinished work; the incidental activity of a population bent on gain, which seeks to amass gold so as to have everything else at once, and, in the interval, mistrusts the niceties of life.
>
> (Tocqueville 1958: 106)

In Manchester, Tocqueville heard 'the noise of furnaces, [and] the whistle of steam' from 'vast structures' which dominated the surrounding dwellings of the poor: 'here is the slave, there the master' (107).

Huge industrial concerns and large towns were major threats to both equality and liberty. The factory master was becoming like 'the administrator of a large empire' and the worker 'like a brute' (Tocqueville 1968: 719). If ever permanent inequality and aristocracy came to America, it would be 'by that door that they entered' (721).

Tocqueville also regarded large cities as a real danger to democratic republics. He predicted that 'through them they will perish' unless their governments created an armed force which 'while subject to the wishes of the national majority, is independent of the peoples of the towns and capable of suppressing their excesses' (343–4).

Tocqueville's 'solution' to the problem of coping with a large urban industrial population within a democracy was no solution at all, as he must have known. In 1831, a New Englander had told Tocqueville that industrial manufacture would be 'fatal' to 'a country as completely democratic as ours'. England and France had effective police able to maintain order 'But with us where is there a force outside the people?' Tocqueville had answered: 'But take care. . . . For if you admit that the majority can sometimes desire disorder and injustice, what becomes of the basis of your government?' (Tocqueville 1959: 68). Ironically, Tocqueville's preferred pattern of democracy – mixing peace, equality, liberty and local government – was incompatible with the most characteristic phenomenon of the world coming into being: the large industrial city.

Mill on Tocqueville

Tocqueville set himself the task of discovering the logic of the unfolding democratic revolution. Democracy was inevitable and potentially unpleasant. He asked: under what conditions might it be bearable, and what could be done to bring about these conditions? Despite moments of hope occasioned by his American trip and the French Revolution of 1848, Tocqueville was ultimately driven to a state of 'melancholy isolation' (Mayer 1968: *xx*).

In contrast, Mill brooded about how social and mental resources could best be deployed to create a civilised society. By 'civilised' Mill did not mean economically developed, but 'advanced in the road to perfection, happier, nobler, wiser' (Mill 1981: 70). Equality was one value to be built into such a society. However, it had to be balanced against other equally important values, including liberty, diversity and individuality. The balancing would be done by intelligent and cultivated men and women at all levels of society, inspired by the words and example of people like John Stuart Mill.

As far as Mill was concerned, the limits on effective action towards his ideal were not set by the democratic revolution. This was less universal and more modifiable than Tocqueville thought. The major constraints derived instead from the laws of political economy and the educational level of the population. He set to work upon them both. Mill killed two birds with one stone by having his *Principles of Political Economy* (1871) printed at his own expense in a cheap 'people's edition' – a good investment in more ways than one since, following its first appearance in 1848, five editions were sold out in his lifetime.

Mill became 'the Great Economist of his day' (Heilbroner 1983: 103). He was very popular among supporters of the working-class adult education movement. His works could be found in the libraries of the new mechanics' institutes. However, he refused to court popular opinion, an attitude which, paradoxically, added to his popularity. A week before his election to Parliament in 1865, he was challenged to confirm whether or not he had written in a pamphlet that although the English working classes were ashamed of lying they were generally liars. As he recalled in his autobiography, 'I at once answered "I did". Scarcely were those two words out of my mouth, when vehement applause resounded through the whole meeting' (Mill 1873: 284).

Some of the differences between Mill and Tocqueville emerge in Mill's review of *Democracy in America*. This appeared in *Edinburgh Review*

Democracy and the Rise of Big Business

in 1840 (an earlier notice based upon the first volume only having appeared in 1835). Mill strongly approved of Tocqueville's methodology, 'a combination of deduction and induction' allied to a sophisticated use of the comparative method (Mill 1976a: 189). These techniques were discussed in Mill's own *System of Logic* (1844) which appeared four years later. Mill also shared Tocqueville's concern with local public spirit as shown in American town meetings. In fact, Mill had advocated a system of local sub-parliaments in Britain some years before (Mill 1833).

However, Mill differed from Tocqueville in three main respects. He queried the plausibility of some of his generalisations. He disputed his logic at crucial points. And he suggested that England provided conditions more favourable than American society for the development of a democracy which was, in the best sense, civilised.

The democratic trend was not as powerful as Tocqueville believed, certainly not in England. The 'passion for equality of which M. de Tocqueville speaks, almost as if it were the great moral lever of modern times, is hardly known in this country even by name' (1976a: 197). Nor were the short-sightedness and agitated character of American government peculiar to an advanced democracy. They had been just as prevalent in the highly undemocratic societies of eighteenth-century France and England. However, what distinguished the United States was that government was practically redundant there. Free from the abuses of an old regime, lacking a large pauper class, untroubled by wars, neighbours and foreign entanglements, American society needed little but 'to be left alone' (113).

Mill argued that Tocqueville had apparently confused the 'effects of Democracy' with 'the effects of Civilization' (236), using the latter term in its narrow sense of growing commerce and increased national prosperity. A tendency to equalisation was one of the important effects of commercialisation. However, the dynamism of American life which so impressed Tocqueville was, Mill insisted, a product of commercial vigour rather than equality.

Mill introduced two other cases to support his point. One, the French of Lower Canada, demonstrated that social equality could be found without a '*go-ahead spirit*'. The other, Great Britain, illustrated a 'progressive commercial civilization' in a very unequal society. In fact, the American people were, in almost all respects, 'an extension of our own middle class' (237–8; original emphasis).

The middle class shaped English public opinion. In turn, public opinion ensured that individuals were very insignificant within the mass. The omnipotence of the majority was a product not of social equality, as Tocqueville would have it, but of population size. Dogmatic common sense, action without speculation, a taste for superficial learning, Nonconformist prissiness: all these marks of democratic America were actually to be found, in a very big way, in bourgeois, class-ridden England.

28

The bias towards mediocrity caused by middle-class influence was just one instance of the deformation imposed upon a society when *any* single class achieved preponderance. This condition led inevitably to uniformity, unoriginality and stasis. In fact, the higher forms of civilisation required social differences, not social uniformity. The commerce and industry of the middle class might indeed contribute to 'improvement and culture in the widest sense' just as long as 'other co-ordinate elements of improvement' existed (243).

In Mill's view, England – unlike America – was fortunate in having a highly differentiated social structure. For example, the existence of a leisured class and a learned class (including Mill himself, of course) was 'one of the greatest advantages of this country over America'. He thought both classes should be made better qualified for the important function of 'controlling the excess of the commercial spirit by a contrary spirit' (246).

However, a truly civilised commercial society needed not just scholars and gentlemen but also an agricultural class. Mill did not mean people like the restless commercial farmers of America, but men and women who have 'attachments to places . . . attachments to persons who are associated with those places' and 'attachment to . . . occupation' (244–5). It was vital that English country folk should be a stabilising influence, counterbalancing the towns (245). This meant that political conflicts between farmers and urban businessmen (such as the dispute over the Corn Laws) should be avoided as far as possible. Above all, a national education system should be organised which would not only check the excesses of the commercial spirit in town, but also raise the intellectual level of the countryside.

To summarise: Tocqueville saw commercial capitalism, the tyranny of the majority and the isolation of the individual as expressions of democratic equality. He found that majority opinion in America was balanced by the influence of the legal profession and that individual isolation was tempered by popular participation in local government. He thought that England was bound to become more equal, democratic and 'American'.

By contrast, Mill saw the tyranny of middle-class opinion and the suppression of individuality as expressions of the commercial spirit, rather than a tendency towards equalisation. He argued that, in the English case, middle-class opinion could be held in check by the learned and leisured classes and the rural population. In other words, cultural differences within an unequal class structure could be manipulated to achieve a healthy balance. Although the English middle class was growing in size, Mill did not think that the aristocracy had so far been seriously challenged. In fact, one of Mill's ambitions was to elevate the learned class at the expense of the leisured class, especially its aristocratic component.

Life as a well-run seminar

By the time he wrote his review of Tocqueville in 1840, Mill was in the last phase of a long period of intellectual exploration. Following the 'crisis' in his 'mental history' during the mid 1820s (Mill 1873: 132–41), he had plunged headlong into the works of Thomas Carlyle, William Wordsworth, and Samuel Taylor Coleridge. He developed an interest in imagination, intuition, and self-cultivation, a feeling for history and a sense of the social importance of the learned class (or 'clerisy').

He soon moved on to Auguste Comte and the Saint-Simonians. After responding positively at first to their holistic approach to social change, he was subsequently repelled by their tendencies towards fanaticism. Another powerful influence, upon him in favour of radical causes such as feminism and the working-class co-operative movement, was Harriet Taylor, especially after their marriage in 1851.

By this date Mill had clarified in his mind the outlines of the civilised society to be argued for, the logical procedures through which such arguments should be conducted, and the principles of political economy to which thought and action had to be adapted.

Mill's ideal society was rather like a well-run college seminar. It envisaged responsible self-development in a context of generous co-operation under the guidance of high-minded and intelligent leadership. Paternalism was, in principle at least, abhorrent to Mill. It led to imposed conformity rather than sincere and freely-given consent to rational rules of conduct. Political and social reforms were required which would foster moral and intellectual education among the population. This meant giving the leisured class an increased sense of responsibility, while giving the working class more leisure.

Principles of political economy

Mill's analysis of contemporary capitalism was grounded in conventional political economy as shaped by Bentham, Ricardo and Malthus. From these beginnings he managed to draw some quite radical conclusions about the reforms which were needed to reduce human subjection to economic oppression and increase the rewards for individual toil. However, his radicalism was strictly limited by the Malthusian fear that society might succumb beneath a rolling tide of brute ignorant humanity.

Mill disliked the idea that 'the normal state of human beings is that of struggling to get on; that the trampling, crushing, elbowing, and treading on each other's heels, which form the existing type of social life, are the most desirable lot of human kind' (Mill 1871: 453). However, any attempt to improve upon the existing situation would have to come to terms with the inherent rhythms of capital and labour. Both were caught up in cycles of perpetual consumption and perpetual reproduction.

Like Thomas Malthus, Mill assumed that unrestricted increases in population would cancel out the benefits of economic growth. However, he thought that through education and social reform the Malthusian trap might be overcome. Mill inherited from David Ricardo the idea that the rate of profit would tend to decline in the course of capital accumulation. Again, however, he modified the argument. If declining profits eventually led to 'a stationary state', that would be 'on the whole, a very considerable improvement on our present condition' (Mill 1871: 453). Economic growth was a false god in Mill's eyes.

Mill was no opponent of private ownership. He clearly saw the value of a property system based upon 'the guarantee to individuals of the fruits of their labour and abstinence' (128). However, there was a sting in the tail. People should not acquire property through the labour and abstinence of others. This meant strongly supporting co-operators and small freeholders, while vigorously opposing the present inheritance laws. Mill favoured radical reform to prevent the large-scale transmission of unearned wealth across the generations.

In fact, there was considerable scope for experimentation with social forms. Although the production of wealth was subject to rigid laws and conditions, the realm of distribution was, in Mill's view, 'a matter of human institution only. The things once there, mankind, individually or collectively, can do with them as they please' (123). This had important implications for industrial organisation.

Mill wanted to see more partnerships of labourers and capitalists, as well as associations of labourers. He approved of the efforts of utopian communities inspired by the ideas of Robert Owen and the work of the co-operative movement. Such schemes based upon the equal division of property and produce were becoming feasible as the labouring population acquired greater political sophistication.

The working class had become 'part of the public' (458). Fortunately, its members could be 'trained to feel the public interest their own' (127). The sense of justice and equality could be fostered further through 'the civilizing and improving influences of association' (461). Two important conditions of communistic experiments were that 'all shall be educated' (127) and that population size should be limited.

As has been seen, Mill was less convinced than Tocqueville about the social value of a landed aristocracy. Five chapters of the *Principles of Political Economy* were devoted to a rural class he considered to be, potentially at least, far superior: the peasant proprietors. The ideal which inspired Mill was drawn from the romantic movement. The independent and public-spirited smallholders of Cumberland and Westmorland were 'the originals of Wordsworth's peasantry' (155). They provided a model which should, as far as possible, be adopted throughout the British countryside.

31

Despite his interest in small-scale socialist experiments, Mill preferred to rely as far as possible upon market mechanisms to discipline and channel behaviour within society as a whole: 'Letting alone . . . should be the general practice: every departure from it, unless required by some great good, is a certain evil' (Mill 1871: 573). Government could intervene when the market failed to deliver individual choices due to externalities or unintended effects. Poor relief came within this category. A further case where government involvement could be justified was in regulating public utilities if competition was impractical.

Above all, diffusion of knowledge by government was desirable in order to remedy ignorance among the population. This would prevent the making of ill-informed choices. The educational function of government was by far the most important to Mill. He was, for example, very keen on increasing public financial support for universities, hopefully the future cradle of a national clerisy.

As far as possible, effective control over public functions should be in local hands: 'the greatest dissemination of power consistent with efficiency; but the greatest possible centralisation of information, and diffusion of it from the centre' (1964a: 168). This quotation from Mill's essay 'On Liberty', originally published in 1859, leads us to his views on the proper balance between individuals, classes and public authority within a democratic society.

The well-tempered bureaucrat

Two dilemmas run through Mill's thoughts on democracy. They are closely related. The first derives from the fact that Mill wanted to maximise the influence of noble minds such as his own upon the population at large. The medium of central authority was the most efficient way to exercise this influence. The analogy of the school comes readily to mind. It is explicit in Mill's essay 'Considerations on Representative Government', originally published in 1861. He wrote that, in the matter of

> the indirect schooling of grown people by public business . . . . A government . . . which neither does nothing itself that can possibly be done by any one else, nor shows any one else how to do anything, is like a school in which there is no schoolmaster, but only pupil teachers who have never themselves been taught.
>
> (Mill 1964b: 359)

The dilemma was that the prestige of central authority might be captured through democratic means by spokespersons for mediocre middle-class values. The benevolent force of an enlightened clerisy might be displaced by the 'tyranny of the majority' (1964a: 68) backed by the full power of the law. In 'On Liberty', Mill mounted a defence of individuality – the condition of creative self-development – against individualism, the self-seeking and unreflective bourgeois mentality conducive to a repressive state of public opinion. Mill wanted to protect the right of people to be different or eccentric. He argued that legal sanctions should only be imposed upon individuals when their conduct was prejudicial to the legitimate rights or interests of others. Where there was no such prejudicial effect, legal coercion was not permissible although other forms of influence could still be applied. Persuasion and inducements were acceptable ways of trying to influence someone to change their mind or alter their behaviour. This approach not only protected intellectual innovators from persecution. It also allowed such innovators, not least Mill, free rein to educate their neighbours through vigorous argument.

There is a great deal more in 'On Liberty' than this. However, the second of Mill's dilemmas is more relevant to the essay on representative government. On the one hand, Mill approved of the increasing involvement of working-class people in the public sphere. This was an important means of educating them in the goals and values appropriate to the individual and society. On the other hand, however, he was concerned about the consequences if they seized the reins of power before they had been properly trained.

Mill accepted that 'the ideally best form of government' was one vesting sovereignty in 'the entire aggregate of the community' and giving all citizens 'the personal discharge of some public function, local or general' (Mill 1964b: 207). However, Mill believed that the British Parliament displayed 'general ignorance and incapacity'. It was in danger of being controlled by 'interests not identical with the general welfare of the community' (243). Parliament might fall under the domination of 'a governing majority of manual labourers' (250). Within such a majority, particular influence would be wielded by 'the most timid, the most narrow-minded and prejudiced, or [those] who cling most tenaciously to the exclusive class-interest' (260).

Mill was not prepared to accept the verdict of Jeremy Bentham in favour of universal suffrage. Bentham's reasoning was that special interests such as the monarchy, the Established Church and the aristocracy would ensure that government served them at the expense of society as a whole, unless all citizens had a vote. This arrangement would ensure the greatest happiness of the greatest number.

The prospect of universal suffrage, except as some distant future prospect, filled Mill with horror. The 'greatest number' were likely, in his view, to behave in ways which would bring misery to minorities, including the intelligentsia. In fact, 'one of the most important questions demanding consideration, in determining the best constitution of a representative government, is how to provide efficacious securities against this evil' (Mill 1964b: 254). His solution was that the wise, educated and responsible part of the society should look after the public interest of the whole. At the same time they should work hard to increase the proportion of society who came into the category of wise, educated and responsible.

The aristocracy certainly had no automatic claim to membership of this privileged category, whatever Tocqueville's view. The most remarkable aristocratic governments in history were, in effect, 'aristocracies of public functionaries, . . . essentially bureaucracies' (245). Tocqueville's distinction between aristocracy and democracy was redundant as far as Mill was concerned. The crucial 'comparison . . . as to the intellectual attributes of government had to be made between a representative government and a bureaucracy'. Not surprisingly, bureaucracy won hands down in Mill's eyes, especially if, as in the spectacularly successful case of the Roman Empire, it was invigorated by occasional infusions of the 'popular element' (246).

Mill admitted that government by 'the most perfect imaginable bureaucracy' would be greatly inferior to 'representative government among a people in any degree ripe for it' (247). However, that certainly was not England's case, in his view. Government was skilled work. Democratic institutions had their work cut out acquiring 'mental capacity sufficient for [their] own proper work, that of superintendence and check' (248).

The danger of a majority class interest getting too much power would be dealt with by a series of measures. Proportional representation would make sure members of enlightened minorities were elected to the legislature. The vote would be denied to any who could not read, write and do sums. Non-tax payers would not be enfranchised. Nor would those receiving poor relief. Additional votes would be given to the better educated, perhaps using as a test 'The "local" or "middle class" examination . . . so laudably and public-spiritedly established by the Universities of Oxford and Cambridge' (285–6). The act of voting 'like any other public duty, should be performed under the eye and criticism of the public'; the secret ballot was not envisaged. Finally, electoral pledges which restricted the representative's independent judgement would be discouraged.

By all these means the special worth in public affairs of the 'better and wiser' would be recognised (288). Such provisions would contradict the view 'imprinted strongly on the American mind that any one man (with a white skin) is as good as another'. In Mill's view, 'this false creed is nearly connected with some of the most unfavourable points in the American character' (289). In effect, Mill did his best to establish the case for inequality based upon education and the social responsibilities accompanying it.

Conclusion

In Tocqueville's view, equality was a fundamental and inescapable aspect of the democratic revolution. Linked with individualism, it seemed to presage an almost inevitable drift towards centralised despotism. However, in the vigorous local institutions of the American Republic, Tocqueville saw the prospect of an alternative future, less disagreeable though far from perfect. Although peace and public spirit were widespread, culture and manners offered little more than comfort and respectability overlaid with nagging frustration and a taste for thrills. However, democratic mediocrity was preferable to democratic despotism. As has been seen, this solution remained viable just as long as manufacturing industry and large towns stayed over the horizon.

In Mill's view, mediocrity was the probable outcome of the steady expansion of middle-class influence in the course of economic growth. However, the tyranny of the majority was a parallel danger, especially as working-class income and political power increased. Mediocrity and despotism were not alternative fates, they were likely to be combined.

In these circumstances, Mill did not turn to the aristocracy as the source of wise leadership, a strategy which might have been attractive to Tocqueville in the English case. Instead, he urged the transfer of social authority from great landowners to educated professional men and women.

Capitalism – in both its urban industrial and agrarian aspects – should be brought under human control. A stationary or no-growth state was within reach. Experiments in communal ownership of industry and an increase in peasant proprietorship would foster a sense of responsible possession. Large bequests of property should be forbidden. Population should be kept in check by self-restraint. Variety and debate should be the catchwords in the sphere of opinion.

A fundamental plank of this programme was a massive effort of national education to counteract the threat of a mediocre middle-class culture. Another was a series of measures to ensure that the democratic revolution should proceed at a slow pace. Both aspects of Mill's approach are illustrated in his enthusiasm for local representative bodies.

At first glance, Mill's support for local government appears to resemble Tocqueville's positive response to the New England town meetings. In fact, it shows how different the two views of capitalist democracy really are. Unlike American local institutions, the English parishes were to be under tutelage: 'The principal business of the central authority should be to give instruction, of the local authority to apply it' (Mill 1964b: 357). Tocqueville presents the American bodies as, in effect, shareholders' meetings. Mill treats the English equivalent as schools which provide for 'the public education of the citizens' (347).

Tocqueville died two years before Mill's 'Considerations on Representative Government' appeared. It would have been interesting to see his review. Would he, perhaps, have recalled this passage in the second volume of *Democracy in America*?

> I am trying to imagine under what novel features despotism may appear in the world. In the first place, I see an innumerable multitude of men, alike and equal, constantly circling in pursuit of the petty and banal pleasures with which they glut their souls . . . . Over this kind of men stands an immense protective power which is alone responsible for securing their enjoyment and watching over their fate. That power is absolute, thoughtful of detail, orderly, provident and gentle . . . . It provides for their security, foresees and supplies their necessities, facilitates their pleasures, manages their principal concerns, directs their industry, makes rules for their testaments, and divides their inheritances . . . . Centralisation is combined with the sovereignty of the people. That gives them a chance to relax. They console themselves for being under schoolmasters by thinking that they have chosen them themselves.
>
> (Tocqueville 1968: 898–9)

Chapter three

Carnegie and Chamberlain

The problem or the solution?

Andrew Carnegie and Joseph Chamberlain came from social classes which caused great anxiety to Tocqueville and Mill, respectively. Carnegie was born into the artisan branch of the urban working class. Chamberlain sprang from the commercial sector of the middle class. While still young men, Carnegie and Chamberlain became successful industrialists, pursuing their careers in ways Tocqueville and Mill would certainly have found repugnant. Subsequently, Carnegie became a prominent ideologue of American democracy, Chamberlain a spectacular practitioner in British politics.

Carnegie and Chamberlain both put enormous effort into image-building. Carnegie presented himself as the noble entrepreneur, product of a near-perfect system of government and economic organisation, an efficient generator of wealth who also had a deep practical concern for the interests of common humanity. Chamberlain's most persistent message was that he knew the people and was ready to express and represent their interests, even if this meant breaking with established traditions and institutions.

According to Mill and Tocqueville, people like Carnegie and Chamberlain represented one of the most serious problems facing capitalist democracy. According to Carnegie and Chamberlain – each taking his own distinctive line – they represented not the cause of contemporary ills, but their solution.

Two businessmen

The ideas of Carnegie and Chamberlain have to be understood in their social and political context. Carnegie, born in 1835, was the son of a poor Dunfermline weaver. Although his father owned his own premises and employed three hands, the family was often near the breadline. The social atmosphere was radical. In 1842, a year of riots, one of his uncles was arrested for holding a Chartist meeting. Six years later, following a winter of very bad trade and near starvation, Andrew emigrated with his parents to the United States.

By the time he was 33 years old, Carnegie had worked his way by shrewd speculation to an annual income of $50,000. The Carnegie steel empire was growing quickly, elbowing out competitors. By the end of the century, Carnegie thoroughly dominated this key industrial sector. Shortly afterwards, he sold up for an enormous sum of money and set about doing good works.

Chamberlain, one year older than Carnegie, came from the social background later to be sarcastically described by Lady Bracknell as 'the purple of commerce' (Wilde 1899: 44–5). His father ran a shoe-making business in London. The family belonged to the Unitarian branch of Nonconformist religion. This religious tendency was mainly nurtured among the better educated Baptists and Presbyterians. It was marked with those Calvinist tendencies which, according to Mill, produced a 'narrow theory of life'. Its adherents developed a 'pinched and hidebound type of human character', hostile to individuality (Mill 1964a: 120).

Chamberlain moved to Birmingham in 1854 to help build up a business based on exploitation of a new American technique for manufacturing iron screws. The firm of Nettlefold and Chamberlain, precursor of GKN, was able to undercut and take over all its smaller rivals. The products of the newly-dominant company 'found a market in every quarter of the globe' (Chamberlain 1886: 607). Chamberlain was not a robber baron on the Carnegie scale. However, his business operations left enough bruises for him to be 'accused of sharp practice, of endeavouring to crush out all minor competitors, and by these means to secure a monopoly in the United Kingdom' (Creswicke 1904: 28).

Carnegie belonged to the industrial aristocracy feared by Tocqueville. So did Chamberlain, before his early retirement from business. Furthermore, when Chamberlain launched himself into local and national politics in the early 1870s, it was at the head of a cause clearly shaped by the 'narrow theory of life' so hostile to liberty in Mill's eyes. Chamberlain was very prominent in the campaigns of the Central Nonconformist Committee and National Educational League. These bodies represented sectarian interests opposed to the 1870 Education Act, a measure extending state aid to a wide range of schools for the working population.

Inherited problems

Despite their sustained self-promotion, by the end of their careers the names of both men evoked an aura of hypocrisy. Carnegie was accused of betraying his principles in dealing with the unions in his own

Homestead plant at Pittsburg. Chamberlain was condemned by his former colleagues in the Liberal party when he refused to support William Gladstone, the Liberal Prime Minister, on the question of Irish Home Rule in 1886. Less than ten years later, Chamberlain was colonial secretary in a Conservative administration.

Carnegie and Chamberlain were both opportunists prepared to put up with a certain amount of inconsistency in their own lives. As original contributors to political theory, they were certainly not in the same league as Tocqueville and Mill. However, they were more than power-hungry tyros hiding their ambitions behind convenient ideological slogans.

Religious belief imposed upon both the American industrialist and his English counterpart the need to justify the pursuit of power and wealth. It also shaped the intellectual and moral content of their distinctive approaches to capitalism and democracy. Both Carnegie and Chamberlain were the products of 'advanced' forms of Nonconformity. The intellectual tendencies produced by this background, especially regarding the role of public opinion and social evolution, will be shortly explored with reference to yet another product of the same milieu: Herbert Spencer.

The young Joseph's religious background has already been noticed. Andrew's parents were, like the Chamberlains, one remove from the Calvinism of Old Dissent. His father left the Presbyterians to become a Swedenborgian; his mother preferred the philosophy of William Ellery Channing, the New England Unitarian.

Not surprisingly, neither Carnegie nor Chamberlain were happy to see themselves presented as brutish self-seekers. The pursuit of wealth and political power had to have a justifiable purpose. In casting round for a set of ideas which would define this purpose, both Carnegie and Chamberlain inherited problems which had faced their predecessors.

As has been seen, Tocqueville warned against urban industrial capitalism. The very large towns contained 'a rabble' whose worst elements included 'freed Negroes' and immigrants bringing to America the 'worst vices' of Europe (Tocqueville 1968: 343–4). Such people could not act responsibly in the public sphere. Nor could factory slaves. Large industrial employers would impose a permanent inequality of conditions by asserting the power of private property. However, instead of assuming corporate responsibility as a class for the interests of the people, it 'abandons them in time of crisis to public charity to feed them' (721). Although he drew very different conclusions, Carnegie was very sensitive to this agenda of problems.

Mill wished to minimise the separation between property and the people by spreading the experience of ownership as widely as possible. He also desired to repel what he believed were improper intrusions into either the private or the public spheres. More generally, Mill wanted the rules governing relations between these distinctive interests and spheres to be adjusted so as to undermine the landed aristocracy and empower the urban professional. Although he was careful never to appear as an enemy of democracy, this mechanism of change and these overall goals were also taken up by Chamberlain.

Herbert Spencer

Spencer's early work was shaped by the English provincial tradition of religious and political dissent. Birmingham's politicians laid a claim to the leadership of this radical movement during the 1830s and 1840s, not least through the campaigns of the Birmingham Political Union and the Complete Suffrage Union. Spencer met Joseph Sturge, the founder of the latter body, while working in the Birmingham area as a railway engineer. He became secretary of the local branch in Derby and helped Sturge to produce a newspaper campaigning against local government corruption. The tone was optimistic and confident.

Although Spencer left the Midlands for London in 1848, the mark of provincial radicalism could be seen in his *Social Statics* (1850). In this work he looked forward to the steady movement of society away from internal conflict, towards willing co-operation between inter-dependent individuals. A spirit of altruism would increasingly dominate people's feelings towards one another.

This book gives an indication of the tone of Birmingham radicalism when Joseph Chamberlain arrived there in 1854. Public opinion was not something to be feared. Tocqueville and Mill had got it wrong. It was not a source of tyranny but a benevolent force, a powerful means of doing good. This spirit was still very much alive in 1868 when Elihu Burritt, the American Consul in Birmingham, published *Walks in the Black Country and its Green Border-Land* (1868). Burritt had known Joseph Sturge 'intimately during the golden autumn of his great and good life' (Burritt 1868: 46). He admired 'the moral influence of the principles and sentiments he put forth in his addresses and speeches' (52).

Sturge was typical of the city. Birmingham and its citizens had shown themselves to be 'intelligent and vigorous-minded' (19) on many occasions. During the days of the national campaign for the 1832 Reform Bill, Birmingham 'organized the force that produced the event, that has governed the governments and guided the people of the kingdom from that day to this. It erected public opinion into a mighty power and enginery for the public good' (21). The organisation of the nation's moral forces was a great antidote to violence, 'rallying aggrieved populations to the platform instead of the barricade' (22).

The capacity to wield this influence was the product of an advance in civilisation as great as James Watt's invention of the steam engine. In fact, 'Not only the moral and material worlds but their prime forces run parallel to each other. What the power of public opinion is in the one, the power of steam is in the other' (Burritt 1868: 23). This was the political atmosphere in which Chamberlain began his political career.

In fact, Chamberlain was not a self-conscious disciple of Spencer. As Beatrice Webb, a woman who knew them both, recorded:

> Herbert Spencer on Chamberlain: 'A man who may mean well but who does, and will, do an incalculable amount of mischief.' Chamberlain on Herbert Spencer: 'Happily, for the majority of the world, his writing is unintelligible, otherwise his life would have been spent in doing harm.' No fundamental personal animus between them but a fundamental antipathy of mind.
>
> (Webb 1971: 146)

Despite the lack of sympathy between Spencer and Chamberlain, it is not difficult to show that Spencerian ideas were influential among some of Chamberlain's Nonconformist allies in Birmingham (see Smith 1977). However, the sole factor relevant here is the influence upon Spencer's earliest writings of radical dissent's sense of confidence in the benevolence of public opinion. It was a progressive force to be wooed, not feared.

Carnegie certainly took a very positive approach to public opinion, not least in Britain. He published a number of books, including his autobiography and a study of James Watt. Between 1882 and 1916 over seventy articles and published addresses appeared under his name. During the 1880s Carnegie provided financial backing for a string of English newspapers. As his biographer disingenuously remarks of Carnegie's visits to one of his papers, the *Wolverhampton Express*, 'He made no pretense of dictating policy, still less of writing leading articles himself, but he liked to assemble the entire editorial force and give them little talks on the great issues then pending in England' (Hendrick 1932: 263).

In Carnegie's case, the influence of Spencer was direct and positive. The latter's comprehensive system of philosophy, biology, psychology and sociology emphasised the beneficial effects of competition. The process of competition permitted the evolution of institutions better adapted to progressive purposes. In this way societies developed while individuals and practices which stood in the way of progress failed to survive.

Carnegie interpreted the several bulky volumes of Spencer's system to mean, in effect, ' "All is well since all grows better" ' (Hendrick 1932: 238). As will be seen, Spencer's approach was modified quite considerably when mixed with Carnegie's other preoccupations. The industrialist got to know Spencer when they crossed the Atlantic together on the same steamship in 1882. Four years later, when Carnegie's book

Triumphant Democracy (1886) was published, the author proudly presented a copy to Spencer with an inscription which described the latter as 'The man to whom I owe most' (239). This work is a good place to start in analysing Carnegie's distinctive approach to capitalist democracy.

Triumphant democracy

Triumphant Democracy was a celebration of the 'fifty years march of the Republic', to quote the subtitle. Carnegie's subject was the half-century that had passed since the Jacksonian years. His book was full of statistics demonstrating its initial proposition: 'The old nations of the earth creep on at a snail's pace; the Republic thunders past with the rush of the express' (1). Faster, taller, deeper, wider, stronger, richer, bigger, better: that was the message. It was repeated in successive chapters: on the American people, the cities and towns, conditions of life, occupations, education, religion, agriculture, manufactures, and so on. The book was, in effect, a report to stockholders telling them that business was great.

It was also a prospectus for potential investors, especially British-born immigrants and the British who remained behind. Carnegie displayed strong but mixed feelings for the country of his birth as hinted in the book's dedication: 'To the BELOVED REPUBLIC under whose equal laws I am made the peer of any man, although denied political equality by my native land'. Like Tocqueville, Carnegie saw America as a more democratic version of Britain: 'The American republican can never be other in blood and nature than a true Briton, a real chip off the old block, a new edition of the original work, and, as is the manner of new editions, revised and improved' (32).

Carnegie shared Mill's hostility to the practice of protecting landed estates through entail and primogeniture. He heartily disliked the landed class, from the monarchy down to 'the narrow, uninformed Tory squire' (68). The essential element in democracy, in his view, was the removal of special titles and privileges. These gave the monarchy, aristocracy and their hangers-on an unfair advantage in the social struggle. By contrast, upon the emigrant from Europe to America

> falls the boon of citizenship, equal with the highest. The Republic may not give wealth, or happiness; she has not promised these, it is the freedom to pursue them, not their realization, which the Declaration of Independence claims; but, if she does not make the emigrant happy or prosperous, this she can do and does do for every one, she makes him a citizen, a *man*.
>
> (Carnegie 1886: 22; original emphasis)

At a number of points Carnegie's analysis agreed with Tocqueville's. They both admired the federal constitution, appreciated the security of property rights, and acknowledged the 'conservative nature of the political institutions of the Republic' (Carnegie 1886: 337). Carnegie also accepted Tocqueville's equation of democracy with equality. However, he did not draw the implication that psychological isolation, neglect of the public sphere and a tyrannical public opinion were potential evils deriving from equality.

Carnegie had no doubt at all that a life largely confined to the private sphere could easily be rich and cultivated: 'certainly not unless the visitor [to America] has access to the homes of those who figure little or none in political life, can he see the best people in the land, or understand the foundations of personal worth upon which the State mainly rests' (344).

The public sphere did not, in the ordinary run of events, require enormous abilities for its management. In moments of great crisis, great men had appeared. Abraham Lincoln had been available in 1860, part of the Republic's 'reserve force' standing by for emergencies. However, 'when the ship of State is in smooth waters more important matters require its attention, and the governing power goes below' (43). In ordinary times politics is routine work 'such as young, briefless lawyers and unsuccessful men of affairs can easily perform. They have to follow public opinion and are mere agents. When great issues no longer divide the British people, the same result may be expected' (327).

As for the charge that American local politics were corrupt, Carnegie argued that the distribution of titles to loyal parliamentarians in Britain was just as bad: 'there is no radical difference whether members' votes are obtained by expected social rank or favor, or expected pecuniary gain' (353). Carnegie had no doubt that in America 'the laws are perfect' (326).

Democratic equality, once established, provided a propitious context for evolutionary processes of the kind described by Herbert Spencer. Cities and towns were a natural result, one which had to be welcomed and certainly not feared, as Tocqueville had done. As far as Carnegie was concerned, the countryside was the place for the very young, the very old and the very dull. Fit, bright young men and women made their way to town. The rapid growth of large cities was a sure sign of progress:

> This is a stupendous change and marks the development of the Republic from the first stage of homogeneity of pastoral pursuits into the heterogeneous occupations of a more highly civilized state. The nation is now complete, as it were, in itself, and ready for independent action. Its mechanical and inventive genius has full scope in the thousand and one diversified pursuits which a civilized community

necessarily creates, and which necessitate the gathering of men together in masses.

(Carnegie 1886: 33)

Tocqueville had associated the city with two perceived dangers: freed slaves and European immigrants. Carnegie accepted that the Republic had faced these 'two sources of great danger' (12) but insisted that the perils had been surmounted.

> The universal testimony is that the former slaves rapidly develop the qualities of freemen and exhibit, in a surprising degree, the ability to manage their own affairs . . . . They are now quite orderly and well-behaved, and much more industrious than before.
>
> (Ibid.: 30)

As for foreign immigrants, the fear had been that they might have 'stood aloof from the national life and formed circles of their own' (13). In fact, the Republic had won these foreigners over by its 'incredible generosity' in offering 'the boon of citizenship' and a good primary education in the public schools:

> The poor immigrant cannot help growing up passionately fond of his new home and, alas, with many bitter thoughts of the old land which has defrauded him of the rights of man, and thus the theatened danger is averted – the homogeneity of the people secured.
>
> (Ibid.: 13–14)

Triumphant Democracy was directed at readers on both sides of the Atlantic, but especially in Britain. To his British readers Carnegie was saying, 'Come in, the water's lovely!' Democratic equality within a republic was the road to progress. All Britons should adopt the pattern of thought Carnegie found in Birmingham. There he had attended a celebration for their Liberal Member of Parliament, John Bright, a staunch supporter of the Union during the American Civil War. The Birmingham audience had sung a hymn to their native land but not 'God save the Queen': 'A royal family is an insult to every family in the land. I found no trace of them at Birmingham' (7).

Carnegie concluded his book with the hope that extension of the right to vote in Britain and the spread of universal compulsory education would soon be followed by the abolition of primogeniture and entail and the disappearance of 'all that remains of feudalistic times' in that society (352). He believed that Britain was steadily moving in the direction of America in respect of its political institutions. In his last paragraph he quoted John Bright's hope that ' "although they may be two nations, they may be but one people" ' (353).

The book was written in dashing style and was a great popular success. It quickly went through several editions and into many languages. A cheap shilling reprint for British working-class readers sold more than 40,000. Critical reaction was mixed. Matthew Arnold, a friend of Carnegie, thought the compilation of factual material useful, although it could not disguise the fact that American life displayed 'a want of the *interesting*, a want due chiefly to the want of those two great elements of the interesting, which are elevation and beauty' (Arnold 1888: 495; original emphasis).

Herbert Spencer's view, in a letter to Carnegie, was that the book was really about the 'triumph of civilization', using the term in the narrow sense of material progress. he added;

> A large part, if not the greater part, of what you ascribe to democracy, is, it seems to me, simply the result of social growth in a region furnishing abundant space and material for it, and which would have gone on in a substantially similar way under another form of government.
>
> (Hendrick 1932: 277)

These comments are highly reminiscent of Mill's critique of Tocqueville on America.

A better title for Carnegie's book would have been *Triumphant Capitalism*. He had convincingly shown the material fruitfulness of American society. He had, perhaps, plausibly argued that democracy, by guaranteeing formal equality and property rights, had contributed to the conditions for capitalist advance.

What he had not done was demonstrate any way in which capitalism contributed to the vigour of democracy. In his chapter on manufactures, the relationship between employer and employee was hidden behind his main subject, which was the relationship between Man and Nature. Carnegie asserted the dignity of labour by free citizens. However, fears about the rise of an industrial aristocracy, such as those voiced by Tocqueville, would not be quelled by any of the evidence produced in *Triumphant Democracy*.

The gospel of wealth

Carnegie attended to the problem of how capitalism fed back into democracy in two articles published in *North American Review* in 1889. They were subsequently published in Britain under the title *The Gospel of Wealth*. Finally, in 1900, they appeared in book form.

The Gospel of Wealth focused upon the consequences of individualism, the trait which Tocqueville had argued was complementary to equality in America. Competition, argued Carnegie, had resulted in enormous improvements in the lives of everybody. As a result of technological advance, the labourer enjoyed material benefits which were denied even to his master in previous generations. However, competition was part of a process of evolution which also brought differentiation and inequality. Specifically, those most fitted to innovate and lead became successful entrepreneurs. With their success came great wealth. Although all benefited from material advances, the gap between rich and poor increased greatly.

To this extent, Carnegie accepted the Spencerian analysis which bundled the costs and benefits of progress together in one package. However, Carnegie was prepared to go further than Spencer and argue that wise individuals could intervene in the evolutionary process, redirecting it somewhat in order to reduce or compensate for its costs. This ambition of rechannelling powerful historical forces within the limits of the possible is similar to the attitude taken by Tocqueville towards the democratic revolution. In Carnegie's case, the historical force was not Democracy, since that had already been largely achieved, but Progress.

The individuals most fitted to intervene in this way were the millionaires who had earned their wealth during active careers in commerce and industry. They were the cream of the system, the pick of the bunch. Their surplus wealth was an enormous burden. Although privately owned, it represented a great public responsibility. It should not be used to provide their heirs with great fortunes, allowing them to become drones. Carnegie once commented: 'I would as soon leave my son a curse as the almighty dollar' (Hendrick 1932: 334). Since he never had a son, no sacrifice was involved. He was all in favour of very heavy death duties.

Carnegie also ruled out the practice of making bequests for public purposes. The argument in this case was that no credit attached to such bequests, since they involved no sacrifice on the part of the deceased. Motives clearly mattered as much as consequences to Carnegie.

A third option was positively recommended by Carnegie. A person who accrued great wealth in life should also distribute it to worthy public causes while still living. As he wrote:

> The fundamental idea of 'The Gospel of Wealth' is that surplus wealth should be considered as a sacred trust to be administered by those into whose hands it falls, during their lives, for the good of the community. It predicts that the day is at hand when he who dies possessed of enormous sums, which were his and free to administer during his lifetime, will die disgraced, and holds that the aim of the millionaire should be to die poor. It likewise pleads for modesty of private expenditure.
> (Carnegie 1891: 371)

Carnegie pointed out that this programme was very similar to the strategy recommended by John Wesley:

Gain all you can by honest industry . . . . Save all you can . . . [then] provide things needful for yourself, food, raiment, &c . . . provide for . . . your household. If you then have an overplus do good to them that are of the household of faith. If there still be an overplus, do good to all men.

(Quoted in Carnegie 1891: 382)

The good that Carnegie particularly wanted his fellow millionaires to perform consisted of helping others to help themselves. In other words, surplus wealth should be spent in creating institutions which would provide aspiring men and women with the means to improve and exploit their talents for the good of themselves and society at large. Special emphasis should be placed upon educational institutions, since they were a long-term social investment. Like Mill, Carnegie was an enthusiastic advocate of heavy spending on schooling for the purpose of expanding the circle of the worthy and responsible within society.

Direct financial aid in the form of massive poor relief was not what Carnegie had in mind. That was better left to the Salvation Army. Charitable payments to the poor on a large scale did little more than alleviate immediate suffering and probably went to the least fit specimens of mankind. As Carnegie once commented, 'I am not so much concerned about the submerged tenth as . . . the swimming tenth' (quoted in Hendrick 1932: 340). The object of his scheme was to make the chance of self-improvement available to a larger proportion of the population. In this way the fruits of capitalism would contribute to the gradual strengthening of democratic equality of opportunity.

Homestead

At this point a slightly longer account of the Homestead strike is appropriate, since it has made such an impact on Carnegie's reputation. Six years before that particular strike, Carnegie had responded to the serious labour unrest of 1886 by proclaiming the value of trade unions as a means of raising the standards of working people. He had written:

The right of the working-men to combine and form trades unions is no less sacred than the right of the manufacturer to enter into associations and conferences with fellows, and it must sooner or later be conceded . . . . My experience has been that trades-unions, upon the whole, are beneficial both to labor and to capital.

(Carnegie 1900: 114–15)

This must have seemed a highly liberal sentiment, especially in the year that a bomb outrage in the Haymarket in Chicago fed widespread suspicions that labour was infiltrated with foreign anarchists.

However, it was a different story when the management of the Carnegie Steel Company dealt with the Amalgamated Association of Iron and Steel Workers in the factory at Homestead in Pittsburg. In 1892 management decided, without securing union agreement, that the tonnage scale (or piece rate) should be reduced. It was made clear that if the union did not accept this, the plant would become non-union. Following a brief lock-out there was a battle between union members and 300 Pinkerton guards, who were trying to bring non-union labour into the plant. Ten men were killed. To cut a long story short, the union was soundly beaten and the Homestead plant became non-union.

During the whole business Carnegie was away in Scotland. However, the local manager at Homestead received his full backing both in public and private. Carnegie was criticised widely in the press. For example, the St Louis *Post-Dispatch* declared that 'In the estimation of nine-tenths of the thinking people on both sides of the ocean, he has not only given the lie to all his antecedents, but confessed himself a moral coward' (quoted in McCloskey 1951: 151). According to his biographer, 'Carnegie was firmly persuaded that, had he been on the scene in July 1892 the Homestead strike would not have taken place. On this point few of his friends or enemies disagreed' (Hendrick 1932: 58).

Between property and the people

Carnegie felt closer in spirit to Birmingham and its politicians than he did to most other English cities. This was reciprocated. The Birmingham Liberals had invited Carnegie to stand as one of their parliamentary candidates in 1885. Although he did not accept, Carnegie admired what he thought was the republican spirit of the city. There was at least some confirming evidence.

During the early 1870s, Joseph Chamberlain's radical reputation caused fears that royalty would not visit the city to open the new municipal buildings while he was mayor. The Prince of Wales did come, however. Proposing the toast at the ensuing banquet, Chamberlain did not deny the label 'Republican', meaning one who had 'a deep unswerving faith in representative institutions'. He held 'as a matter of theory at all events, that that is the best government for a free and intelligent people in which merit is preferred to birth'. However, he was not one to advocate violence or go against overwhelming popular opinion in favour of monarchy. In any case, the defenders of the Prince of Wales need not have worried. It was perfectly possible that 'a man might be a gentleman as well as a Republican' (Chamberlain 1914: 47–8).

That last phrase captures quite nicely the balance Chamberlain tried to achieve in his political activity. From the perspective of the House of Lords or the upper ranks of his own party, he liked to appear as the man in close touch with the wishes of the people, prepared to argue for the rights denied them. As Cooke and Vincent put it, within the parliamentary field 'He liked to be felt as a threat, and could not quite see himself in other roles' (Cooke and Vincent 1974: 13).

In his dealings with the electorate and with non-electors, at Birmingham and up and down the country, Chamberlain emphasised his determination to ensure that, despite its previous failings, any governing power to which he belonged would behave handsomely in dealing with its clients, the community. In other words, looking 'upward' he asserted the rights of the people on their behalf; looking 'downward' he promised the fulfilment of neglected obligations on the part of property.

Chamberlain first made his name in politics as an articulate Nonconformist radical in the early 1870s. He was a skilled organiser equipped with a shrewd business brain. Liberal voters and activists were organised through the Birmingham Liberal Association, which had been founded in 1865. By 1873 Chamberlain was chairman of the Birmingham School Board, and Mayor of Birmingham.

During the mid 1870s, Chamberlain adopted a broader radical strategy. The education issue was merged into a concern for the conditions and rights of ordinary people. In a parallel process, the National Education League was superceded in 1877 by the National Liberal Federation. This body was dominated by Chamberlain. All its leading officials came from Birmingham.

The NLF provided an organisational focus for Liberal voters and activists. After the 1880 general election it provided the victorious Liberals with an instrument of party discipline at Westminster. Its influence was greatly exaggerated by supporters and opponents alike. The former claimed it was a thoroughly representative democratic body. The latter condemned it as a vile American import, liable to corrupt influence. It was dubbed the 'caucus', implying dirty deals, smoke-filled rooms and a spoils system.

This discussion of Chamberlain's approach to capitalist democracy will concentrate upon the period between 1870 and 1885 when he was building himself up to a position so apparently strong that Carnegie could describe him as being 'certainly nearer to the Premiership of Britain than any one except Mr Gladstone' (1886: 344). Chamberlain's actions and advocacy on behalf of imperialism and protectionism during the twenty years after 1886 are mentioned in a later chapter but are not relevant here. The object is not to summarise, still less to rationalise or justify, a whole career. At this point the main concern is the strategy of political discourse adopted during the 1870s and 1880s by a man who was, according to a parliamentary colleague, 'the hope of decided, consistent, and intelligent Liberalism (Rogers 1903: 254).

It would be unrealistic to expect a fully worked out or consistent theoretical position from Chamberlain. His significance is that in his forays into national politics, especially during the early 1880s, he found – and irritated – the sensitive spots in British politics with respect to the relationship between the public and private spheres, and between property and the people. By contrast, in Birmingham during the 1870s and 1880s he developed and expounded a form of local politics which appeared to reconcile tensions between these spheres and interests.

A paradox

When Chamberlain arrived at Birmingham in 1854, the local balance of power was shifting on a number of axes. It was moving away from business and professional cliques closely associated with the county squirearchy, and towards other cliques, also rich and respectable, who cultivated their links with artisans, office workers and small traders within the city. Influence was flowing away from the Church of England and towards Nonconformism; away from the Tories and towards the Liberals; away from a politics which defended privilege and exclusivity in the name of Church and Monarchy and towards the politics of democratic gestures, large town meetings, freedom, righteousness, and the power of public opinion. As a successful business man, a Nonconformist, a Liberal and a brilliant public speaker, Joseph Chamberlain was in the right place at the right time.

He began as a one-issue politician, expressing the resentment of Dissenters over the fact that the 1870 Education Bill would strengthen the influence of the Established Church. However, he was soon moving towards a broader social analysis, telling his fellow Nonconformists at Manchester in 1872 that 'Special privileges in ecclesiastical matters have their counterpart in political monopolies and social class distinctions; they react injuriously on all progress and reform' (Chamberlain 1914: 20). The political implications were spelt out to the Sheffield Reform Association the following year:

> The cardinal principle of Liberalism is this – that the people shall be assisted to govern themselves; and the principle which underlies Toryism is the principle of patronage – the principle that the poor can best be governed by those who style themselves their betters.
> (Chamberlain 1914: 26)

These particular thoughts were not new. Chamberlain's originality and skill was in pushing through a reform programme in Birmingham which appeared to put his type of Liberalism into practice; and then making sure that everybody knew about it. He also attempted to carry his message to a national audience. At this point a paradoxical shift occurred. In Birmingham Chamberlain was able to present himself as the leader of a wise and civic-minded propertied class caring for the people's needs. When the same set of principles was projected on the national stage, Chamberlain appeared to be a rabble-rouser whipping up the people's anger against the establishment.

The civic gospel

During Chamberlain's three years at the head of the municipal corporation and the Birmingham School Board, a great deal was done. The city's gas and water supply was taken into public ownership, the corporation acquired a large amount of land in central Birmingham, the local school building programme was considerably speeded up and a start was made on laying out a great new central thoroughfare, aptly named Corporation Street. These innovations were helping to create a large administrative vested interest for the corporation, which appeared set to be under Liberal domination for several years. However, more benevolent motives also operated. The philosophy behind all this activity was set out in 1874 by Chamberlain in a speech at Hurst Street Chapel in Birmingham:

> The Corporation of Birmingham is engaged in a great struggle to promote the welfare, health and happiness of the population over which it rules, and its labours are supplemented by the individual efforts of such institutions as this. . . . I am a Radical Reformer because I would reform and remove ignorance, poverty, intemperance, and crime from their roots. What is the cause of all this ignorance and vice? Many people say . . . intemperance [but] . . . I believe that intemperance itself is only an effect produced by causes that lie deeper still. I should say these causes, in the first place, are the ignorance of the masses; and, in the second place, the horrible, shameful houses in which many of the poor are forced to live.
>
> (Chamberlain 1914: 42–4)

In practice, a great deal more emphasis was placed upon schools and libraries than improving the dwellings of the poor. Chamberlain, like Carnegie, was more interested in the 'swimming tenth' than the 'submerged tenth'. He also agreed with the American industrialist that individuals who achieved great material success also acquired great public obligations. However, unlike Carnegie, Chamberlain argued that the best way to serve the community was in the public sphere. There was no better occupation than council work for any man with ambition or a philanthropic turn of mind.

Chamberlain made his position clear enough in 1876. He had 'no sympathy at all with superior persons who sneer at municipal work. . . .

We have seen in the United States of America how the withdrawal of men of character and of ability from all concern and interest in local work has depreciated the standard of public morality.' He argued that 'our local parliament' should include 'men of the highest ability and culture' while also remaining 'in close sympathy and relationship with the mass of the people whose daily needs and common wants should find fitting and frequent expression in our midst' (Chamberlain 1914: 71-3).

As has been argued, Carnegie's 'gospel of wealth' created separation and hierarchy. It reserved to the richest owners of private property the privilege of investing surplus wealth for the good of the people as a whole. This approach clearly ranked private enterprise above the public sphere of government. It also set property, which 'knew best', in authority over the people. Chamberlain was exploring another way which became known as the 'civic gospel'. Its overt intention was to bring the energies of the private sphere into the public realm and reduce the potential for division between property and the people.

The intellectual groundwork had been laid by an influential local minister, George Dawson, who in 1861 had argued that although 'the old guilds and the old corporations had declined, we [in Birmingham] had found a new plan of forming ourselves together more in accordance with the thought and feeling of the time, and capable of bringing together a better union of classes'. In Dawson's view, adopted by Chamberlain, a town like Birmingham was 'a solemn organism through which should flow, and in which should be shaped all the highest, loftiest, and truest ends of man's intellectual and moral nature' (quoted in Dale 1898: 101).

Property and the people were to be drawn together in two ways. First, professionals, business people and ministers of religion were morally exhorted to take a leading part in managing the community's affairs through voluntary work and local government. Above all, they should take care of education and community health through municipal institutions which 'represent the authority of the people' (Chamberlain 1914: 41). This would encourage the growth of a responsible and knowledgeable citizenry who would model themselves upon, rather than becoming dependent upon, the civic establishment.

Second, through its public agencies the community as a whole would own property and enterprises, such as the gas and water supply operations mentioned previously. These would be managed by the establishment for the good of the community as a form of 'municipal socialism'.

This was indeed how Birmingham presented itself to the world during the last quarter of the nineteenth century and the early decades of the next. There was an element of self-deception in it, but the system was by no means entirely sham. It had a number of structural supports. An important material consideration was that several of Chamberlain's local Liberal allies were important local employers. Authority in the private sphere carried over into public business. Trade unions were relatively weak on the shop-floor, though treated with flattery on the political platform. The network of educational institutions developed by the new regime created a large sympathetic clientele among the lower middle class. The Liberals had important friends in the local press. They also had the 'caucus'.

The caucus, officially the National Liberal Federation, had some of the functions and organisational trappings of a modern party machine. It was a useful means of influencing opinion among the faithful. Chamberlain stressed its representative function. His message was that it supplied the democratic element in Liberal hegemony, concentrating the people's power. He insisted in 1884 that such an organisation was 'worthy the support of every true Liberal, of every man who trusts the people' (Chamberlain 1914: 118). It is worth contrasting this view of Liberal organisation with the recollections of George Holyoake, an activist from the days of the Birmingham Political Union in the 1830s:

> The famous Birmingham Political union of 1832 was 'hung up like a clean gun' . . . and never taken down again. Many years later a new Union was projected. Mr Joseph Chamberlain was in the chair. I was on the platform, and the only person present who was a member of the former union. I had no opportunity of speaking — nor indeed had anyone, save movers and seconders of motions. There was nothing radical about the proceedings. Nobody's opinion was asked. No opportunity of discussion was given. The meeting was a mere instrument for registering the business of the chair. The impression that afternoon made upon me has never left me. Nothing afterwards surprised me in the performances of the 'quick-change artiste' of the Parliamentary music hall.
>
> (Holyoake 1905: 69–70)

These comments justify a brief digression.

The importance of performance

Holyoake's observations, although jaundiced, make two points. First, they indicate the degree of dominance Chamberlain was able to achieve through efficiency and organisation. Second, they give an insight into an important mode of dialogue in the public sphere between political representatives of the propertied establishment and ordinary people, with or without the vote. Holyoake used the metaphor of a music hall or theatre. The relationship between public figure and people was indeed like that between artiste and audience.

Communication between political leaders and the people at large occurred in the theatrical context of campaign oratory. The politician's task was to represent to the population their values and prejudices. While for Carnegie the performance which justified power was measured in the seclusion of the counting house, for Chamberlain it was judged on the public stage. On the one hand, performance meant achievement; on the other hand, it meant enactment.

The prize obtained by performance in Carnegie's world was surplus wealth; in Chamberlain's world it was trust. The dynamics of trust were not the same in Britain as in the United States, as Vivien Hart has pointed out (Hart 1978). In America, the sovereign people distrusted their politicians as a matter of course. The latter had an uphill struggle to prove themselves.

In Britain, the political culture was very different. It was the ruling establishment of substantial property owners who distrusted the people at large outside the pale of full citizenship. Chamberlain's message to the people was that he trusted them. Unlike his opponents, he was ready to give them tickets for the show. In 1884, a year of electoral reform, he told an audience at Denbigh:

> Well, for years the Tories resisted every extension of the suffrage; they were consistently opposed to the introduction of political power to the masses of the people. Now . . . they are seeking by pretexts and pretences to delay what they dare not any longer deny. They are in the position of the owner of a place of entertainment who should say to a great crowd outside, 'You are, we admit, entitled to admission to the performance; you have as much right to be there as those who are now enjoying what is going on, but we have not made up our minds whether we will put you in the galleries or the pit – until we do that, and we shall not hurry ourselves, you must wait outside in the cold, and the play must go on without you.
>
> (Quoted in Creswicke 1904: 161)

To continue the analogy, in a speech like this Chamberlain was putting himself outside the theatre with the waiting crowd, playing the political busker. It was not a role which endeared him to the management.

The national stage

In Birmingham Chamberlain dominated public opinion. He had helped a new propertied establishment into power and enjoyed their support. Although many leading Liberals were Anglican (including the leading local newspaper editor), tap roots were sunk deep into local Dissent. There were ties of interest and, perhaps, even idealism with the beneficiaries of local public education. In this context, Chamberlain could afford to talk like a democrat or even a republican.

Outside of Birmingham, the same rhetoric made property owners uncomfortable, especially in rural areas and in Westminster. In those contexts Chamberlain sounded radical and did not look like a gentleman. When he first spoke in Parliament, one Tory member murmured that he seemed like 'a head clerk at a West End draper's' (McCarthy 1904: 80).

The discomfort generated by Chamberlain among property owners reached a peak during the early 1880s, culminating in his speeches in favour of his own 'unauthorised' programme for Liberalism. The latter was a radical manifesto issued without reference to the party's national leadership.

It was not pleasant for landowners to read in their newspapers that Chamberlain believed 'the rights of property have been so much extended that the rights of the community have almost altogether disappeared', or that 'the prosperity and the comfort and the liberties of a great proportion of the population have been laid at the feet of a small number of proprietors who "neither toil nor spin" ' (Chamberlain 1914: 171).

Chamberlain deliberately evoked memories of the English Civil War, of Puritan grievances and the enclosure of common land. He declared:

> I hold that the sanctity of public property is greater even than that of private property, and that if it has been lost, or wasted, or stolen, some equivalent must be found for it, and some compensation may be fairly exacted from the wrongdoer.
>
> (Chamberlain 1914: 155)

Anxiety was especially intense when Chamberlain reminded his audience that 'Society is banded together in order to protect itself against the instinct of those of its members who would make very short work of private ownership if left alone' and asked: 'what ransom will property pay for the security which it enjoys?' (137).

No one would pretend that Chamberlain's speeches were finely-argued treatises in political philosophy. His thinking veered between natural rights theory and utilitarianism and, in the latter case, between James Mill and John Stuart Mill. The latter would probably have sympathised with Chamberlain's regret that in agriculture, 'There has been no force tending to dispersion and subdivision' since there was a great need for 'the re-establishment upon the land of the old class of yeomen who were at one time the most independent and the most prosperous class in the kingdom' (157–8).

Chamberlain also wanted to reduce the political power of large landlords by setting up a rural system of local government. Extensive government intervention to promote universal education was also on his agenda. In fact, Chamberlain was never given the opportunity to put his manifesto into practice.

Conclusion

To summarise, Carnegie argued, first, that 'triumphant' democracy created the conditions for capitalist growth; second, that the market selected winners, such as himself; third, that their wealth and moral fitness gave these winners the duty to sponsor the spread of educational opportunity among the people (thus strengthening democracy); and, fourth, that social leadership should be provided by the sphere of great private wealth, leaving politicians in the public sphere with the secondary task of following the dictates of a public opinion elevated by the influence of industrialists and bankers.

Given his assumptions about the ethical character of the market's judgements and the beneficial tendency of evolution, Carnegie's paternalism has a certain coherence. Criticism has mainly fastened upon his apparent hypocrisy, for example, over the Homestead strike. Compared to Carnegie, the case of Chamberlain is more complex.

Chamberlain is commonly regarded as having been a failure when it comes to national politics. However, in Birmingham it was a different story. The Liberal establishment which he led to power – a mixture of businessmen, professionals and bureaucrats – achieved the kind of central dominance over a specific local polity that John Stuart Mill had hoped might be possible nationally. This was done in the name of the people. More precisely – and it slightly changes the tone – in the name of the people of Birmingham.

The civic leadership straddled the public and private sectors and, for a while at least, maintained sympathetic two-way communication with the more articulate and organised part of the local working class (see Smith 1982). During the last quarter of the century, especially after the party split over Irish Home Rule in 1886, the Liberal establishment gradually merged with its Conservative Anglican counterpart. The Chamberlain clique remained dominant, however. Joseph's son, Neville, became mayor in 1915.

Despite his 'Jack Cade' image, Chamberlain 'never thought it possible or expedient to bring everything down to one dead level. . . . The strong man and the able man must always be first in the race' (Chamberlain 1914: 142). Furthermore, although the local caucus went in for its share of jobbery and political favour-mongering it was never capable of imposing the kind of blanket repression of thought that Mill feared.

When Julian Ralph, a New Yorker, visited Birmingham in 1890, he was informed that Birmingham was

> a city that builds its own street railroads, makes and sells its own gas, collects and sells its water supply, raises and sells a great part of the food of its inhabitants, provides them with a free museum, art gallery, and art school, gives them swimming and Turkish baths at less than

cost, and interests a larger proportion of its people in responsibility for and management of its affairs than any city in the United Kingdom, if not the world. It is [he concluded], above all else, a business city, run by business men on business principles.

(Ralph 1890: 99)

Birmingham Liberalism never really lived up to its own propaganda. However, it provided one working model, on a very small scale, of the successful transfer of political power from a gentrified Tory regime to a relatively enlightened urban patriciate prepared to experiment with 'socialistic' schemes in a spirit of community improvement. The extensive scheme of educational institutions was eventually crowned by the inauguration of Birmingham University, aided by a massive endowment from Andrew Carnegie. Joseph Chamberlain was the university's first chancellor. In terms of Mill's ideas these were all substantial moves in the right direction. In the light of Mill's social anxieties, it is ironic that the dominant figure should have been a Dissenting industrialist proud to declare 'I belong to the middle class' (Chamberlain 1914: 23).

Chapter four

Ostrogorski and Bryce

Law, politics, and democracy

Large-scale industrial capitalism and mass party organisation were both relatively new phenomena in late nineteenth-century America and Britain. Not surprisingly, the points where they intersected were of special interest to analysts of the developing forms of capitalist democracy in the two societies. This chapter focuses upon the work of Moisei Ostrogorski and James Bryce, both of whom considered the implications of the transformation of democratic forms under the influence of industrial capitalism.

Not very much is known about Moisei Ostrogorski, despite the substantial monument he left behind in the shape of his two-volume work entitled *Democracy and the Organization of Political Parties* (1902). We do know he was born in 1854 at Grodno in Russia, studied law at St Petersburg, and took a job at the ministry of justice. Later on, he studied in Paris and also spent a great deal of time in Britain and America researching his major work. By 1906 he was back in Russia where he served as a representative of the Constitutional Democratic party in the Duma of 1906, elected following the Revolution which had occurred the preceding year. As far as we know, Ostrogorski died in 1919.

Ostrogorski's major work, an examination of British and American political organisation, contained a preface by James Bryce. At the end of his 'Author's preface' Ostrogorski thanked Bryce who 'initiated me into several points of English political life and gave me valuable introductions' (1902a: *lvii*). Bryce was an appropriate contact. He had published *The American Commonwealth* in 1888. Many years later he produced a comparative study of six societies, entitled *Modern Democracies* (1921).

James Bryce (or Lord Bryce of Dechmont as he eventually became) is less elusive than Ostrogorski. Born in 1838 of sternly Presbyterian parents, he migrated at an early age from Belfast to Scotland, his family's ancestral home. His father was a schoolmaster and a distinguished geologist. Bryce was educated at Glasgow University and subsequently at Oxford, where he successfully resisted swearing allegiance to the Thirty-Nine Articles, the usual test of Anglican orthodoxy. His obvious academic brilliance helped him over this hurdle.

Within a short time, bolstered by a first class degree and a clutch of academic prizes, Bryce became recognised as a leading light. His first career was made in the Law. However, he abandoned the Bar in 1882 after being elected to the House of Commons. Before this date he had served as Regius professor of civil law at Oxford. He later became a member of Gladstone's cabinet. Between 1907 and 1913 Bryce was British ambassador to the United States. He was very familiar with that society, having made extensive visits in 1870, 1881 and 1883.

Bryce was a busy man all his long life. His interests included mountaineering (he once nearly fell into a volcano), extensive travelling (he was an expert on the Near East), the classics, botany, geology, history and political science. He inspired mixed feelings among those who encountered him. To university teachers who caught the lash of his Presbyterian rectitude, Bryce was 'that awful Scotch fellow' (quoted in Fisher 1927: 43). By contrast, according to Albert Dicey, one of his student companions, Bryce's

> most valuable quality is his childlike 'life' and go. His kindness and friendship is beyond praise. He stirs us up, rushes about like a shepherd's dog, collects his friends, makes us meet, leads us into plans and adventures, and keeps everything going.
>
> (Fisher 1927: 59–60)

In later years, however, Members of Parliament looking for lively debate or an early division often found speeches from the red-bearded member for Tower Hamlets rather unwelcome. His 'little blemishes of manner and method' included

> A certain lack of pliability, an insistent voice, a temperament somewhat deficient in . . . good-humoured composure . . ., a turn of phrase incisive rather than humorous, a prevailingly serious outlook coupled with . . . excessive indulgence in historical disquisitions and analogies.
>
> (Ibid.: 176)

Nevertheless, if you could stand his pace and match his range of interests – or if you excited his curiosity – Bryce was evidently charming.

Getting the facts

As an undergraduate at Oxford, and later as a don, Bryce belonged to an extensive network which included A.V. Dicey (political theorist),

T.H. Green and Edward Caird (philosophers), J.R. Green and E.A.
Freeman (historians) and, from an older generation, Matthew Arnold.
By the 1850s, John Stuart Mill was the single greatest intellectual
influence upon university men such as these.

Mill was 'regarded . . . as the ultimate court of appeal for all moral,
political or philosophic questions'. Mill's Oxford admirers had not been
soaked in Benthamism the way Mill was, 'but the dislocation he suffered
after his breakdown resembled as well as anticipated their own situation
a decade or so later, with one significant difference: Mill's own prescription for recovery was available to them' (Harvie 1976: 38-9).

Wordsworth, Coleridge, Carlyle and radical politics were part of the
cure. So was a concern with well-grounded generalisations about society
and culture. The implications of systematic and objective empirical
research for ethical beliefs, and vice versa, remained a troublesome area.
At this point Mill was not very helpful. However, in the meantime, Bryce
and his friends were quite ready to follow Mill to Tocqueville where
they found a practical guide to scholarly research.

Ostrogorski had little time for Mill, but a great deal for Tocqueville.
He opened his book with a quotation from *Democracy in America*: 'A
new political science is wanted for an entirely new world' (*li*). Ostrogorski
may have developed his admiration for Tocqueville – some of whose
passages 'can never be forgotten' (Ostrogorski 1902b: 633) – while working in Paris during his late twenties at the École Libre des Sciences Politiques. Ostrogorski studied under Emile Boutmy, a disciple of Hippolyte
Taine. The writings of the latter on French history were, according to
A.V. Dicey, 'nothing but studies in the school of Tocqueville (Dicey
1893: 772; quoted in Mayer 1968: *xxxi*).

Tocqueville's message was this: gather facts, collate them, experiment with them, and extract the general truths they contain. As
Christopher Harvie comments, such an approach was typical of 'Bryce,
Dicey, J R Green, George Otto Trevelyan and John Morley in their
scholarly work, and of British historians of the late nineteenth century
in general' (Harvie 1976: 44).

It was also Ostrogorski's approach. He spent fifteen years researching
Democracy and the Organization of Political Parties. Much of his
material, neglected by historians and political thinkers, 'had to be
gathered from real life and not libraries' so that it could be brought 'for
the first time within the purview of science' (*liv*). Several towns were
visited in 'a long and minute enquiry' conducted with 'absolute independence of mind and perfect sincerity in the statement of its results'
(*lv–lvi*). Subsequently,

> The facts and the impressions as well as the few documents which
> I obtained led me to generalizations which I constantly verified by

putting myself in touch with men and things. I broke up my generalizations into concrete and often very matter-of-fact questions which I put to my interlocutors, whom I treated not only as witnesses, but also as subjects of direct observation . . . . Then I recast my generalizations by adding to them or pruning them in accordance with my new impressions. After operating in this way for years in various parts of the country, without neglecting the literary research required for the historical part of the subject, I seemed to have arrived at conclusions worthy of being presented to the public.

(Ostrogorski 1902b: *lv*)

This is similar to the strategy adopted by Tocqueville as shown by the notebooks from his American and British trips. In Ostrogorski's case, the result was a closely-argued treatise drawing upon historical, philosophical and comparative analysis.

Emancipation of the individual

Ostrogorski believed that when a gentlemanly ruling class based upon land had governed England, society had been homogeneous and stable. However, the masses and the middle class rose up to destroy the old unified hierarchical society. They replaced it with a new regime, radically individualistic and egalitarian. These same forces were also very powerful in the United States, a society which provided Britain with a model of its future. There is evidently a broad similarity with Tocqueville's approach to the transition from aristocracy to democracy.

In Ostrogorski's opinion, this transition had disrupted the unity between society and state which existed when nobles and gentlemen dominated all major institutions. The 'time-honoured social ties that bound the individual to the community were severed' (3). Methodical organisation of the modern electorate was being carried out by 'disciplined and permanent parties'. He was not sure whether they would be able to reunite the individual with society, producing 'a new synthesis' (4).

England had been 'aristocratic and feudal' two generations before; 'at the present moment . . . [it was] completely drawn into the democratic current' (4). This particular example therefore allowed the transition process to be observed 'working out its logical development . . . and presenting an orderly sequel of premise and conclusion' (4). The American part of his study gave Ostrogorski a means 'to see a little more clearly and a little farther . . . . What appeared to us in England as a germ, blossoms in the United States, thanks to conditions which are unfortunately too favourable, into a luxuriant plant' (1902b: 603).

Ostrogorski did not approve of the effects of modern political parties.

They were the product of individualism, industrialisation and the growth of large cities. These trends, which made Carnegie proud of his 'triumphant democracy', were, in Ostrogorski's opinion, crushing underfoot individual conscience and responsibility. They had produced not triumph but disaster.

Carnegie's idol, Herbert Spencer, was also dismissed: 'It is absolutely false that there is any analogy between social phenomena, in which free will plays such an important part, and biological phenomena' (Ostorgorski 1902b: 697).

The emancipation of the individual from the repressive bonds of the old society was due to a number of factors. Methodism and the Evangelical movement stirred the individual conscience into action on behalf of prisoners, slaves, oppressed peoples and other 'fellow-creatures' (Ostorgorski 1902a: 29). Adam Smith asserted the individual's right to pursue his own interests. Tom Paine insisted upon the rights of man. So did revolutionaries in France and America.

The utilitarians denied the existence of natural rights but fortified the sense of individuality. Bentham regarded every citizen as his own legislator guided by his sovereign conscience. Philosophical Radicals campaigned against the corrupt old regime. The romantic movement pitched the individual soul against the world's dull routine. A new 'social cosmogony' emerged 'in which the starting point as well as the goal is the individual and not society' (38).

Technological progress, industrial advance and a new spirit of individual enterprise complemented these philosophical developments. The middle class became more powerful and self-aware. Marching behind the banner of the Birmingham Political Union it claimed the franchise, which it finally won in 1832. Municipal reform, religious toleration, the new Poor Law, the coming of the railways and the repeal of the Corn Laws, all undermined the special position of the landed ruling class.

As the individual was set free and society was levelled down, relationships became more abstract, organised into formal categories imposing distance: workmen/capitalists, tradesmen/customers, and so on. The particular gave way to the general. Public opinion became a mighty force. The individual became isolated. Interest in local affairs diminished. Personal loyalty ceased to be a strong motive for action in politics as elsewhere.

Attempts at reaction – the Oxford movement, Disraeli's Young England, the protests of Thomas Carlyle and the propaganda of the Christian Socialists – all failed. They could not re-establish authority, duty or a sense of community as social principles. However, John Stuart Mill caught some of the spirit of these movements:

> The feelings awakened by Carlyle, Dickens, and others were led by Mill into the channels of logic and science. This was his great

achievement, and this was what gave him his power over opinion, and in particular his influence with the rising generation, which combines the enthusiasm of the intellect and the heart, or, to put it another way, thinks it is following reason when it is really only obeying its emotional impulses.

(Ostrogorski 1902a: 74)

Mill emphasised quality of experience, as opposed to mere quantity, and postponed the utilitarian millenium until everyone had been properly educated. However, according to Ostrogorski, his 'doctrine was in substance the same as Bentham's' (Ostrogorski 1902a: 74): the same emphasis on utility, observation and experience, the same individualism.

Mill's works appealed to emotion as much as to reason. His treatise on utilitarianism (Mill 1964c) was 'the philosophic hymn of a mystery' (80), the essay on liberty 'another hymn, . . . an anthem of love' (81). Mill supplied a gospel for the new intelligentsia and political class. His peculiar power to charm derived from his readiness to yield considerable ground to the enemies of utilitarianism while retaining its basic individualism:

> In every department, in politics, in morals, in political economy, Mill makes very extensive concessions to his adversaries, and by these very inconsistencies in his doctrine he accentuates its success; he not only conveys to the public the seductive impression of impartiality and sincerity, of boldness and openness of mind, but he allays discontent and silences the misgivings aroused by the uncompromising character of Bentham's doctrines, and wins the sympathy which was being attracted towards his opponents.
>
> (Ostorgorski 1902a: 79)

In 1867, when there was considerable pressure for a further extension of the franchise, Mill argued in Parliament for a system of proportional representation along the lines described in his *Representative Government*. Mill's object was to guard the rights of minorities. His particular proposal was not accepted but another amendment protecting minorities was successful.

This amendment decreed that in the large urban constituencies where three Members of Parliament were to be elected under the expanded franchise, each elector should only be able to vote for two candidates. Under this arrangement, one of the three seats in such constituencies was likely to be won by a minority interest – as long as that minority amounted to at least one third of the local voters. To a substantial degree Mill's specific objective was achieved. Ironically, however, the minority clause in the 1867 Reform Act gave a substantial boost to an organisation which, in Ostrogorski's view, became a profound threat to liberty.

Democracy and the Rise of Big Business

The caucus in England

Like Tocqueville and Carnegie, Ostrogorski found Birmingham in the vanguard of political innovation. The minority clause was nullified by disciplined strategic voting directed by Liberal political managers: "'Vote as you are told" was the password' (Ostorgorski 1902a: 162). Coordination was organised through the Birmingham Liberal Association. In the early 1870s this body was run by men 'little inclined to philosophic doubt' who 'did not understand the scruples of a John Stuart Mill' (164). At the head of these men, Joseph Chamberlain became the Baron Haussman of Birmingham.

The 'sectarian . . . and . . . intolerant' spirit (194) of the 'Birmingham plan' (172) spread through the national Liberal party. So did its organisational techniques. Following the Liberal general election victory of 1880, the National Liberal Federation attempted to manipulate both public opinion and the political behaviour of Liberal MPs. The Conservative party copied this approach. Both parties built upon their substantial experience of local canvassing and close monitoring of local electoral registers.

The caucus as developed in Birmingham had a pyramidal organisation of elected and co-opted committees. It represented Liberals from all parts of the city. The one shilling fee was waived if necessary. In the early days, Chamberlain successfully persuaded 'the best men' to join the 'Six Hundred', as the total committee membership (of 594) were known. In this way 'They maintained uninterrupted relations with the masses by means of public assemblies, informal meetings, and personal communications on questions of general interest, and thus kept up a current of public spirit' (167).

In the longer term, the caucus nationally became a means by which the middle class could retain the position it had won in 1832 in spite of the further extension of the franchise in 1867:

> pretending to bow down before the masses, [the middle class] let them say what they liked, allowed them the satisfaction of holding forth and of voting extravagant resolutions in the caucuses, provided that it [i.e. the middle class] was allowed to manage everything; and to cover its designs it developed the practice of wire-pulling.
>
> (Ostrogorski 1902a: 581)

The middle class worked its will through the ward leaders – 'shop-keepers, clerks and superior artisans' (346) – who devoted themselves to the organisation. These small fry seized the chance to raise themselves socially through the caucus. Some even became town councillors or local magistrates. Bill Smith might become 'William Wellworth Smith, Esq.' (356). Ostrogorski balanced these comments by noting that English municipal administration was generally efficient and uncorrupt.

Ostrogorski emphasised the theatricality of political meetings. Just as churches lead their congregations in ritual observances, so 'the Caucus inculcates their duty on its members by, to use a more profane term, regular performances' ranging from extraordinary meetings on specific issues to 'fêtes and entertainments'. On all such occasions the main object for participants was not intellectual debate but 'to feel that they are a crowd, to lead each other on, to rouse and excite each other' (Ostorgorski 1902a: 354).

In the 1820s, Tocqueville had seen Birmingham as an English outpost of democracy based upon equality and liberty. Seven decades later, Ostrogorski identified this city as the immediate source of a corrupt democratic regime combining social snobbery and the cynical manipulation of public opinion. It was going the way of America.

The caucus in America

By the mid-1820s, Aaron Burr, Martin Van Buren and Andrew Jackson had emerged as leading figures in a local and national 'spoils' system. The strategy of the successful politician was to reward his friends and punish his enemies. By the 1840s the system of party conventions dominated by professional politicians was well established.

Most citizens neglected politics and concentrated upon their private concerns. Full-time mercenaries held the field. Lincoln himself became caught up in the spoils system. Following the civil war, political and economic life became more centralised. As has been seen, business empires such as Carnegie Steel were one outcome. Ostrogorski stressed another, the development of city political machines giving the professional politicians even tighter control. Presidents were weak. Some, like Ulysses S. Grant, headed scandalous administrations. Even Grover Cleveland could do little to stop the widespread corruption.

Machine politicians in the cities fought to get their hands on the public purse. They used patriotic rhetoric, fraud, ethnic appeals and respectable front men as means to win votes at election time. Politics was regarded by most citizens as a disreputable money-making exercise. Ostrogorski gave details of machines and 'rings' in many cities. He reported, for example, the comment of a Midwestern reformer in 1895:

> the city hall of Chicago [was] an asylum of party retainers, who live on the public revenues, control party management, and stand between the people and their government. It culminated in . . . a common council which was literally a den of thieves. Some three fourths of the members banded themselves together to plunder the public and blackmail corporations.
>
> (Smith 1896: 7; Ostrogorski 1902b: 175)

At the centre of the machine was the boss. Typically, he was self-made, usually Irish, perhaps an ex-waiter or one-time newspaper boy who had graduated to 'repeater' (fraudulent voter) and then precinct captain-cum-saloon keeper. He would have built up his own local machine and got himself elected to the city council, that 'promised land' of contracts, franchises and monopolies. Avoiding gaol (perhaps for homicide), such a man would strive to become 'the Caesar of the Machine and of the city' (Ostrogorski 1902b: 402).

The supreme talent of the boss was 'skill in the management of men. . . . To some he offers the solid food of places, of money and of pulls; to others the unsubstantial diet of promises' (403). Cool, calculating and taciturn in his political dealings, the boss would be full of homespun oratory on the public platform. However, his object was not to shape but to monitor public opinion as part of his pursuit of money and power. He was like a feudal lord managing a crowd of vassals. The crowd 'recognise in him a master spirit. . . . One would almost think that they are proud of their bosses' (407).

Private affluence, public apathy

Behind the American political machine were to be found the moneyed men. The machine 'smoothed the way for what is called plutocracy' (572). Machine politics permitted the trusts and corporations to win franchises and protective tarrifs from the public authorities. In fact, 'the Organization has served as a lever to all the great private interests in their designs on the public weal' (574).

This was done with impunity. The regime of the caucus in both England and America depended upon the withdrawal of much of the middle class from active and direct involvement in public affairs. Machine politics extinguished the spirit of the New England town meeting. Ostrogorski argued that in the United States the most common form of idealism was patriotism, a poor substitute for civic conscience. The closing of the frontier, the impact of immigration, materialism, the growing complexity of society and government, and increases in regulation: all added, directly or indirectly, to the power of the machine.

The growth of large towns in America, as in England, separated the masses from the influence of well-intentioned opponents of the machine, now dispersed to the suburbs. In England, the increase in socialist agitation towards the end of the century made it uncomfortable for better-off people to take an active part in politics. The agitation was not strong enough to make them feel they had to be involved directly in order to protect their interests. In the case of America, Ostrogorski confirmed Carnegie's view that most people thought that the pursuit of private material advancement was the best expression of true freedom under a perfect constitution.

A possible cure

Political parties filled a gap in modern democracies by taking over the task of organising the electorate. In doing so they undermined the individual citizen's independence, energy and autonomy in public life. The parties perverted the operation of public opinion. Instead of being a legitimate mode of 'social intimidation' (Ostorgorski 1902b: 626) exercised by citizens against each other and their government, public opinion was taken over and processed by party bosses for their own purposes.

Ostrogorski deplored the 'fatalism of the multitude' (631) – a concept borrowed from Bryce (1894b: 344) – by which he meant an extreme aversion to being out of line with the majority. In Ostrogorski's view, Tocqueville failed to grasp the full significance of the omnipotence of the majority; in particular, 'the consequences which it may entail for the working of the political order' (Ostrogorski 1902b: 634). Specifically, the dominance of permanent political parties encouraged 'cowardice' (635) among rulers and ruled.

For example, 'It keeps the force of public opinion in the condition of brute force' and prevents the expression 'of manifold and divers opinions which can hold one another in check and evolve a moral force capable of quelling or intimidating brute force' (636). The 'political formalism' of party organisation also prevented the free emergence of an elite based upon 'the natural inequality of brains and character'. Democracy needed such 'guides' (640), prepared to show their fellows how to exercise moral liberty and decide each public issue for him or herself without fear of majority opinion.

Ostrogorski recommended two remedies for the degrading influence of party government, especially in the more desperate case of America. One was 'the improvement of . . . general culture'. In other words, education. At this point, his views are broadly similar to those of his contemporary, John Dewey. Ostrogorski insisted that the task of the universities in a democracy was 'not so much to reproduce their own species, as to make men and citizens' (601).

His other remedy was 'the improvement of . . . political methods' (601). Ostrogorski favoured 'decentralization of the power of opinion' (663), partly by an autonomous provincial press, partly by a multitude of political organisations with overlapping memberships focused upon several specific issues. Ostrogorski called this a 'league system' (689). Citizens would not have to be on the same side on every question, following a party line. This would mean the end of 'permanent parties with power as their end' (658). A better model for public life was provided by the reform leagues, civic federations and committees of one hundred springing up to campaign for specific reforms in American cities.

Ostrogorski argued that this form of political organisation should be supplemented by proportional representation and 'preliminary pollings' (Ostorgorski 1902b: 709), by which he meant initial tests of electoral preference which would guide citizens when casting their votes. Finally, the existing party system should be abolished inside the national legislature, allowing members genuine independence. Above all, the civic mind of the individual should be given free expression.

Strikingly absent is any real consideration of the need for a complex democracy to have a thoroughly competent bureaucracy. The preparation of legislation was to be the task of standing committees chosen from the legislature. They would include 'champions of every different view' (723). These champions would have the backing of the campaign organisations within the league system. One can imagine the comments of an old India hand like Mill on this proposal.

In view of his sharp words upon the part played by Mill's writings in legitimising the corrosive force of individualism, Ostrogorski was sensitive to the suggestion that he was reproducing utilitarian ideas. In an appendix on 'the power of social intimidation as a principle of social life' he insisted that resemblances to 'the doctrines of the English utilitarians . . . are superficial and illusory' (752).

The utilitarians believed in 'the identification of private interest with public interest'. By contrast, he wished 'to subordinate the former to the latter' through the use of a variety of social sanctions. Ostrogorski did not rely like Mill on 'the association of ideas in the human mind. As a practical moralist, I know no human mind in the abstract. I know only human minds, some base, others mediocre, others noble' (753). Mill and he had both found a way from selfishness to disinterestedness. However, he twitted Mill for being 'obliged to make dialectical, not to say sophistical jumps, whereas I proceed from one stage to another, slowly but surely' (754).

In the case of Tocqueville, Ostrogorski's sympathy was overt, as already seen. However, despite carefully distancing himself from Mill, Ostrogorski incorporated a number of ideas which demonstrate an acute sensitivity to the problems which haunted the latter. Four ideas in particular from Ostrogorski's work come into this category. First, the need to have a variety of opinions in vigorous contention within a democracy. Second, the insistence upon raising the level of political culture through education. Third, the view that brains and character should form the basis of social inequality. And fourth, support for proportional representation as a means of guaranteeing the representation of minorities.

The professional optimist

In his preface to *Democracy and the Organization of Political Parties*,

James Bryce felt 'bound to utter a note of mild dissent' from Ostrogorski's thesis. Bryce did not question the facts as presented, but he did not agree with the conclusions. In particular, Ostrogorski had exaggerated the part played by the caucus in England and failed to allow for 'healthy influences' correcting any ill effects it might have. More specifically, party organisation in England was in the hands of 'a different class of men' from the American wire-pullers. It was 'almost wholly free from the more sordid elements' (Bryce 1902: *xliii*).

Ostrogorski had made a valuable contribution. However, it was to 'the *pathology* of party government' (*xliv*; my italics). The forms of party organisation he examined were far removed from 'the democratic ideal of the intelligent independence of the individual voter' (*xliv–xlv*). England was nearer than America to this ideal. This was because the one legitimate form of party influence – 'an appeal to the intellect and conscience of the voters through speeches and literature' – was more common in the former society than the latter. It would become even more common with the support of party chiefs guided by a 'sense of public honour and duty' (*xlvi*).

Above all, however, 'it is public opinion which must keep the party organizations in check'. Ostrogorski had feared the parties were corrupting public opinion. Bryce argued that public opinion could cleanse the parties. These were the words of 'an optimist, almost a professional optimist', criticising a work which was, perhaps, 'overcharged with gloom' (*xlii–xliii*).

Ostrogorski thought party organisation was preventing the emergence of a natural elite who would guide their fellow citizens. Bryce believed such 'independent citizens' – truth-loving, moral, public-spirited – were already available: 'It is they who keep the parties in order by casting their weight, now on the side of one party, now on the other, according to their judgement of the merits of each.' Such people were present in force in England. In the United States, also, 'independent citizens' were 'more active and more sensible of their duty at this moment than they were thirty years ago' (*xlvii*). The clear implication was that Ostrogorski had got it wrong. England was not becoming more like America. In fact, the reverse was more likely to be true.

Bryce was a copper-bottomed Liberal, not given to intellectualising his doubts and fears. He was no armchair philosopher but a Victorian man of action. Education was important in his scheme of things – so he headed a royal commission on secondary education. Politics mattered – so he made his way into Gladstone's cabinet. Volcanoes were fascinating – so he spent a night or two on the edge of the great crater of Kilauea in Hawaii. America was interesting – so he became British Amabassador in Washington.

His response to moral and political puzzles was twofold. First, he collected information. As he wrote in *Modern Democracies*, 'It is Facts that are needed: Facts, Facts, Facts. When facts have been supplied, each of us can try to reason from them' (Bryce 1921a: 13). Second, he relied upon the love of truth supposedly inculcated by free institutions. This would yield the closest possible approximation to a good and workable solution for the relevant problem.

National character was a major determinant of this process. Bryce argued that 'A people through which good sense and self-control are widely diffused is itself the best legislator, as is seen in the history of Rome and in that of England'. National character and national institutions act upon each other. The best institutions are those which help 'men to goodwill, self-restraint, intelligent cooperation [and] form what we call a solid political character, temperate and law-abiding, preferring peaceful to violent means for the settlement of controversies' (11). In Bryce's hands the concept of 'people' does not mean 'all humankind' but a 'national population'.

Englishness was, in Bryce's view, the best guarantee of freedom. He wrote that

> The traditional love of liberty, the traditional sense of duty to the community, be it great or small, the traditional respect for law and wish for serious reforms by constitutional rather than violent means – these were the habits ingrained in the mind and will of Englishmen.
> (Bryce 1921a: 160; D. Smith 1986: 254–5)

When he wanted to compliment the Americans, he called them 'the English of America' (Bryce 1894a: 358).

Bryce was not very sympathetic to Tocqueville's treatment of democracy in America: 'Democratic government seems to me, with all deference to his high authority, a cause not so potent in the moral and social sphere as he deemed it' (4). In fact, Bryce thought the term 'democracy' had in recent years 'been loosely used to denote sometimes a state of society, sometimes a state of mind, sometimes a quality of manners'. Cutting through all these associations, variously 'attractive or repulsive, ethical or poetical or even religious', Bryce argued that 'Democracy really means nothing more or less than the rule of the whole people expressing their sovereign will by their votes' (1921a: *viii*). The practice of democracy in this sense would produce few benefits if the population lacked education and political maturity. He thought, for example, that the history of Latin America during the nineteenth century abundantly proved this point: 'Why confer free self-governing institutions on a people unfit to comprehend or use them?' (328).

The American commonwealth

Bryce's *The American Commonwealth* (1894a; 1894b) has become an institution rather like the Washington Monument: much admired, but rarely examined in detail. There are good reasons for this. Much of it is boring. With stupendous bad judgement, Bryce placed the most tedious subject matter – four hundred pages on the federal constitution – right at the beginning and left the most interesting – on the party system and public opinion – until the second volume. Bryce was evidently reluctant to compress his material. In fact, it grew, haphazardly, from one edition to the next. Just as states were added to the Union, so chapters were added to *The American Commonwealth*. Between 1888 and 1910 the length of the work increased from 1,400 to 1,700 pages.

The book presents a panoramic photograph, with the political system looming very large in the foreground. Bryce guides you amiably and sometimes tediously around the landscape, demonstrating vast knowledge about the things that come into view. There are frequent historical and comparative illusions, especially to England, France and the classical world, but the book does not present a systematic historical or comparative argument.

Bryce did not so much argue a thesis, as convey a mood. The very depth of his knowledge transmitted a feeling of great affection for America. He obviously loved it, warts and all. Furthermore, he believed that having gone through a bad patch, the country was on the way up in terms of its public life: 'the downward tendency observable since the end of the Civil War seems to have been arrested . . . . Good citizens are beginning to put their hands to the machinery of government' (Bryce 1894b: 75).

It would be impossible to reproduce the observations and arguments in their entirety. Bryce's treatment of party organisation broadly agreed with Ostrogorski's. Three other points relevant to the interplay between capitalism and democracy are also worth mentioning. First, Bryce had a relatively high opinion of the political judgement of ordinary working-class people: 'they have often been proved by the event to have been right and their so-called betters wrong' (251). English working-class support for the North in the American Civil War was one example mentioned. Bryce was sympathetic to experiments in direct legislation, especially in the United States, since 'The legislator can be ''got at'' . . . [but] the people cannot' (472). In his view, the late nineteenth century had been a period of 'immensely extended and popularized culture and enlightenment' (342). As a result, 'the tyranny of the majority is no longer a blemish on the American system' (343). It was important that Negroes and central European immigrants also be educated to a similar level of political sophistication.

Second, Bryce argued that the range of political skills required differed between England and America. Only two types of statesmen were needed in America. One was 'the parliamentary tactician' (229) who could handle his fellows in cabinet and in the representative chamber. The other was 'the leader of the masses' (Bryce 1894b: 230) who could arouse crowds with eloquence. Although these were needed in Europe, three other types were found there also. They were: first, the 'diplomatist with a wide outlook over the world's horizons'; second, the statesman with 'an aptitude for constructive legislation'; and third, 'the administrator who can manage a department with diligence and skill and economy'. These last three types were not required in America, since that society had very little foreign policy, no 'mistakes of the past to undo' and no large permanent civil service (229).

Third, Bryce betrayed a fascinating ambivalence when dealing with the large capitalists in America. They displayed no special political insight or moral elevation. Indeed, they were 'uninteresting . . . [and] intellectually barren outside the sphere of their business knowledge' (301). More candid than Carnegie, Bryce recognised that they used politics to defend their own interests. The heads of the railroad corporations impressed him: 'These railroad kings are . . . the greatest men . . . in America' (653). In fact, they illustrated a conspicuous tendency in American life whereby 'the principle of monarchy, banished from the field of government, creeps back again and asserts its strength in the scarcely less momentous contests of industry and finance' (654).

This obviously recalls Tocqueville's warning several decades before. However, Bryce was remarkably sanguine about this danger. There was little possibility of 'a new aristocracy of rich families, and therefore a new structure of society'. There was no sharp division between rich and poor. Average living standards were high. And 'the faith in equality and love of equality are too deeply implanted in every American breast to be rooted out by any economic changes' (865). It is during passages like this that the astringency of Ostrogorski's analysis is most missed.

Modern democracies

Bryce was, indeed, a professional optimist. His confidence in the virtue of Englishness and the good sense of Americans – 'no nation better understands its own business' (Bryce 1894a: 34) – was quite relentless. This confidence had to overcome some mighty onslaughts. For example, in 1893 his old Oxford friend Charles Pearson published *National Life and Character: A Forecast*. In this book Pearson argued that the progress of the white race was reaching its climax. Europeans could not easily spread beyond the temperate zones. The balance of power between white and non-white was likely to turn against the former. Once the physical expansion of the white race was stopped, their whole civilisation would be under threat.

A stationary society would develop bringing with it lower ideals, apathy, weakened character and acquiescence in a state-run society providing order and modest comfort. A further consequence would be that the 'inferior' non-white races would assert their independence, adopt European material civilisation and use its techniques unscrupulously and effectively against the whites. European labour markets would be flooded with non-white immigrants.

The argument of this fascinating book, a sort of modified 'frontier thesis', was apparently supported by the spread of socialist ideas within the labour movements of both Britain and the United States. Like many of his circle, Bryce was deeply impressed by the case made out in the book. He wrote to Pearson, 'Gloomy your forecast certainly is: but I know of nothing in Europe and not very much in America to make me think it too despondent' (quoted in Harvie 1976: 234). During the next quarter of a century a great deal happened to stir up these anxieties, including the collapse of the Chinese Empire, demands for self-government in India, the industrialisation of Japan, the First World War and, not least, the Russian Revolution.

It was against this background that Bryce, at the age of eighty-three, published the two hefty volumes of *Modern Democracies* (1921). New thoughts were perhaps not to be expected in such a work. In fact, parts of it are much more interesting than *The American Commonwealth*. Bryce's last book is an intriguing study of liberalism at the end of its tether.

Modern Democracies was based upon notes made by Bryce during travels in France, Switzerland, the United States, Canada, Australia and New Zealand before the First World War. These six cases were examined in some depth in the book. The case studies form a lengthy middle section of the work, preceded by some abstract observations on the nature of democracy and followed by some empirical generalisations about the present and future of this form of government. This third part is the most worthy of study, seven decades later.

Bryce found that with respect to domestic administration 'democracies have nothing to be ashamed of' (Bryce 1921b: 401). Furthermore, the goals of foreign policy were determined by democracies 'at least as wisely as [by] monarchies or oligarchies' (419). Study of their judiciaries yielded 'nothing to discredit democratic governments' (426). He favoured the extension of direct legislation (e.g. referenda) since it was 'unequalled as an instrument of practical instruction in politics' (477). Unfortunately, opportunities for direct participation in the preferred setting of small self-governing communities were greatly reduced because of the 'industrial and commercial forces which draw men together into larger aggregations' (489).

On the other side of the matter, legislatures were losing their 'sense of social responsibility' (371). They were plagued by filibustering, the splitting and multiplication of parties, the determined schemes of 'small sections which exercise a power disproportionate to their numbers' (Bryce 1921b: 383), and the tendency for members to act as mandated delegates rather than responsible representatives. All modern democracies faced the danger of allowing 'self-interest to grasp the machinery of government' and use it for 'ignoble ends'.

Propaganda was another threat, a result of 'the irresponsible power wielded by those who supply the people with the materials they need for judging men and measures' (505). These were serious concerns since they marked the point where 'the spirit of Faith in the people and the spirit of Liberty part company' (436). A majority might be subverted. Law and opinion were 'The two safeguards on which democracy must rely' (534). Their strength depended upon 'the character of each people' (435). Equally needed were 'more insight . . . sympathy . . . energy [and] patriotism' from 'the so-called upper and educated classes' (505).

Capitalist pressures made themselves felt strongly. 'Democracy has no more persistent or insidious foe than the money power.' Its corrupting influence was greater 'where authority is vested in the multitude' than in 'a well-organized bureaucracy' (533). Equally disturbing was 'Class War' (638) which fed on the feeling that democracy should be valued not for the opportunities it gave for uplifting participation in public business, but for the material benefits it provided. The outcome might be revolution:

> Strange and unexpected evolution! Democracy overthrows the despotism of one man or the few who ruled by force, in order to transfer power to the People who are to rule by reason and the sense of their common interest in one another's welfare; and after two or three generations there arises from the bosom of democracy an effort to overthrow it in turn by violence because it has failed to confer the expected benefits. The wheel has gone its full round; and the physical Force which was needed to establish democracy is now employed to destroy it.
>
> (Bryce 1921b: 639)

Communism would probably be run by 'an industrial bureaucratic oligarchy' (664). Under such a system the nation would be regarded as 'an economic whole, existing for the purposes of production and distribution'. By contrast, democracy regarded the nation as 'a Moral and Intellectual whole, created for the sake of what the ancient philosophers used to call the Good Life' (654). This latter concept was becoming less appealing as ordinary people felt increasingly secure in the economic fruits they had won by using their civil rights. Why keep up public meetings, elections and debates just for their educative value? Such a way of thinking did not necessarily lead to communism. But there were other undesirable fates on offer.

For example, popular apathy might deliver political power to 'an intelligent bureaucracy capable of giving business men the sort of administration and legislation they desire, and keeping the multitude in good humour by providing comfort and amusements' (Bryce 1921b: 663). The bureaucrats would not, 'if wise', change the constitution but free self-government would be nevertheless lost.

The 'physiological factor which we call Heredity' had to be considered also. The numerical superiority of the 'Backward races' need not be discouraging. Some of them, argued Bryce, were intellectually equal to the Europeans and might renew the energies of 'the advanced races whom luxury has enervated'. In any event, the fate of democracy depended upon the 'moral and intellectual progress of mankind as a whole' (665–6).

Conclusion

James Bryce and Moisei Ostrogorski both clearly saw historical tendencies at work which they did not like. These tendencies offended the liberal values they shared. Ostrogorski responded by offering an unrealistic prescription for producing a better future. It envisaged a system of multiple political groupings without taking into account the practicalities of *realpolitik*. Bryce viewed such a prospect with considerable disapproval. One of his complaints against modern democracy was its tendency to generate a multitude of minor parties any one of which might acquire an influence far beyond its numbers.

Ostrogorski's prescription, ironically enough in view of his overall pessimism, expected far too much of human nature. By contrast, Bryce, the 'professional optimist', offered not a prescription but a prognosis. This prognosis was, with equal irony, a generally gloomy one.

Democracy was under threat. Its essence, as far as Bryce was concerned, was the active participation of citizens in their government. This emphasis distinguished him from Tocqueville and Carnegie. Both the latter had used the word 'democracy' to mean social equality in terms of the market and legal rank. In contrast, Bryce meant by 'democracy', first and foremost, political liberty.

Historically, political liberty had been fought for as part of a battle against political and economic oppression. Unfortunately, the economic benefits of equality undermined the very basis of political liberty. This was because the foundation of a democracy was located, in Bryce's view, in the national character of the people concerned. Prosperity weakened character and hence undermined democracy itself.

The Nonconformist conscience of Bryce the Presbyterian brought him to the same conclusion as Tocqueville, though by a different route. Both believed that equality was liable to undermine liberty. As has been seen, Ostrogorski's argument led him down similar paths to Mill, though he perhaps wished to disguise the fact.

Chapter five

Veblen and Hobson

Two economic heretics

The rise of the large-scale industrialist within capitalist democracies was closely related to the emergence of more powerful central government bureaucracies. Thorstein Veblen and John Hobson both agreed that the key relationships were those between big business, the state and the people. Hobson argued that with support from the state, democratic forms could be strengthened in a way which would humanise capitalism. Veblen had a different view. In his opinion, the only hope was that capitalism would destroy itself and at the same time make the existing state redundant. Democracy would arise from the ashes.

John Dos Passos was an admirer of Veblen:

At Carleton College young Veblen was considered a brilliant unsound eccentric; nobody could understand why a boy of such attainments wouldn't settle down to the business of the day, which was to buttress property and profits with anything usable in the debris of Christian ethics and eighteenth century economics that cluttered the minds of college professors, and to reinforce the sacred, already shaky edifice with the new strong girderwork of science Herbert Spencer was throwing up for the benefit of the bosses.

People complained they never knew whether Veblen was joking or serious . . . .

Even in Chicago as the brilliant young economist he lived pioneer fashion. [The valley farmers had always been scornful of outlanders' ways.] He kept his books in packing cases laid on their sides along the walls. His only extravagances were the Russian cigarettes he smoked and the red sash he sometimes sported. He was a man without small talk. When he lectured he put his cheek on his hand and mumbled out his long spiral sentences, reiterative like the eddas. His language was a mixture of mechanics' terms, scientific latinity, slang and Roget's Thesaurus. The other profs couldn't imagine why the girls fell for him so.

(Dos Passos 1933: 97–100)

Thorstein Veblen was born in 1857 into a prosperous farming family which held a prominent position in Manitowoc County, Wisconsin. His parents had emigrated to the United States from Norway ten years previously. A precocious lad, his way of settling a dispute with a neighbour over a dog was to write 'anathemas in Greek on the neighbor's fence' (Veblen 1931: 192).

As an adult, he combined 'impenetrable personal reserve' with contempt for convention. Dr Veblen never used his title. Once, during an ocean voyage, a fellow passenger discovered his status and asked him what sort of a doctor he was: 'Well', he replied gravely, 'I am a horse doctor, but I would rather you wouldn't mention it, as I don't want it known' (193). The passion and acuteness of Veblen's critique of capitalism often recalled Karl Marx. In style, he sometimes anticipated Groucho.

Veblen arrived at the University of Chicago in 1891 and was appointed to a fellowship in economics the following year. He stayed in Chicago for fourteen years, his longest period of continuous academic employment. His free and easy disregard of convention regarding relations with women eventually made it difficult for him to stay there. He subsequently held posts for short periods of time at Stanford University, the University of Missouri and the New School for Social Research in New York.

During the First World War Veblen wrote some reports for the Food Administration and for President Wilson's inquiry (co-ordinated by Walter Lippman) into the terms of a possible peace settlement. In 1918 he began to write for *Dial*, a New York journal. His readers appreciated his critique of Wilsonian policies and his enthusiasm for the Bolshevik Revolution. However, Veblen and his readers soon lost interest in each other.

Despite these professional involvements, for most of his adult life Veblen with his 'wrinkles, . . . vandyke beard and yellow teeth' (Dos Passos 1933: 101) was a bit of a gypsy, something of a hermit, living in cellars and shacks. The result of these isolated months and years was a formidable collection of works: eleven books and over one hundred and fifty articles and reviews.

In *The Big Money*, published in 1933, four years after Veblen's death, John Dos Passos summarised, in his own distinctive prose, Veblen's intellectual legacy:

> he established a new diagram of a society dominated
> by monopoly capital,
>   etched in irony
>   the sabotage of production by business,
>   the sabotage of life by blind need for money
> profits,
>   pointed out the alternatives: a warlike society strangled by

the bureaucracies of the monopolies forced by the law of diminishing returns to grind down more and more the common man for profits, or a new matter of fact commonsense society dominated by the needs of the men and women who did the work and the incredibly vast possibilities for peace and plenty offered by the progress of technology.

(Dos Passos 1933: 101–2)

John Hobson was born a year later than Veblen, and survived until 1940. During his life he published even more than Veblen: over forty books – including a sympathetic study of Veblen (Hobson 1936) – and roughly the same number of articles, chapters, reviews and pamphlets. This remarkable productivity was in spite of (or, perhaps, because of) the fact that Hobson never became entrenched within the academic world, even to the small extent achieved by Veblen.

On the face of it, Hobson had a more promising start for a budding academic. He was born in Derby 'in the middle stratum of the middle class of a middle-sized industrial town in the Midlands' (Hobson 1938a: 15) Derby was Herbert Spencer's home town also. In fact, the young Hobson often used to meet Spencer walking into town with a local bank manager. Hobson knew the bank manager slightly but never exchanged a word with Spencer.

Hobson's father, who ran the local Liberal newspaper, sent him to Derby Grammar School and then on to Oxford. After leaving university with a disappointing lower second, Hobson tried a bit of sub-editing back in Derby, and then some schoolmastering in Faversham and Exeter. In 1887 he moved to London and got a job as a university extension lecturer. Two years later he published, jointly with A.F. Mummery – 'a business man [and] . . . great mountaineer' (30) – a book entitled *The Physiology of Industry* (1889). The authors argued that saving was not, as the classical economists had assumed, a key to national prosperity. On the contrary, excessive thrift was a major cause of the underemployment of labour and capital.

This line of argument was quite inconsistent with the tenets of political economy. The latter assumed capitalist production depended upon 'a constantly increasing provision of new capital and, therefore, . . . the willingness of an increasing number of persons to save and invest income which they might have spent in raising their standard of comfort and luxury'. By arguing that saving was not a virtue, Mumford and Hobson 'contravened the one claim which political economy had to ethical respectability' (32).

Hobson's punishment followed swiftly. He was barred from teaching economics by the London Extension Board. An invitation to give a series of lectures on economic subjects for the Charity Organisation Society was suddenly withdrawn. Hobson had become an economic heretic. In the long run, one compensation for this miserable treatment by the establishment was that John Maynard Keynes later acknowledged the publication of the offending book as marking 'an epoch in economic thought' (Keynes 1973: 365). Although Hobson was offered posts in America, he never returned to academia. Like Veblen, he developed a dislike of the university world and an abiding interest in the sociology of knowledge.

Hobson married the daughter of a wealthy New Jersey lawyer, which must have helped financially. He also enjoyed some inherited wealth. As an independent writer, he became a central figure in the conflict-ridden circles of the New Liberals. Around the turn of the century men such as L.T. Hobhouse, Herbert Samuel, Graham Wallas and Ramsay MacDonald were trying to come to terms with the inadequacies of Manchester School economics and the increasing significance of collectivist politics. Hobson contributed to this work, not least as a member of the staff of the *Nation*, a journal he joined in 1907. A colleague, H.N. Brailsford, later described him in this period:

> Rather older than most of us around the table, Hobson looked the student he was, sparely and slightly built, rather tall and in his later years very frail . . . . When he spoke . . . it was usually to give a new turn to the discussion, often a rather startling and original turn. He generally spoke as he wrote, soberly weighing his words, but he would express himself at times with a blunt violence that was not wholly humorous. Under the balanced, objective manner of his books . . . there burned strong and deep feelings. What I recall most vividly of his part in our talks was the brilliance of his wit. We always knew when something good was coming. He raised his right eyebrow, and paused to indulge in a peculiar stammer, which one rarely noticed at other times, while he was giving his epigram the neatest possible shape. He had a formidable gift for irony and satire.
>
> (Brailsford 1948: 4)

Hobson and Veblen have evident similarities. The manners and ideas of each created a distance between the man and the society to which he belonged. They were as much rejecting as rejected. Veblen laughed off his doctorate. Hobson refused a peerage from Ramsay MacDonald in 1931. Each man used the distance created as a protective shield behind which he could cast a new model of capitalist democracy.

Reconstructing economic man

The hedonistic conception of man is like a homogeneous globule of desire of happiness under the impulse of stimuli that shift him about the area but leave him intact. He is neither antecedent or consequent. He is an isolated, definitive human datum, in stable equilibrium except for the buffets of the impinging forces that displace him in one direction or another. Self-imposed in elemental space, he spins symmetrically about his own spiritual axis until the parallelogram of forces bears down upon him, whereupon he follows the line of the resultant.

(Veblen 1963: 52)

Veblen rejected utilitarian psychology and the ahistorical models of classical political economy. He adopted a view of human nature similar to the pragmatists': in his view, a human being was 'a coherent structure of propensities and habits which seeks realisation and expression in an unfolding activity' (52). Desires and inclinations were, in fact, a complex product of heredity, experience, tradition, convention and material possibilities.

Human habits and desires were aspects of an unfolding historical process. In the course of this process the economic interest shaped and was, to some extent, shaped by other human interests: 'aesthetic, sexual, humanitarian, devotional'. Veblen was keen to develop 'an evolutionary economics' based upon 'the theory of cultural growth as determined by the economic interest' (54–5).

Veblen was much closer to John Dewey than he was to Jeremy Bentham. However, he was not prepared to emulate Dewey's faith in professionals and educators as guardians of democratic values within an unequal society. Such guardians were liable to be subverted by the pecuniary interests and values of the business class. By contrast, Veblen believed the interests of democratic communities would be best served by the strong communal orientations and matter-of-fact scientific attitudes of skilled operatives at the heart of the new industrial order (see Smith 1988: 65–73).

Similarly, Veblen was much closer to Herbert Spencer than he was to Adam Smith. But, unlike Spencer, he did not believe that the waste and misery generated by competition were inevitable by-products of evolution. On the contrary, industrial evolution was changing mental habits and getting people used to thinking in terms of scientific fact and causal sequence. Armed with a more rational disposition, human communities would be able to reduce waste and misery.

Veblen was merciless in his attacks upon conventional economic and political morality, especially in America. The natural rights theory of property based upon the owner's input of labour was an outmoded relic of the handicraft era. Public opinion, shaped by the prejudices of small-town shopkeepers, continued to reflect this theory. In one of his last books, written after the First World War, Veblen commented that 'The retail trade, and therefore in its degree the country town, have been the home ground of American culture and the actuating center of public affairs and public sentiment throughout the nineteenth century'. (1923: 151)

The post-war world was different. Veblen noted:

> it is now recognised, or at least acted on, that the salvation of twentieth-century democracy is best to be worked out by making the world safe for Big Business and then let Big Business take care of the interests of the retail trade and the country town, and much else.
>
> (Veblen 1923: 151–2)

Democracy was a sham. Writing in *Dial* immediately after the war, Veblen described 'democratic sovereignty' as 'a cloth to cover the nakedness of a government which does business for the kept classes' by consistently maintaining 'the rights of ownership and investment' (1969: 125).

The most convenient way to indicate the wide range of Veblen's critique of modern capitalism is to focus upon two of his books which encompass his views on culture, economics and the political sphere. They are *The Theory of the Leisure Class* (1970) and *The Theory of Business Enterprise* (1965).

Both these books were written during Veblen's long stay in Chicago. The first originally appeared in 1899, the second in 1904. It is likely that conditions in that rapidly growing industrial metropolis provided a large part of Veblen's background evidence. Chicago was the scene of dramatic demonstrations in favour of both labour and capital. It witnessed experiments in civilising both the masses and their masters. The Haymarket outrage in 1886, during a strike at the McCormick works, had strengthened middle-class anxieties about violence in the labour movement. The Columbian Exposition or World Fair seven years later had, by contrast, asserted the organising capacity and material power of American big business. The centrepiece was a magnificent fountain representing the Goddess of Liberty on a splendid vessel steered by Father Time.

Shortly afterwards, the Nonconformist conscience pulled off a wonderful *coup de théâtre* with the publication of William T. Stead's magnificent broadside *If Christ Came to Chicago!* (1894). Stead mixed his fire and brimstone with tables giving sensational details of the highly respectable Chicago landlords who drew rent from the city's multitudinous whore houses, gambling joints and other resorts of low entertainment. The very same year the town of Pullman, just south of Chicago, famous for the heavy-handed paternalism of its master George Pullman, was riven by a bitter strike as the residents joined a national stoppage against their landlord and employer. This was hardly the outcome that Carnegie had predicted for the carefully-costed benevolence of his business associate and friend, the railroad coach-maker.

Meanwhile, a vast army of men were busy disassembling a never-ending parade of livestock at Chicago's stockyards. Not too far away, Jane Addams and the well-born ladies at Hull House on Halstead Street offered elevating sociability, practical advice and intellectual sustenance to the surrounding ethnic communities.

The rewards of making it in Chicago were huge. At the centre of society around the turn of the century was Mrs Potter Palmer, the wife of a success-ful real estate developer. The entrance hall of her lake-side mansion was three storeys high, its walls covered with marble mosaic and tapestries. From this hall, you could step into a French drawing room, a Spanish music room, an English dining room, a Moorish corridor or a Japanese parlour. The mistress of this sumptuous palace slept in a Louis XVI bed ten feet high.

Mrs Palmer had imitators and rivals. Her eventual successor as queen bee was Mrs Harold McCormick, born Edith Rockefeller. Emmett Dedmon described the McCormick life style:

> Mrs McCormick carried out her social program in a regal manner; no queen or ruler of a court could have been more rigid in attention to protocol. Even her children, when they were grown, could see her only by appointment . . . . Her large household staff included a first and second butler, two parlor maids, a coachman, footman, houseman and six detectives. Her personal maid had a helper, a sewing woman, who in turn had an assistant . . . . Mrs McCormick allowed herself to speak to only two servants – the chief steward and her personal secretary. Through these she ruled her entire household.
>
> (Dedmon 1953: 303)

Veblen emphasised the high level of theatricality and display in the domestic and social activity of rich American business families. The expectation of performance in this sense was, in his view, focused upon the private sphere, rather than upon the public sphere as in Britain.

The theory of the leisure class

In Veblen's view, the ways of thinking characteristic of business in his day were the product of previous historical stages. During the barbarian epoch of medieval feudalism the institution of property came into existence. Predatory warriors acquired property by, quite simply, taking it and making it their own. One typical form of property acquired by seizure was women. The institution of marriage had its roots in this practice. Possession of property was regarded as an indication of successful exploits and of superior prowess. Property ownership was a sign of masculine aggressiveness and a mark of social status.

The ideology of natural rights which developed in the early modern era of domestic industry – and which still figured in the speeches of contemporary business people – presented a misleading picture of the cultural dynamics of property as a social institution. Property in modern America was still strongly marked with the barbarian heritage. The prestige flowing from property was undermined if the owner appeared to be engaged in any form of useful toil. Self-respecting predatory warriors (or business men) would not be caught 'mixing their labour' with the soil or its industrial equivalent.

The barbarian culture of the business class was a competitive one, organised around conspicuous consumption, including highly visible leisure activities. Pecuniary emulation between individuals was preferred to communal co-operation. Deliberately wasting money and time, the leisure class of large property owners distorted or repressed in themselves an even more basic human trait, one whose historical origins lay in a savage (in the sense of primitive) era before the feudal period. This was the 'instinct of workmanship' (Veblen 1970: 75), in other words the inclination to engage in purposeful activity for the benefit of the whole community. This had predominated in the peaceful neolithic age and was being reinvigorated, in Veblen's view, by the complex machine technology of modern industry. Skilled engineers were developing scientific habits of thought organised in terms of impersonal material causes and effects. Their natural disposition was to use the power of technology for the good of all.

The culture of the leisure class was expressed in the forms of contemporary sport and religion. Higher education provided both to the leisure class. College athletics developed 'truculence and clannishness' (175) as well as an inclination to 'Chicanery, falsehood . . . [and] browbeating' (181). The academic, like the priest, existed in order to enjoy leisure on behalf of the leisure class. The latter were not able to display unaided the capacity for leisure which their station in life commanded. They had to employ others to be leisured on their behalf. Within the home, a man's wife and servants carried out a similar function.

The norms of taste reflected this adoration of the useless and artificial, whether in the form of cast-iron rustic fences, debilitating female forms of dress or, on a grander scale, Chicago's Columbian Exposition. According to Veblen, the ostentatious classicism of the world fair demonstrated that 'The sense of beauty in the population of this representative city of the advanced pecuniary culture is very chary of any departure from its great cultural principles of conspicuous waste' (101).

Impressive as Chicago's pecuniary culture was, the leisure class in America remained in its infancy, compared to its counterpart in Britain. Veblen treated the United States as 'essentially a mature colony, a branch of the British colonial system and of British culture' (Dorfman 1970: 352).

As Veblen put it in *Imperial Germany and the Industrial Revolution*, 'The development of the perfect gentleman (and of the perfect gentlewoman) in any given case takes time.' These institutions were 'a complex affair of usages, distinctions, cultivated tastes, worked out under the general surveillance of the principle of conspicuous waste'.

Specifically, the gentleman and gentlewoman should not in any way be useful. They should certainly not contribute to anyone else's 'physical well-being . . . or . . . pecuniary gain'. By these standards, England was a magnificent success:

> the English community has grown slowly and symmetrically to the highest and most substantial maturity attained by the pecuniary culture within the bounds of Christendom. The other English-speaking peoples have been doing well, but they have come into their heritage too late to have worked out this knotty problem of how to dispose of their disposable margin of goods and energies without leaving a materially serviceable residue.
>
> (Veblen 1964: 140–1)

In *The Theory of the Leisure Class*, Veblen noted two movements in American life which counteracted pecuniary culture. One was the feminist movement arising in the domestic heartland of the leisure class. Upper-class women were more protected than their menfolk from the full blast of pecuniary culture. Within their ranks some were beginning to think that existing arrangements were mistaken. They were demanding emancipation and work. The other contradictory force was the resurgence of the spirit of workmanship among the industrial vanguard of scientists and engineers. Their field of action was the business enterprise to which we now turn.

The theory of business enterprise

The argument of *The Theory of Business Enterprise* (1965) turns around two distinctions. The primary distinction is between the economic, cultural and political tendencies associated with, respectively, business enterprise and the machine process. A secondary distinction is made between the standards of economic behaviour in the age of domestic industry and handicrafts and those in operation at the time Veblen was writing. It is convenient to begin by briefly considering the latter distinction.

In the old days, the producer and the customer had close personal contact. Craftsmen were careful of their reputation for workmanship. The 'adage that "Honesty is the best policy" seems on the whole to have been accepted and to have been true' (Veblen 1965: 52). In more recent times,

personal contact with customers had been minimised. Misleading advertising and widespread profiteering had become normal: 'Business
management has a chance to proceed on a temperate and sagacious
calculation of profit and loss, untroubled by sentimental considerations
of human kindness or irritation or of honesty' (Veblen 1965: 53).

The purposes underlying economic life had changed:

> Under the old order, industry, and even such trade as there was, was
> a quest for livelihood; under the new order industry is directed by
> the quest for profits. Formerly, therefore, times were good or bad
> according as the industrial processes yielded a sufficient or an
> insufficient output of the means of life. Latterly, times are good or
> bad according as the process of business yields an adequate or
> inadequate rate of profits. The controlling end is different in the pre-
> sent. . . . Prosperity now means, primarily, business prosperity;
> whereas it used to mean industrial sufficiency.
>
> (Veblen 1965: 178)

The distinction between industrial processes and business operations
was central to Veblen's analysis of modern capitalism. The former was
based upon the operation of machinery and relied upon 'a reasoned
procedure on the basis of a systematic knowledge of the forces employed'
(6). The mechanical basis of modern industry was complex. Complementary processes and sectors interlocked closely. The system depended upon
the constant 'running maintenance of interstitial adjustments between the
several sub-processes or branches of industry' and 'unremitting . . . quantitative precision' (8) with respect to materials and machinery. The
pressures for uniformity and standardisation were great. They extended
from the mechanical operations themselves to the producers and consumers of industrial goods.

The task of regulating this system fell upon those who conducted
business transactions: 'It is at this point that the business man comes
into the industrial process as a decisive factor' (18). However, the transactions of such men were carried on 'for business ends, not for industrial
ends' (27). Their whole object was pecuniary gain. Ironically, these gains
were greatest when there were large and frequent disturbances of the
industrial system. The business man's special skill consisted not in the
efficient management of a particular industrial process but in 'an alert
redistribution of investments from less to more gainful ventures, and
. . . a strategic control of the conjunctures of business through shrewd
investments and coalitions with other business men' (24–5). Such people
had a vested interest in sabotaging the smooth running of industry (see
Veblen 1919).

Business operations consisted to a great extent of struggles between
rival groups of business men using the weapon of 'pecuniary coercion'.

Typically, such operations involved 'a derangement, more or less extensively, of the industrial system at large' (Veblen 1965: 32). The exigencies of business prevented the potential benefits of technological advance from being realised. The plutocrats were too busy putting each other out of business and establishing large combinations run by fewer and fewer bosses. Veblen pointedly remarked that

> probably the largest, assuredly the securest and most unquestionable service rendered by the great captains of industry is . . . this sweeping retirement of business men as a class from the service and the definitive cancelment of the opportunities for private enterprise.
>
> (Veblen 1965: 48)

This process was far from complete. In the meantime, the community as a whole was subsidising, in the form of high prices, the enormous costs of competitive selling. For example, advertising was an expensive input intended to create 'vendibility' (59) – rather than usefulness to the consumer. In order to conduct his strategies, the business man created a mountain of credit on the basis of 'good-will'. For example, 'The "good-will" of Mr Carnegie and his lieutenants, as well as of many other large business men connected with the steel industry, has also no doubt gone to swell the capitalization of [the United States Steel Corporation]' (172–3).

Borrowed funds eliminated the need to wait until existing capital had been turned over, but they did not represent or bring about any increase in industrial capacity. In fact, they created a large gap between the true value represented by industrial equipment and the fictitious value expressed by credit ratings. The pressure of interest payments stimulated further borrowing. When the gap became too wide, credit was withdrawn, companies were revalued downward and liquidation often ensued.

Capital in business corporations was an object of trade. Ownership and management were, as a consequence, widely separated. The links made by Adam Smith between the enterprise of the business man, the efficiency of industry and the good of the community no longer applied. The business man could end up rich while the corporation he had invested in went into liquidation. The community bore the expenses of his wheeler-dealing and suffered the ensuing loss of industrial production.

Two powerful movements were undermining the dominance of business enterprise. One, already briefly mentioned, was the cultural impact of machine technology. Unlike Tocqueville, Mill, Bryce and Ostrogorski, Veblen believed that the advance of industrialism had a positive civilising effect. It cleared the mind of myth. It raised intellectual and moral standards. Not through the mediation of successful entrepreneurs (in spite of what Carnegie thought), but directly through machinery's matter-of-fact character. This left little room in the minds of its operatives for the conventional falsehoods of business men.

The industrial working class was decreasingly influenced by the false notion of property based upon natural rights. Individual property ownership had little hold on the mind of a workman who had to be geographically mobile to meet the demands of industry. It was pointless to settle down in his own house. In any case, thrift was a useless exercise in his condition of life. His trade union resisted the pecuniary coercion exercised by bosses in the name of property rights. Socialistic notions were becoming appealing. More generally, 'the cultural growth dominated by the machine industry is of a sceptical, matter-of-fact complexion, materialistic, unmoral, unpatriotic, undevout' (Veblen 1965: 372).

Another powerful movement ran in the opposite direction. It drew its strength from the entrenched position of business within the polity: 'Representative government means, chiefly, representation of business interests' (286). Popular acceptance of the principles of property and patriotism was under threat in ways already noticed. Nevertheless, by a 'happy knack of clannish fancy' the 'common man' still felt he had 'some sort of metaphysical share in the gains which accrue to the business men who are citizens of the same "commonwealth"' (289). Perhaps the use of that particular term was a quiet dig at Bryce's *The American Commonwealth*, which had gone through several reprints in the decade before *The Theory of Business Enterprise* appeared.

In any case, the beneficiaries of business enterprise still had powerful cultural and political resources upon which to draw. They defended their interests through the medium of political parties. Veblen went further than Ostrogorski. He did not just argue that business interests used political parties intermittently to achieve specific favours. According to Veblen, business interests organised the parties as a permanent means of ensuring favourable government policies:

> The business interests domiciled within the scope of a given government fall into a loose organization in the form of what might be called a tacit ring or syndicate, proceeding on a general understanding that they will stand together as against outside business interests. The nearest approach to an explicit plan and organization of such a business ring is the modern political party, with its platform, tacit and avowed. . . . The ring of business interests which secures the broadest approval from popular sentiment is, under constitutional methods, put in charge of the government establishment.
>
> (Veblen 1965: 294)

Since the 1870s, capitalists had confronted a serious problem of ' "Overproduction" or "underconsumption" ' (214). Many businesses had become over-capitalised relative to their profit-earning capacity. A major culprit was 'the advancing efficiency and articulation of the processes of the machine industry' (Veblen 1965: 254). One response had been the development of pools and trusts to regulate price and inhibit cut-throat competition. Another response had been imperialism. For example, in the early twentieth century 'it was the Spanish–American War, coupled with the expenditure for stores, munitions, and services incident to placing the country on a war footing, that lifted the depression and brought prosperity to the business community' (251).

The 'current policy of war and armaments' was an 'extreme expression of business politics' (292), one which shifted pecuniary competition to the international sphere. International policy was directed at advancing 'the frontiers of pecuniary culture among the backward populations. There is commonly a handsome margin of profit.' Since these peoples 'do not willingly enter into lasting business relations with civilized mankind', armaments were needed to make trade lucrative (295).

There was a clear danger that resources would be drawn away from industry into war, leaving nations ruined by 'a policy of emulative exhaustion' (299). In fact, imperial policies were likely to be justified increasingly in terms of dynastic goals. Furthermore, it was quite possible that dynastic considerations, or the pride of governments, might take the leading part. Business interests might become a means rather than an end.

In fact, there was no escape. One way or another, business enterprise was doomed. It would be cast down at the hands of an insurgent scientific machine culture, oriented to the needs of the community and heedless of private property. Or it would succumb to a resurgent old regime of 'status, fealty, prerogative, and arbitrary command' enforced by 'a militant, coercive home administration' (398–9).

Veblen's discussion of imperialism and underconsumption drew straight from and explicitly upon John A. Hobson's recently-published work. It is time to examine this work directly.

The need for a new liberalism

Hobson regarded Veblen as 'essentially a powerful exploratory thinker' who was able 'to discover and reveal the structure of modern society and some of its operative tendencies more truthfully than any other thinker of his age' (Hobson 1936: 22). Although it is unlikely that they ever met, the two writers did exchange letters. Hobson's visits to the United States gave him first-hand experience of that society's distinctive 'blend of ruthless competition and equally ruthless monopoly'.

Democracy and capitalism were at the centre of Hobson's concerns. He acknowledged the 'clear and comprehensive exposure of the corruption of democratic institutions in American states and cities . . . given by Ostrogorski'. However, he believed that in England 'the play of social–economic forces is more obscure and more impeded by traditional and humane considerations' (Hobson 1938a: 68). Hobson's intellectual objective was to provide a theoretical means whereby the 'humane' could slip free of the 'traditional'.

Hobson wanted to bring in the state to tame the excesses of capitalism and strengthen the basis of collective and public life. Individual development would then be possible in the context of an intelligent and caring democracy. Ironically, this programme has some superficial resemblances to the 'municipal socialism' of Joseph Chamberlain. Ironic, because around the turn of the century Chamberlain became the major political spokesman for the policy of imperialism. Hobson made his name by a series of whole-hearted attacks upon this policy, especially during the Boer War in South Africa. At the time of this war, Chamberlain was Colonial Secretary in the Conservative government.

Imperialism

Chamberlain's overall strategy of imperialism was neatly expressed in a speech he made in 1895:

> I regard many of our colonies as being in the position of undeveloped estates, and estates which can never be fully developed without Imperial assistance. . . . It is only in such a policy of development that I can see any solution of those great social problems by which we are surrounded. Plenty of employment and a contented people go together, and there is no way of securing plenty of employment except by creating new markets and developing the old ones. . . . If the people of this country are not willing to invest some of their surplus wealth in the development of their great estate, then I see no future for those countries, and it would have been better never to have gone there.
>
> (Quoted in Garvin 1934: 19–20)

Chamberlain's promotion of colonial development as a means of achieving social betterment recalled his enthusiasm for property development in central Birmingham on similar grounds. In both cases, opponents complained that the supposed beneficiaries of his policies – the slum dwellers of inner Birmingham in one case, the British working class and the native population in the other – were, in fact, the victims. Slum dwellers were not rehoused by the city when their homes were demolished. Imperialism, Hobson argued, inhibited social reform at home and encouraged despotic policies on the part of business and government.

Few politicians were more implicated in the politics of the Boer War (1899–1902) than Joseph Chamberlain. In 1899 Hobson went to South Africa for several months on behalf of the *Manchester Guardian*. He examined the tensions that developed between the Boers and the British inhabitants, following the discovery of gold in the Transvaal. Hobson interviewed a wide range of key politicians and business people, including Cecil Rhodes and General Smuts. In Hobson's view, the Boer War was the result of a conspiracy organised by financiers with capital tied up in the gold mines.

Imperialism: A Study (1938b) first appeared in 1902, a revised edition following three years later. The material on South Africa was woven into a more general argument based upon the mechanism of oversaving – in other words, overinvestment or underconsumption – that had originally got him into trouble with the academic establishment fifteen years before. Lenin later drew upon Hobson's work in his own *Imperialism. The Highest Stage of Capitalism* (1964a). To have been praised by both Lenin and Keynes is no mean recommendation.

Hobson argued that since 1870 British overseas expansion had undergone a transition. Before this date, colonialism had involved white migration to sparsely populated territories. Full British citizenship was enjoyed by settlers who, in some cases (e.g. Australia) set up a separate nation. After this date, a new imperialism appeared, especially in Africa and Asia. Britain, France, Germany and other advanced societies competed to establish control over new territories in these continents. In these territories, the white settlers were a small but dominant minority. The oppressed native majority, forced to work for foreign business interests, were 'too foreign to be absorbed and too compact to be crushed' (11). Injustice and hostility were the outcome.

According to Hobson's calculations, one third of British imperial territory and a quarter of its population were acquired during the last three decades of the nineteenth century. The new acquisitions brought few trading opportunities to Britain. They were not to be explained by the need to find outlets for the British population. Its rate of increase was apparently tending to fall. Equally unconvincing was the suggestion that military and diplomatic competition between nations for imperial territories was a means of maintaining national vigour and ensuring 'social efficiency' (155). This form of Social Darwinism, encouraged by, for example, Benjamin Kidd (1894), turned might into right. In Hobson's view, art, literature and science were far more rational fields of international competition.

The high costs of imperialism were not justified by economic or political returns. Jingoism, the spirit of 'my country right or wrong', overrode this difficulty. Capitalist interests encouraged this spirit through the media. In particular, public opinion was manipulated by the press. In Hobson's view, modern newspapers combined the vices of 'a Roman arena, a Spanish bull-ring and an English prize fight all rolled into one' (1901: 29). They were brutalising, peddling vicarious violence to a receptive public. Imperialism fed upon irrationality and atavism.

As long as the population at large accepted the costs of imperialism, benefits flowed to a number of vested interests. Financiers profited from a perpetual climate of speculation. Service personnel, the armaments industry, shipping magnates, missionaries, engineers and civil servants all found profitable employment in the empire. So, indirectly, did the religious and education institutions which depended upon their patronage. Democracy suffered. The despotic tendency of imperial administration was re-imported into the home country. Capital was diverted from social reform towards the empire.

The pressure for imperialism stemmed from the 'chronic congestion of productive power and of production' (Hobson 1938b: 84–5) unmatched by consumption. Trusts were formed within some industries to reduce their total output, a tendency noted by Veblen also. However, this manoeuvre failed to solve the problem of what to do with excess funds within the system as a whole. Hobson commented:

> Thus we reach the conclusion that Imperialism is the endeavour of the great controllers of industry [i.e. the financiers and trust-makers] to broaden the channel for the flow of their surplus wealth by seeking foreign markets and foreign investments to take off the goods and capital they cannot sell or use at home.
>
> (Hobson 1938b: 85)

Wasteful and parasitical, imperialist entrepreneurs preferred extensive to intensive development, seeking quantitative success at the expense of qualitative advance.

Hobson became a strong advocate of international organisation. This would supply 'some organised representation of civilised humanity' (1938b: 232), enforcing peace and justice. In the early phases of the First World War, Hobson joined a 'small Neutrality group' in an effort to keep Britain out. In fact, he claimed, 'My only contribution to this cause was the annexation of Lord Bryce, just returned from America, whom I tracked on Saturday afternoon to a place in Camden Town where he was personally engaged in unpacking trunks of books' (1938a: 103).

When the war was over, Hobson served on the Bryce Committee which drew up initial plans for a League of Nations. He published his own minority view in *Towards International Government* (1915). Such a government should have an armed force at its disposal. Backed up by favourable world opinion it would be able to stop the rich nations from oppressing the poor. International peace would not be soundly based, however, until individual societies had developed satisfactory forms of capitalism and democracy.

Welfare and the market

Hobson wanted a theoretical and practical alternative to the existing system. This alternative was based upon an incisive critique of capitalism, focusing upon the limitations of economics as a discipline, the unjust nature of the market and the causes of recurrent trade depressions.

John Ruskin provided Hobson with a fundamental insight. In the latter's words: 'A subdivided routine-producer could not be an efficient consumer of any of the more worthy sorts of wealth. Nor could an idle consumer, living not by his labour but on his "means" ' (Hobson 1938a: 41). Hobson, like Ruskin, wanted to restore to economics the moral dimension it had lost since Adam Smith's time.

Like Veblen, Hobson thought of 'homo economicus' as active, purposive and, increasingly, humane and rational: 'the barriers against the social control of economic processes by human intelligence and will are continually being weakened' (1930: 125). Increasingly, society would be able to minimise the material and psychic costs of production and maximise the utilities available to the consumer. Producers would perform tasks for which they were psychologically fitted. Consumers would become capable of appreciating their own higher needs.

Organic unity would be brought about not only between human beings as producers and consumers but also between individual and social beings. Both would be achieved through the development of a more rational and moral human consciousness. Hobson shared with his contemporary, L.T. Hobhouse, the view that the evolution of such a consciousness could be moulded by reformers such as himself.

Capitalism interfered with the achievement of organic unity. Advertising created false needs. Many things bought and sold in the market were valueless: they represented not wealth but (Ruskin's word) 'illth' (*viii*). Drawing upon Veblen's argument in *The Theory of the Leisure Class* – 'a work of profound and penetrating power' (1914: 142) – Hobson condemned 'the inevitable effects of easily-gotten and excessive wealth upon the possessors. So far as they operate, they induce futile extravagance in expenditure. Instead of making for utility, they make for disutility of consumption' (144).

In fact, society's contribution to production gave it a proper claim upon the income and wealth of individuals. This contention was 'the lynchpin of Hobson's critique of classical economics' (Allett 1981: 71). Exchange depended upon a price system which summed up the needs and capacities of a vast network of human beings. Productivity gains and profits achieved through the market were, in part, a social product. Part of the surplus wealth created should return to society as public property. It should be part of the 'commonwealth' (Hobson 1938a: 190) – a word which Hobson, unlike Veblen, could use without irony.

In fact, the market operated unjustly. It failed to distribute wealth according to either needs or maintenance costs. Society's claims were ignored. Force and bluff prevailed, for example in relations between big business and labour. In such a society, Say's Law – that income creates its own demand by way of incomes earned in production – did not apply. When huge inequalities of private wealth existed, the rich could not spend all they had and the poor could not buy all they needed. As has been seen, one response by capital to this situation was imperialism. An alternative response, more favourable to society's interests, was available.

A new democracy

> The pretence that capitalism is consistent with a real democracy in which the organised working classes can take their part in Government . . . wears thinner and thinner . . . . To present the appearance of democracy, without handing over the reality of government to the people, has long been the unchallenged achievement of the upper classes in Britain and America.
>
> (Hobson 1938a: 119)

To repair the damage, Hobson proposed a more active role for the state.

On the one hand, negative freedoms should be maintained – insofar as they did not interfere with the collective interest. Hobson erected a less formidable barrier than did J.S. Mill around individual liberty. He was prepared, for example, to consider 'rational control of parentage, at least to the extent of preventing through public education, or if necessary by law, the propagation of certain surely recognized unfitnesses' (1938a: 173).

On the other hand, the state should advance positive freedom by creating a moral environment conducive to self-development and social awareness on the part of the citizen. This environment would be founded upon resources provided by public property rights. Exponents of the liberal tradition had forgotten how important these rights were:

> In earlier civilisations, where there was little opportunity to utilise the surplus productive power of the people for capitalistic enterprises . . . the right and power of the community to direct what surplus energy was available into . . . common services were supported by a very real sentiment of the people. The individualistic trend of modern times has largely stifled this active sense of community.
>
> (Hobson 1930: 162)

Individual and social activity would intermingle, each supported by distinctive forms of property, one public, the other private.

Like Tocqueville, Hobson approved of the habit of human association. It served the evolutionary process of fostering higher, more rational, socialised ideals:

> the evolution of the mind of man into a fuller rationality means the strengthening and clarifying of those relations of feeling and thought which bind him to his fellows and to his world and which are rooted in the 'blind' instincts of gregarious, superstitious, curious man.
>
> (Hobson 1914: 356)

Referenda and other forms of democratic participation would help this process along. Hobson agreed with Bryce rather than Mill at this point. However, like Mill, Hobson thought the details of government should definitely be in the hands of experts. In fact, at the very end of his autobiography, the final point he makes is that:

> the general standard of intelligence and knowledge must rise to a level where a reasonable acceptance [by the less educated classes] of special cooperation and expert directness is attained. The old notion that any ordinary man is equal to the doing of any job, or at any rate to judging how it should best be done . . . must be displaced by a clear conviction that an effective operative democracy requires close attention to the inequalities of men in order that special abilities may be utilized for the common welfare.
>
> (Hobson 1938a:212)

Unfortunately, the community's wealth was being taken over by the forces of 'improperty' (Hobson 1917: 52), especially the military and profiteering capitalists. In *Democracy After the War* (1917), Hobson argued that the poker-table ethics of capitalism had to be countered by a series of measures. These should include: functional representation of the major economic interests in a national industrial council; a minimum wage; and a redistributive income tax.

Especially important would be a new system of regulating the main industries producing standardised goods needed by all. These would be run by 'a minority of trained specialized brain and hand workers' with a view to maximising efficient production. There would also be trade-union organisations, joint councils of managers and workers, and conciliation boards including consumer representatives. Private enterprise would continue to run industries supplying specialised or idiosyncratic needs which could not be standardised.

Hobson was not an old-style liberal after the fashion of James Bryce. Nor was he quite a socialist. He shared Richard Cobden's vision of international prosperity and civilisation based upon free trade. However, the main enemies of this vision, in his view, were not the aristocracy (the object of Cobden's anger) but the manipulators of finance capital.

Hobson favoured an increase in the state's role, but he did not wish to abolish the market.

Individual freedom was valued, but it had to be very heavily supplemented by a positive freedom enacted by the state for the community as a whole. Just as J.S. Mill worked hard to shake himself free of the ethical assumptions of Benthamism, so Hobson struggled to move beyond the economic assumptions of Mill, whose treatment of supply and demand, encountered as a student, 'seems even at that early age to have stuck in my gizzard' (Hobson 1938a: 25).

Conclusion

Hobson concurred with Veblen in the main outlines of his analysis of industrial capitalism. However, he differed from Veblen on how the development of democracy was related to the progress of capitalism.

For Hobson, the extension of democratic participation within a capitalist society would foster the evolution of human reason and morals towards a higher plane. A more organic economic order could then be built upon the principles of human welfare, sustained by enlightened consent. In other words, democracy would humanise capitalism. In fact, universal manhood suffrage was not finally achieved in Britain until after the First World War. By contrast, Veblen lived in a society which had much longer experience of something approaching universal suffrage. In Veblen's view, democracy was not likely to reform capitalism.

Generally more pessimistic than Hobson, Veblen concentrated upon the deforming contradiction between industry and business, between the matter-of-fact scientific spirit and the predatory or pecuniary animus. A true democracy concerned for the best interests of the community could not appear until after capitalism underwent a final crisis. This would destroy the system of business enterprise. At this point a syndicalist regime organised through soviets of engineers, scientists and specialised operatives would be able to assume control of industry. Guided by the instinct of workmanship such a regime would employ economic resources in the interests of the community as a whole. Instead of being the agency through which capitalism was reformed, democracy in this syndicalist form would emerge to fill the vacuum left by the latter's demise.

That possibility lay in the future. By 1914 the key configuration of forces had become the interplay between big business, the state and the people. Veblen and Hobson both asserted that the first had subverted the second and duped the third – with potentially disastrous results. The cataclysm of the First World War appeared to justify their arguments, giving history's stamp of approval to the intellectual work of their most creative years. However, the period 1914–18 was a beginning as well as an end. It brought a new international order into being and enforced a new reckoning of the issues.

Chapter six

Who rules?

Replacing the nobility

All the writers discussed in the first part of the book assumed that as a result of the increasing influence of democracy and capitalism, both as ideas and ways of life, the aristocracy's influence was bound to decline. Some of them qualified the point. For example, Veblen argued that feudal values still lived on, temporarily, in the form of the captain of industry's predatory and pecuniary instincts. Carnegie found kings and dukes convenient punch bags. By re-fighting old battles on behalf of republicanism, he gave his message a radical air. Chamberlain whipped up puritan fervour by summoning up memories of the English civil war. Ostrogorski was still hankering nostalgically for the good old days as late as the 1900s.

However, despite the sound and fury, Tocqueville already knew by the 1830s that the game was up for the class to which he belonged. He thought the loss – in terms of wisdom in the public sphere, culture in the private sphere and enlightenment in both – was considerable. Even Mill, far less impressed by the aristocracy, recognised that a void had been created which needed to be filled.

The question was: who would take the aristocracy's place as the dominant influence upon the public sphere, providing wisdom and good judgement? Tocqueville, the lawyer, was very impressed with the successful way legal professionals played this part in American society. Mill, the bureaucrat, not surprisingly found that he had to recommend the state bureaucracy for the job. Carnegie, the plutocrat, saw very clearly that only industrialists could fill the gap. In fact, it is a little glib to put it quite like that.

Apart from the lawyers, whom Tocqueville perhaps admired more for their conservatism than their intelligence, four interests were put forward as candidates for the task of providing public virtue and enlightenment. First, *the people*. Tocqueville was surprised how well ordinary Americans coped with running public business for themselves.

However, he was not confident it would last, in view of the danger of a despotic form of rule exploiting the tyrannical potential of public opinion. Chamberlain often spoke about 'the people', but he wanted them to stay in their proper place as an appreciative audience, grateful to be allowed into the theatre.

More wholehearted confidence in the good sense and capacity for judgement of the people – or at least some of the people – came from James Bryce and Thorstein Veblen. The first used the term to refer to nationality, the second to indicate class. Specifically, Veblen placed his hope in a resurgence of the community-oriented 'instinct for workmanship'. However, this was to be found not among the working class as a whole, but in the section of this class most closely involved with engineering technology.

Bryce was certainly not drawing upon any notion of the universal rights of humanity. He would, for example, have been quite happy to see the democratic revolutions in Latin America reversed. Bryce distinguished between different 'peoples' according to the strength and bent of their national character. The English were a splendid breed, by his account. The point is that by 'the people', Bryce meant 'the national population'. In his view, Englishness was soaked with the finest essence of liberalism and therefore could be trusted – up to a point at least.

The people were at their best, according to Bryce, when they were leavened by a strong minority of 'independent citizens' – by implication, well-educated property owners (education and property ownership almost invariably went together) who would act in a rational, moral and public-spirited way. These independent and civic-minded people, rising above party and prejudice, would treat each issue on its merits, without fear or favour. *The independent citizen* was the second candidate for the position of wisdom's guardian in a capitalist democracy. Ostrogorski placed his reliance almost entirely upon this hidden army.

Two other candidates remained. The third was *a public bureaucracy* whose highly educated leadership would be drawn from the universities and would have close links with the national intelligentsia. Mill and Hobson both regarded such a bureaucracy as essential. The former saw it as a means of holding the line until the educational level of the population was sufficient to permit greater participation in government by the people. The latter wanted the bureaucracy to be much more interventionist, regulating the commanding heights of the economy and creating positive freedoms through a wide variety of state services. He saw a place for referenda and a degree of worker representation in industry, but this fell far short of direct or fully participatory democracy.

The fourth candidate was *the industrialist*. Carnegie and Chamberlain presented themselves as exemplary instances of what could be done to provide democracy with intelligent leadership. Both accepted that success in the market place was an indication of very good character. It marked a person out as both qualified and obliged to use the same talents for the public good. Chamberlain believed the proper way to do this was by holding public office. The industrialist would work alongside successful and public-spirited people from the professions, religious bodies and other adjuncts of bourgeois society. Carnegie preferred a more direct use of personal power, by-passing public institutions.

In practice, the dramatic impact of industrialisation during the nineteenth and early twentieth centuries, combined with the relatively sluggish response of central government, meant – as has been seen – that this final candidate received the lion's share of attention. The bureaucratic agents of government – the official, the planner, the scientist – received more sustained attention after the First World War.

Models of capitalist democracy

The transatlantic debate as expressed in the contributions so far examined can be summarised in terms of the following five models of capitalist democracy:

The *participatory* model of capitalist democracy assumes that individuals will invest their time and energy as fully in the public as in the private sphere and that private property will not provide the basis for domination by a powerful minority.

The *mediatory* model of capitalist democracy assumes that an educated and propertied minority will complement its dominance in the market with intelligent and humane leadership in the public sphere.

The *paternalistic* model of capitalist democracy assumes the priority of the private over the public sphere but recommends that the most successful business people should use their superior judgement and wealth to provide services to the community.

The *manipulatory* model assumes the improper and generally covert dominance of private interests, especially business people, within the public sphere. This influence is exercised partly through the promise of jobs and favours.

The model of *hegemonic* capitalist democracy assumes that the public sphere is managed by agents who use their relative autonomy to advance, directly or indirectly, the interests of capital at the expense of the interests of the people as a whole, especially the working class.

No one favoured the *participatory* model without major reservations. For example, Tocqueville and Bryce both believed that its success depended upon the national character of the people concerned. Even then there were serious doubts. On the one hand, Tocqueville argued that municipal duties were many and widely shared in New England towns, because 'Americans rightly think that patriotism is a sort of duty strengthened by practical service' (Tocqueville 1968: 83). The chances for participatory democracy in Jacksonian America were strengthened by the broad spread of property ownership among citizens who were equal before the law. On the other hand, the pursuit of personal comfort by citizens might, in his view, undermine active popular participation in public affairs. The gap might too easily be filled by a despotic minority manipulating public opinion. Bryce, also, believed the pursuit of private affluence was deadly for public spirit.

Bryce and Veblen were both writing several decades after Tocqueville's time. Political equality persisted in America and had advanced in Britain. However, in both societies inequalities in the industrial sphere had increased considerably. Veblen looked forward to the self-destruction of hegemonic capitalist democracy to be replaced by a participatory form of democracy. However, the condition was that capitalism would cease to exist. The evils represented by the party system, the selfish leisure class and capitalist propaganda would all be swept away. Industrial production would be organised efficiently for the good of the community as a whole.

Bryce thought revolution relatively unlikely and expected that if it did occur, it would bring new evils. His main hope was the emergence of a form of capitalist democracy mixing participatory and mediatory aspects. In some respects, this compromise solution had been anticipated by Tocqueville who approved of the role played by the American judiciary in guiding participatory democracy.

Two advocates of the *mediatory* form of capitalist democracy were Mill and Chamberlain. Both argued that a leading position in government should be taken by people who had demonstrated their competence by becoming leaders in other spheres. Mill emphasised the role of the educated university graduate within the central bureaucracy, Chamberlain the successful industrialist or professional practitioner in municipal government. Both placed great importance upon the expansion of educational facilities in order to raise the intellectual and moral standard of the citizenry.

They each supported gestures towards establishing in Britain the close harmony between property and the people that Tocqueville believed existed in America. Mill was an enthusiast for co-operative schemes in industry, an expansion of peasant proprietorship, and reform of the inheritance laws. Chamberlain's exercises in municipal socialism allowed him to claim that the people of Birmingham owned their own basic utilities. Some of the formal mechanisms of participatory democracy were maintained within the Liberal party through the organisation of the caucus. Chamberlain parted company at this point with Mill who, in common with many other educated gentlemen, thought party politics a disreputable business involving jobbery and doing favours for your friends in return for political services. This critique – basic to the manipulatory model – was developed further by Ostrogorski.

The *paternalistic* model of capitalist democracy was promoted by Carnegie. As has been seen, Carnegie elevated the private sphere above the public sphere and ranked the wealthy entrepreneur above the people at large. In both respects, he favoured symbiosis rather than overlap and interpenetration. Party politics was beneath his contempt. In times of national emergency, great leaders would emerge for a brief while from the private sphere to serve the public interest; their service in the public sphere would guarantee the continued security of private transactions. Meanwhile, the very wealthy would pour resources into popular institutions to encourage further recruits to their number from below.

The paternalistic and mediatory models were two responses to the absence or (perhaps in America's case) the passing away of the conditions that made participatory democracy possible. The revolt at the company town of Pullman in 1894 showed that attempts to implement the paternalistic model on any large scale were probably doomed in America (athough paternalism lasted a little longer in Britain, especially at the local level). The other two models – of the manipulatory and hegemonic forms of capitalist democracy – contained critiques which undermined the claims of the mediatory and paternalistic models (see Diagram A, p. 194).

The *manipulatory* model was set out by Ostrogorski. Political parties of the kind organised by Chamberlain and his more evil counterparts in America were engaged in nothing less than organised deception, bribery and corruption of the public. A few 'front men' from the respectable part of society provided some flimsy support for the claims made in the mediatory model. However, the main object of party organisation was to maintain the influence and wealth of the party's private backers.

The model of *hegemonic* capitalist democracy, as developed by Veblen and Hobson, started from the manipulatory model but went much further. Political parties were now seen as part of the systematic subversion of government and people by the agents of capitalism. The object was not just to line the pockets of unscrupulous opportunists but to maintain an oppressive and exploitative social organisation in being. Educational institutions, so strongly touted by Mill, Chamberlain and Carnegie, were thoroughly woven into the capitalist net. They offered no hope of civilisation or reform. Both Hobson and Veblen believed that a more rational consciousness was developing in spite of, rather than because of, the schools and universities.

It is very noticeable that the positive models of capitalist democracy – participatory, mediatory, paternalistic – and the negative models – manipulatory, hegemonic – placed the same set of values at the centre of their vision. Party politics were treated with a varying mixture of suspicion, fear and contempt. Chamberlain covered his own position by claiming (without very much justification), first, that the moral strength of the cause of Liberalism found legitimate and spontaneous expression in the banding together of citizens and, second, that his power base, the Birmingham Liberal party, represented the traditional sentiments of almost the whole of the city. All the people discussed accepted the ideal of the active, educated citizen deeply involved in the public sphere and none of them, least of all the plutocrat Carnegie, had much time for a life mainly directed by the pursuit of private affluence.

Part two

Capitalism and the Rise of Big Government

Chapter seven

Laski and Lasswell

A new world

The First World War undermined the empirical basis for two articles of nineteenth-century liberal faith: the utility of *laissez-faire* as a means of advancing peace and prosperity; and the fundamental rationality of humankind. Following the dismemberment of the Austro-Hungarian Empire and the defeat of Imperial Germany, Central Europe was in ferment between the wars, a highly unstable mix of nationalities, ideologies and classes. One consequence was a migration of European intellectuals across the English Channel and the Atlantic Ocean. New ideas came with them, including the work of Sigmund Freud. He offered a new and powerful model of man to compete with the partly discredited assumption of universal human rationality.

The Russian Revolution of 1917 also had profound consequences. For example, it provided a dramatic example of a rapidly modernising society dominated by public officials. The Soviet case suggested that control by the state might be an alternative to control by big business. The Russian Revolution did for Karl Marx what the French Revolution had done for Tom Paine and Jean-Jacques Rousseau. It gave his ideas the immense prestige of being associated with the overthrow of an old order and the creation of a new one.

Nineteen seventeen changed the context of the debate on capitalist democracy. The nineteenth century had been dominated by the American experiment. Exponents of a European liberal tradition fashioned in societies where aristocratic influence, though declining, remained power-ful, had anxiously looked on as Andrew Carnegie's world took shape. By contrast, the twentieth century was to be dominated by the Russian experiment. Increasingly, big business in the United States took up the role of anxious spectator. It hoped for the disintegration of the Soviet Union as ardently as the British aristocracy had cheered on the seceding South during the American Civil War.

The two men whose writings are examined in this chapter had to come to terms with a very different world from the one in which Bryce, Veblen and Hobson had grown to maturity. Their distinctive approaches to capitalist democracy were developed during the 1920s and 1930s at a time when the United States and Britain were both 'in between'. Despite its international decline, the patina of aristocratic grandeur and the trappings of imperial power still clung to British society. In spite of its tremendous economic capacity and potential, America had not yet taken up a global role.

The politics of experience

Harold Laski and Harold Lasswell were born in 1893 and 1902 respectively. They both had strong links with Anglo-American liberalism of the pre-war period. Lasswell's teacher at Chicago, the political scientist Charles E. Merriam, had been a great admirer of James Bryce (Karl 1974: 36, 40). At Oxford, Laski was taught history by H.A.L. Fisher and constitutional law by A.V. Dicey, respectively Bryce's biographer and one of his closest friends.

Laski taught at Harvard University between 1916 and 1920. His American friends included Oliver Wendell Holmes of the US Supreme Court. Another was the journalist Walter Lippman, a past pupil of Graham Wallas, Laski's predecessor as Professor of Political Science at the London School of Economics and Political Science. Laski took up this post in 1926 upon Wallas's death, and held it until his own death in 1950.

Laski held radical views. He ran into trouble at Harvard in 1919 for some remarks he made which were sympathetic to the Boston policemen, then on strike. He later wrote for the Labour party's newspaper, the *Daily Herald*, and was active in the British general strike of 1926. Laski advised the Labour government of 1929 on various matters, served on the London County Council's education committee, became an alderman on Fulham's borough council and sat on the National Executive Committee of the Labour party. In the victorious year of 1945 he was party chairman.

Lasswell was a graduate student at the University of Chicago in the early 1920s. He was particularly influenced by Robert Park, the sociologist, and Charles E. Merriam, 'the father of the behavioral movement in political science' (Karl 1974: *viii*). Lasswell began his teaching career at Chicago and remained there until 1938 when he moved to Yale as Professor of Law and Political Science. He regarded Laski as

[an] articulate and devoted teacher . . . . There was no doubt in [his] mind that, unless an intellectual bridge was built between the dogmatisms of conservative capitalism and the collectivizing trends of the age, there would be a catastrophic age of terror and

revolutionary violence . . . . For a vast congregation of former students Laski personified an informed intelligence and a sympathetic personality attuned to the major issues of his day and concerned with clarifying and affecting history by reaching the minds and consciences of everyone within the sound of his persuasive voice or able to read his unceasing flow of books, articles and declarations. He brought to the forum of learned debate the policy issues of the moment. For him, they were framed in the great tradition of the perpetually oscillating balance between the claims of order and liberty.

(Lasswell 1963: 168-9)

Harold Lasswell's praise was directed at a man who had felt, like himself, that democracy was both incomplete and endangered. Both men rejected theories based upon the supposed preferences and actions of rational individuals and a sovereign state. Their immediate intellectual predecessors had defined the 'task of the hour'. In Lasswell's words, this task was

the development of a realistic analysis of the political in relation to the social process, and this depends upon the invention of abstract conceptions and upon the prosecution of empirical research. It is precisely this missing body of theory and practice which Graham Wallas undertook to supply in England and which Charles E Merriam has been most foremost in encouraging in the United States.

(Lasswell 1951a: 46)

It is worth pausing, briefly, at the names of Wallas and Merriam. In *Human Nature in Politics* (1948) and *The Great Society* (1914), Graham Wallas produced a psychological interpretation of contemporary politics. He dismissed the assumption that human nature normally exhibited decency and rationality. Ostrogorski's regret at the worldly naughtiness of machine bosses caused Wallas to comment: 'One seems to be reading a series of conscientious observations of the Copernican heavens by a loyal but saddened believer in the Ptolemaic astronomy' (Wallas 1948: 125). James Bryce was likewise committed to an old-fashioned idea of democracy formulated as if 'human nature were as he himself would like it to be, and as he was taught at Oxford to think that it was' (127). Without actually saying it outright, Wallas condemned Bryce, the self-proclaimed 'professional optimist', as unscientific. If Bryce's 'hope-for-the-best' approach to contemporary politics were adopted it would be as if 'an acknowledged leader in chemical research . . ., finding that experiment did not bear out some traditional formula, should speak of himself as nevertheless "grimly resolved" to see things from the old and comfortable point of view' (129).

Charles E. Merriam of Chicago University agreed with Wallas's view

109

that the non-rational side of human nature should be accepted as a datum and built into the theories of political science. However, 'Wallas found it difficult to put into actual practice the doctrines he preached, and never made much use of the experimental or statistical methods' (Merriam 1925: 73). Merriam contributed to the latter of these tasks by helping to build up a tradition of well-funded political science research in the United States. He was, for example, a powerful figure in the dealings of the national Social Science Research Council and the Local Community Research Committee at Chicago University.

Merriam also got involved in Chicago politics. He campaigned for the position of mayor in 1911 and 1915, arguing for efficiency and planning in local government. On neither occasion was he successful, although he blamed ballot rigging for his defeat in 1911 (Karl 1974: 71). Merriam makes a nice contrast with an earlier figure. If Joseph Chamberlain of Birmingham was a highly effective local politician who did not quite make it as a practitioner of political theory, Charles E. Merriam of Chicago was a very successful academic who failed to establish himself in the real world of politics. Neither made a satisfactory fusion between theory and experience. This last point returns the argument to the main theme.

Laski and Lasswell had both been strongly influenced by the distinctive American philosophy of pragmatism. This approach, developed by John Dewey, William James and C.S. Peirce, laid stress upon the special validity of learning acquired through experience. According to this approach, thought is stimulated when practical activities are frustrated in some way. For the pragmatist, the 'truth' of an idea or concept is best tested by seeing if it 'works' in the sense of solving specific practical problems. From this common beginning, Lasswell and Laski moved in very different directions.

Both were interested in the complex interplay of perception, personality and power. However, while Lasswell focused upon 'the private basis of public acts' (Lasswell 1951a: 7), Laski emphasised the public context of private lives. He sought a way of 'making the State find place for the personalities of ordinary men' (Laski 1980: 15).

Lasswell developed a 'manipulative' political science based upon 'contemplative' analysis of political and psychological aspects of the social order (Lasswell 1951b: 318). He drew heavily upon the work of Freud. Laski set out to provide 'A new political philosophy' for 'a new world' (1980: 15) and drew from it a series of practical proposals for social and political reconstruction. He became increasingly reliant upon a Marxian perspective.

The good life

The intellectual consequences of the break-up of the old central European empires in 1918 have already been mentioned. In fact, the influx of German ideas into the English universities had begun long before the First World War. One major manifestation during the late nineteenth century was the idealism of T.H. Green and, a little later, Bernard Bosanquet. Green drew upon Hegel and Kant to criticise, among others, J S Mill. Breaking with the individualism of the utilitarian approach, Green argued in *Prologomena to Ethics* (1883) that self-realisation is achieved only through relations with others. You transcend your individual consciousness and contribute to a higher morality through participation in the wider consciousness which permeates society and its institutions. In his *Philosophical Theory of the State* (1899) Bosanquet stressed that all human achievement depends upon shared activity which draws people outside themselves. The isolated individual could achieve nothing worthwhile. It was necessary to participate in the encompassing spirit of the group.

By the early twentieth century, many English intellectuals were turning away from idealism. Some, like Laski, retained its sense of moral purpose but adopted a revised epistemology. Others rejected the demand that you should merge the self in something higher and deeply spiritual. Among the latter, G.E. Moore, author of *Principia Ethica*, told his readers that the most valuable things they could know or imagine were 'the pleasures of human intercourse and the enjoyment of beautiful objects' (Moore 1962: 188).

Moore's message was much welcomed among the Cambridge and Bloomsbury sets to which John Maynard Keynes, among others, belonged. They were a powerful antidote to puritan demands that you should make the best of yourself and do your social duty. Whatever the strengths and weaknesses of Moore's philosophical approach, Keynes was later to write that it had the negative effect of protecting his friends and himself from 'the final *reductio ad absurdam* of Benthamism known as Marxism' (quoted in Skidelsky 1983: 143).

Keynes did not stray as far from the world of Bentham and Ricardo as that comment implies. In fact, although he found Say's Law a convenient straw man, Keynes insisted that his own 'general theory' did not dispense with the classical economics of the Manchester School. He advocated a large extension of central state controls over taxation and interest rates, but argued that if such controls succeeded in establishing full employment 'the classical theory comes into its own again from that point onward' (Keynes 1973: 378). The result of increasing the powers and functions of the state would be to preserve an economic system which gave ample scope for individualism, 'the best safeguard of personal liberty' (380).

Capitalism and the Rise of Big Government

The grammar of politics

Harold Laski proposed a much more radical reordering of economic and political institutions. In *The Grammar of Politics*, which first appeared in 1925, he joined the revolt against English idealism. He turned Green and Bosanquet on their heads, substituting for their idealism 'a purely realistic theory of the state' (Laski 1980: 29). At its centre was the proposition that the state's purpose was to enable men and women to express their personalities and satisfy their impulses within a shared life. The citizen's capacity to apply reason and sound judgement should be developed to the greatest extent possible. The shared life of society should have the benefit of the most expert advice and the widest range of experience available.

Laski's approach to rights, duties, liberty, equality, property and authority was shaped in accordance with the purpose just stated. The key test was functionality. For example, 'By a functional theory of rights is meant that we are given powers that we may so act as to add to the richness of our social heritage. We have rights, not that we may receive, but that we may do' (40–1). The action required of citizens was that they should fulfil the best in themselves. They should contribute their individual experience and 'instructed judgement to the public good' (29).

Three important conditions were attached to this formulation of citizenship rights and duties. First, individual personality was not to be subsumed within some overriding 'general will'. Differences among people and the variety of their individual experiences were precious resources for the state. In Laski's view, 'since the State is seeking to realise the fruits of social experience, it must clearly act upon the largest interpretation of experience that is open to it. It can neglect no source that, even potentially, has hints and ideas to contribute. That is the real case for democratic government' (36).

Second, it was the responsibility of the state to ensure that 'avenues of creative service' were available to 'any who were willing to utilise them' (41). This responsibility included the task of providing citizens with the means to develop their intellect and powers of judgement. An efficient and open education system was desirable, as was a press which supplied 'an honest and straightforward supply of news' (147).

Third, the obligation upon any citizen to obey the state depended upon that citizen's assessment of the extent to which the state was fulfilling its responsibility to him or her. In order to command our obedience, the state had genuinely to seek to achieve the purposes outlined. Furthermore,

> We are the judges of that achievement. What it is, and the difference therein from what it has the actual power to be, is written into the

112

innermost fabric of our lives . . . . Power is thus morally neutral; what gives it colour is the performance it can demonstrate.

(Laski 1980: 26–7)

For Laski, citizens were not passive spectators at a drama. They were active participants, awarding credits and demerits to the producer. If the state performed in a way which frustrated the efforts of an individual to realise his or her best self, that individual had no obligation to obey the state.

A major casualty of Laski's theory was the concept of irresponsible, unlimited state sovereignty. Authority in the polity envisaged by Laski was decentralised, consultative and conditional. Unity was to be achieved by 'a process of so associating interests that each, in the solution effected, finds sufficient concession to itself to experiment with the result' (263). Creative obedience resulted from self-imposed discipline. Authority was to be federal in the sense that it acquired legitimacy and elicited consent because it 'coordinates the experience of men into solutions that harmonise the needs they infer from those experiences' (224).

Laski supported a positive form of liberty built upon economic and political equality. He was uncomfortable with Mill's attempt to define strict limits to state interference since 'All conduct is social conduct in the sense that whatever I do has results upon me as a member of society'. In Laski's view, liberty was society saying to the individual 'do the best you can'. In his words: 'Freedoms are . . . opportunities which history has shown to be essential to the development of personality' (144). They should be available in both the political and the industrial spheres, for example in the form of works councils.

Liberty implied guaranteed minimum levels of income, education and political rights for all. This was because no individual could achieve self-realisation except in cooperation with others who are also making the best of themselves. Where power and property were divorced from legitimate functions they should be abolished, whether in the House of Lords or the City of London. The actual amount of wealth enjoyed by an individual should reflect his or her value to society: 'My property is, from the standpoint of political justice, the measure of economic worth placed by the State upon my personal effort towards the realisation of its end' (87–8).

Under the general supervision of central government, much greater powers could be transferred to local government than had been customary. This would 'revivify the quality of local life' (427). The distribution of powers between local and central government should be roughly equivalent to the relation between the states and the federal government in the United States.

Within a democracy the political parties played a vital role. Laski did

113

not adopt the hostile line of Ostrogorski or express the suspicions of Bryce and Veblen. In his view, the parties provided 'the most solid obstacle we have against the danger of Caesarism' (Laski 1980: 313). The first line of defence against the threat of despotism and its corollary, a completely passive electorate, was not the town meeting (Tocqueville), enlightened and independent gentlemen (Bryce) or proportional representation (Mill). It was a two-party system:

> The life of the democratic State is built upon the party-system . . . .
> [For example], parties arrange the issues upon which people are to vote. It is obvious that in the confused welter of the modern State there must be some selection of problems as more urgent than others. It is necessary to select them as urgent and to present solutions of them which may be acceptable to the citizen body. It is that task of selection the party undertakes. It acts . . . as the broker of ideas . . . . What, at least, is certain is that without parties there would be no means available to us of enlisting the popular decision in such a way as to secure solutions capable of being interpreted as politically satisfactory.
>
> (Laski 1980: 312–13)

Laski acknowledged the tendency of parties to stimulate pugnacious conflict, group separatism, falsification and personalisation. However, 'the services they render to a democratic State are inestimable' (313). Such views may not be surprising in a book published very shortly after the Labour party achieved office for the first time in 1924.

The rule of the 'elected amateur' would ensure 'a direct and continuous relation between government and public opinion' (424). However, party government, argued Laski, should be supplemented by expert advice and administration. Contact with ordinary people was equally desirable for administrators and the judiciary. Government would also benefit from the expertise and experience of social scientists, professional bodies and other experts, organised through a panoply of commissions, advisory committees and so on. The machinery of representation and consultation should combine both the territorial principle (e.g. the interests of Scotland) and the functional principle (e.g. the interests of the coal industry).

Laski's approach to political economy – especially with respect to imperialism, state control of industry, inheritance and redistribution – owed a great deal to John Hobson, his colleague on the editorial board of the *Nation*. However, Laski paid more attention than Hobson to the need for a balanced mix of professional expertise and representative democracy within industrial structures. He was in favour of employees helping to set work standards within their own industries although he did not go down the syndicalist path taken by Veblen. Laski preferred a system of vocational associations regulating their function in conjunction with central government, a pattern reminiscent of Emile Durkheim's *Professional Ethics and Civic Morals* (1957).

In *The Grammar of Politics* Laski proposed using the resources of capitalism to raise minimum economic standards throughout the population while also introducing democratic practices into industry on a large scale. The problem with this approach was that the main beneficiaries of capitalism were opposed to an extension of democracy while the principal beneficiaries of democracy had very serious reservations about the existing economic order. In Laski's words:

> The working-classes of the world have no longer any faith in capitalism. They give it no service they can avoid. It implies a distribution of property at no point referable to moral principle. It means waste and corruption and inefficiency. Nor, historically, can it avoid the difficulty that political power has now been conferred upon those who least share in the benefits it secures; there is not, I think, any evidence of men coming to the possession of political power without trying, as a consequence, to control economic power also. This may, of course, be resisted. But the result of such resistance on any large scale will inevitably be revolution, and there will then be precipitated exactly the situation predicted in the communist analysis.
>
> (Laski 1980: 507)

Capitalism and democracy were, potentially, in open conflict. Laski continued:

> I do not say that revolution will be successful. I do, however, urge that even its defeat will destroy the prosperity of capitalism, on the one hand, and imply such an iron dictatorship of the capitalist, on the other, as to usher in a period of guerrilla warfare almost certain to ruin the prospects of civilisation. It is to the avoidance of such a dilemma that the view here urged is directed.
>
> (Ibid.)

During the next decade Laski became increasingly aware of the obstacles to be overcome before the kind of society he had envisaged in *The Grammar of Politics* could actually be achieved.

Democracy in crisis

In *Liberty in the Modern State* (1930) Laski turned away from the positive view of liberty adopted in *The Grammar of Politics*. He was less sure that the state would encourage the development of its citizens' capacities and inclinations. On the contrary, individuals needed protection from the state.

Laski drew closer to Mill's approach. Like Mill in the 1860s, Laski in

115

the 1930s had little confidence that political power would be exercised in a civilised way. Like Mill, he responded by insisting that a strong barrier should be erected around the individual. People should learn to value this protection of their individuality since

> liberty is essentially an expression of an impalpable atmosphere among men. It is a sense that in the things we deem significant there is the opportunity of continuous initiative, the knowledge that we can, so to speak, experiment with ourselves, think differently or act differently, from our neighbours without danger to our happiness being involved therein. We are not free, that is, unless we can form our plan of conduct to suit our own character without social penalties.
>
> (Laski 1930: 35)

Laski did not relinquish the objective of a social order driven by the 'instructed judgement' of all its citizens. However, three aspects of such a social order were emphasised. First, active consent by the people was a necessary condition, implying relative equality: 'the absence of such consent is, in the long run, fatal to social peace' (214). Second, empathy and effective two-way communication were essential. Political leaders have to be able 'to interpret the experience of their subjects as these read its meaning' (223). Third, people had to overcome the dogmas and stereotypes which bedevilled rational thought: 'I do not know how to emphasize sufficiently the quite inescapable importance to freedom of the content of the educational process' (183). Laski placed his faith in reason since 'Where there is respect for reason, there, also, is respect for freedom' (256).

The fate of the 1929 Labour government showed that the opponents of reason were not just ignorance and dogma but also economic interest. In 1931, during the severe economic depression, the Labour Prime Minister Ramsay MacDonald agreed to accept cuts in unemployment benefit in order to preserve Britain's international creditworthiness. Only four Labour ministers accepted this policy. However, MacDonald agreed to implement it at the head of a National government dominated by Conservatives. It was a severe blow to Laski's hopes. In a pamphlet entitled *The Crisis and the Constitution* (1932), he admitted that 'the road to power is far harder than Labour has, so far, been led to imagine' (9).

Laski's subsequent reflections on the condition of capitalist democracy were contained in *Democracy in Crisis* (1933). In two further books – *The State in Theory and Practice* (1935) and *The Rise of European Liberalism* (1936) – he developed this argument further. In his view, liberalism as a doctrine was 'a by-product of the effort of the middle class to win a place in the sun' (Laski 1936: 258). Under pressure from socialism and the trade unions, as well as thinkers like Green, Arnold and Tocqueville, liberals had adopted a positive conception of the state in the late nineteenth century: 'The revolutionary challenge was to be avoided by the gospel, as Mr Chamberlain termed it, of "ransom" ' (241). However, the 'social service state' arrived too late. The share of capitalist wealth expended on social objects had been insufficient to 'assure itself against attack' (1933: 165).

Until 1914, the socialist critique of liberalism was typified by the Fabians. Their hopes for a gradual transition to a socialist state were shattered after the First World War. Capitalists began to question the viability of a democratic order which demanded high spending on amenities for the masses. The economic depression severely limited the tax-raising capacity of a system based upon private profit:

> Capitalist democracy worked admirably so long as the environment was stable enough to maintain the self-confidence of its governing class. But inherent in it was a new struggle for power. It offered a share in political authority to all citizens upon the unstated assumption that the equality involved in the democratic ideal did not seek extension to the economic sphere. The assumption could not be maintained. For the object of political power is always the abrogation of privilege.
>
> (Laski 1933: 53)

The First World War had disrupted the psychological conditions underlying popular acceptance of nineteenth-century liberalism. In Keynes's words, it had 'disclosed the possibility of consumption to all and the vanity of abstinence to many' (quoted in Laski 1936: 257). Laski pointed out that despite scientific advances which greatly expanded the productive capacity of the industrial system, the capitalist regime after the First World War lowered the living standards of the people in order to preserve itself. Laski moved beyond the analyses of Hobson and Veblen towards a Marxist approach:

> The basic factor in any given society is the way it earns its living. . . . Changes in the methods of economic production appear to be the most vital factor in the making of change in all the other social patterns we know . . . . In any society . . . in which there are groups whose relations to the productive process is fundamentally different, conflict is inherent in the foundations of the society.
>
> (Laski 1935: 108–12)

After 1931 Laski was convinced that 'A capitalist democracy will not allow its electorate to stumble into socialism by the accident of a verdict at the polls' (Laski 1933: 77). The opposition of the US Supreme Court to President Roosevelt's New Deal supplied American evidence for this point. A future Labour election victory in Britain would probably be followed by a flight of capital and, soon afterwards, the suspension of the parliamentary system either by the defeated

Conservative administration or the incoming Labour regime.

Fascism offered a way for capitalism to hang on to political power and suppress democratic opposition from the working class in the political and economic spheres. Such an authoritarian regime would not prevent a serious split emerging between finance capital on the one side and, on the other, the technicians (here resembling Veblen) and *petite bourgeoisie*. Both groups would become proletarianised.

Revolution was a very likely outcome, although it was hardly guaranteed success. The Russian Revolution of 1917 had occurred under very special circumstances, including a defeated and divided army. These were unlikely to be reproduced in Britain or America. In view of this analysis, it was 'essential that any party which is seeking to transform the economic foundations of society' should 'maintain as long as it can a constitutional order which permits it openly to recruit its strength' (Laski 1935: 320).

In *The Rise of European Liberalism*, he had considered an alternative approach which contradicted his own argument:

> If it is demonstrable that capitalism can always find a practicable way out of its crises, that a depression like that by which the world has been afflicted since 1929 is merely a halt on the road to recovery rather than a symptom of a fatal disease, then, clearly, it becomes possible, with recovery, to transcend the immediate contradictions of the system by moving to a new productive equilibrium in which the demands of the working-classes for material benefit can be satisfied at a new high level. Where this can be effected it is unlikely . . . that there will be an effort by the working class to re-define the class-relations of the society.
>
> (Laski 1936: 183–4)

According to Laski, two schools made this alternative argument. One was the Keynesian school, which assumed an extension of state intervention in the economy as 'an impartial arbiter' concerned with optimising 'total well-being'. Such a scheme envisaged 'a *via media* between capitalism and socialism . . . without any change in the essential structure of class-relations' (185–6). The other school assumed the abandonment of a great deal of social legislation and a return to 'a rigorous policy of *laissez-faire*' (184). Ironically, although Laski thought that neither approach was likely to succeed, they summarise the main themes of capitalist democracy since the Second World War.

In *Reflections on the Revolutions of Our Time* (1943), Laski suggested that the war against Hitler provided an opportunity for a non-violent democratic revolution, permitting the abolition of capitalism. He argued that 'The possibility of evolution by consent' existed for a short period at least while 'the drama of war makes the common interest more compelling than the private interest' (161). In fact, the policy of the 1945 Labour government fell far short of Laski's ambitions. To a great extent this was because it

> was bound to look to the United States for aid in its attempt at revolution by consent . . . . It could not avoid becoming the apparatus for defending middle-class supremacy in America and maintaining it against the challenge of socialism in Western Europe.
>
> (Laski 1952: 110–11)

Promise and performance in America

Following the Second World War it was clear that 'World history is more likely to be shaped by American history than by any other element in its making; [and] how it is to be shaped depends on how Americanism is shaped' (Laski 1948: 751). Laski had been deeply familiar with Americans and America since the First World War. These were the subjects of his longest book, *The American Democracy* (1948) which was 'written out of deep love of America' (*ix*). He gave the object of his affection a pretty hard time.

In between two introductory chapters on the tradition and spirit of America, and a concluding chapter on Americanism as a principle of civilization, Laski provided chapters on a series of interlocking themes. These included political institutions, business enterprise, labour, religion, education, culture, minorities, international relations, the professions and the media.

Despite its promising theme and the great knowledge of its author, the book is a disappointment. It reveals more about Laski's aspirations and frustrations than about the nature of American society. In brief, his argument was that America confronted a serious crisis of national purpose, compounded by internal divisions. Businessmen were the principal source of America's ills. They still represented 'the problem foreseen by Tocqueville' (52). As Veblen had pointed out, they were wedded to a wasteful culture of conspicuous consumption and an antiquated economic philosophy. They were hardworking, optimistic, apolitical, conformist, hospitable and ignorant.

By contrast, labour offered the potential basis for a decisive movement beyond *laissez-faire* and towards socialism. In particular, Laski hoped for the creation of an independent political party representing this emancipatory force. Its opportunity might be at hand, because America was at a crossroads in the 1940s. In Laski's view,

> the factor which is going to alter the whole basis of the party system in America is the twofold coincidence that the conclusion of the pioneering age is accompanied by its need to accept the

responsibility of leadership in an interdependent world . . . it is, I think, certain that [the United States] will become altogether a society which tries to fulfil the democratic ideal or a society which tries wholly to deny it.

(Laski 1948: 82)

America was faced with 'a grave choice between a profound diminution in its standard of living and an embarkation on a policy of economic imperialism'. Before either course was well advanced a successful challenge to the existing party structure was likely. There would be reactionary tendencies but 'impersonal forces' seemed to be moving America 'in a democratic direction which no party can deny and yet survive. Here is the real promise of American life' (82).

So far, promise was not being matched by performance. Sadly, organised labour in America was divided and unable to see clearly the fundamental contradiction between capitalism and democracy. Despite the fact that 'America stands on the threshold of its third great revolution' – Laski meant the revolution leading to democratic socialism – 'the psychological preparation of its people has been declined by the very agency which should be taking the lead in its making' (262). Unfortunately for Laski, the unions were too American to see his point.

Subjectivity and the state

In the same year that *The American Democracy* was published, Harold Lasswell presented his own analysis of the problems confronting democratic societies, including the United States. Like Laski, he focused upon the dimension of political power. However, as the title of his book *Power and Personality* (1948) implied, the other dimension of his analysis was not economic, but psychological. In order to make democracy work, the key issue was not to put the economic structure right but to get personality right. Scientists paid considerable attention to shifts in the physical environment, but:

Our self-observatories are in a less-advanced state . . . . We need a never-ending inventory of the character–personality structure [with special reference to the requirements of democracy] of our one-year olds, our two-year olds and so on up. These annual cross-sectional patterns can be chosen by proper sampling methods throughout all accessible cultures, all strata in society, and hence during all crisis and intercrisis situations.

(Lasswell 1948: 169)

Lasswell proposed that cross-sectional reports on 'environmental and predispositional factors' should be made. These would permit experiments to be carried out for the sake of determining the relative usefulness of different ways of changing the environment to help in 'the formation of the democratic personality' (Lasswell 1948: 169). Taken by itself, this example makes Lasswell seem rather like Dr Strangelove. However, it should be seen in the context of Lasswell's earlier career.

Lasswell began by focusing upon the political impact of individual and collective attitudes, moving beyond formal political theory and traditional political biography with the help of pragmatism and Freud. He moved the armoury of scientific detachment into an arena heavily occupied by interest and emotion. The style is sometimes faintly reminiscent of Machiavelli, at other times it recalls Clausewitz.

Later in his career, Lasswell placed more emphasis upon the role of political science as one of the 'policy sciences' whose 'function is to provide intelligence pertinent to the integration of values realized by and embodied in interpersonal relations' (Lasswell and Kaplan 1950: *xii*).

When Lasswell wrote his most renowned book - *Politics: Who Gets What, When and How?* (1951b) - in the mid 1930s he 'was concerned with sketching a "general physiology" of the political process rather than working out the strategies appropriate to any postulated system of public order. This task was deferred' (1958: 210). The task of the policy science developed by Lasswell was to show how democracy could be made to work as well as possible. Lasswell took up this task following the Allied victory in the Second World War. The 1940s were as crucial for Lasswell as the 1930s were for Laski.

In fact, it is convenient to think of Lasswell's career in three phases. First, during the 1920s he was developing a distinctive methodology. A colleague from those days recalls his versatility and brilliance:

> Merriam sent him to England and he came back with an English accent, he sent him to Vienna and he came back with a full-grown psychoanalytical vocabulary, he sent him to the Soviet Union and when he came back he showed that Marx could be reconciled with Freud.
> (Harold Gosnell, quoted in Bulmer 1984: 194)

Major works from this phase are *Propaganda Technique in World War I* (1971), originally published in 1927 and *Psychopathology and Politics* (1951a), which appeared in 1930.

Second, during the 1930s he sketched out his model of the relations between personality, politics, society and the international order. The most interesting books from this phase are *Politics: Who Gets What, When and How?* (1951b), originally published in 1936, and - not so well known but equally fascinating - *World Politics and Personal Insecurity* (1965), which appeared in 1935. They are both more readable than the highly abstract 'summa theologica' entitled *Power and Society* (Lasswell and Kaplan 1950) which summarised the concepts and assumptions embedded in Lasswell's approach.

In the third phase following the Second World War, as has been noticed, the emphasis upon policy science became strong. A key text is *Power and Personality* (1948).

Tension and fantasy

Tocqueville and Mill had feared the irrationality of public opinion. Through its agency, prejudice was liable to challenge the rule of the rational. Lasswell demonstrated that nearly a century later the tables had been turned. The rational procedures of science and bureaucracy were fully equipped to create fantasy and strengthen prejudice within public opinion. In his study of propaganda during the First World War he showed that this function was systematically organised by the state. By directing a flow of signs and symbols for the attention of the target audience at home or abroad, the propagandist sought 'the instigation of animosity toward the enemy, the preservation of friendship between allies and neutrals, and the demoralisation of the enemy' (1971: 46).

Lasswell concluded that propaganda by print, screen and so on was the modern substitute for the tribal tom-tom: 'print must supplant the dance' (221). He suggested that in order to create the unity and determination needed for war, irrational forces within the psyche had to be mobilised. However, the appearance of reason had to be maintained. Preachers, lecturers, journalists and other professional word-spinners were brought into play: 'All is conducted with the decorum and the trappery of intelligence, for this is a rational epoch, and demands its raw meat cooked and garnished by adroit and skilful chefs' (221).

The skill of the propagandist consisted not only in bedecking his or her appeals with the garnish of rationality, but also in working out where the most combustible 'reservoir of explosive energy' was to be found within a society. This expertise consisted in knowing about the society's 'tension level' (190). (As was seen in an earlier chapter, Chamberlain's speeches on property and the people showed him to be a gifted practitioner in this area.) The propagandist concerned with stirring passions in wartime typically wanted to put a match to the bonfire. The peacetime politician was usually more interested in pouring water over the danger area. This was a central theme in *Psychopathology and Politics* (1951a).

In this book Lasswell dismissed the idea that politics was about rational discussion and democratic consultation. In a passage which took a point of view diametrically opposed to the line adopted by Laski in *The Grammar of Politics*, Lasswell complained about the 'vast diversion of energy towards the study of the formal etiquette of government'. He added:

In some vague way, the problem of politics is the advancement of the good life, but this is at once assumed to depend upon the modification of the mechanisms of government. Democratic theorists in particular have hastily assumed that social harmony depends upon discussion, and that discussion depends upon the formal consultation of all those affected by social problems. The time has come to abandon the assumption that the problem of politics is the problem of promoting discussion among all the interests concerned in a given problem. Discussion frequently complicates social difficulties, for the discussion by far-flung interests arouses a psychology of conflict which produces obstructive, fictitious, and irrelevant values.

(Lasswell 1951a: 196–7)

In Lasswell's view, the problem of politics was less to solve conflicts than to prevent them occurring. Political activity should direct society's energy at 'the abolition of recurrent sources of strain in society'. The tension level should be reduced as far as possible through 'preventive politics'. This should be guided by 'the truth about the conditions of harmonious human relations, and the discovery of the truth is an object of specialized research; it is no monopoly of people as people, or ruler as ruler' (197).

The covert analogy is with medicine. Medical researchers develop the knowledge necessary for applying preventive medicine to the human constitution. Political scientists provide a similar service enabling preventive politics to be applied to the political constitution.

By the use of a psychopathological approach relying on evidence such as individual life histories and techniques such as free-fantasy, the personality systems of both rulers and ruled could be analysed. Careful analysis of childhood experience could reveal typical patterns producing, for example, the agitator and the administrator.

Lasswell concluded that 'Agitators as a class are strongly narcissistic types. Narcissism is encouraged by obstacles in the early love relationships, or by overindulgence and admiration in the family circle' (125). By contrast,

As a class the administrators differ from the agitators by the displacement of their affects upon less remote and abstract objects. In the case of one important group this failure to achieve abstract objects is due to excessive preoccupation with specific individuals in the family circle, and to the correlative difficulty of defining the role of the self.

(Lasswell 1951a: 151)

Lasswell proposed a general formula for the developmental history of political man. It was $p \} d \} r = P$. In this formula, p represents private motives, d equals displacement on to public objects, r means rationalization in terms of public interest, P refers to the political man and the sign $\}$

indicates 'transformed into'. Lasswell argued that the political man has similar private motives to everyone else in early life. Like some of his fellow men he displaces these private motives on to public objects. What marks out the political man as singular, however, is 'the rationalization of the displacement in terms of public interests' (Lasswell 1951a: 262). For example, a political agitator is, in fact, looking for love or 'response' to himself as an individual, but he is likely to present himself as, say, the saviour of his class or country.

Ironically, although this was very much opposed to the spirit of Laski's work, Lasswell's approach overlapped with his at a key point. Laski had made the subjective experience of the citizen a litmus test which determined the legitimacy or otherwise of the state. He abhorred the idea of the state making overriding and irresistible claims upon the individual on behalf of society. Lasswell was sympathetic to such a view, for he argued that an observer might choose 'specific subjective experiences, such as a sense of loyalty to the community, and say that all who have this experience [and/or certain others] under specified conditions make up the state' (241).

Such a method assumed (as Laski assumed) that 'The group is not a superindividual phenomenon but a many-individual phenomenon' (241). One consequence of this approach was that although the state was 'independent of any one individual . . . it ceases to exist when enough individuals change their minds or die without procreating' (242). Building upon a similar assumption, Laski had argued that politicians and officials should, on the one hand, become as familiar as possible with the experiences of ordinary people and, on the other hand, cultivate knowledge and rationality ('instructed judgement') among the population at large.

Lasswell certainly accepted the first point. Social administrators and social scientists should 'mix with rich and poor, with savage and civilized, with sick and well, with old and young' (201). However, in doing this Lasswell's expert would be not so much obeying the injunction to 'educate and be educated by his clients and constituents' (as Laski might have said) but the command to get into 'direct contact with his material in its most varied manifestations' (201).

Laski supported reason in the sense of informed discussion among interested parties. By contrast, Lasswell backed reason in the form of scientific intervention eased by the acquiescence of those who constituted the scientists' 'material'. As he put it: 'The preventive politics of the future will be intimately allied to general medicine, psychopathology, physiological psychology, and related disciplines. Its practitioners will gradually win respect in society among puzzled people who feel their responsibilities and who respect objective findings' (203).

Elites and the mass

In *Politics: Who Gets What, When and How?* (1951b), Lasswell's interpretation was based upon 'the working attitude of practising politicians' concerned with 'influence and the influential' (7). The book is organised in three parts. The first part distinguished between the elite and the mass according to their success in obtaining values such as deference, income and safety within the social order. Elites could be analysed in terms of their capacity to manipulate a variety of techniques which kept them at the top of the pyramid of values. Their economic and other characteristics could also be considered. Most of the book is devoted to an exploration of these two dimensions of elites.

In the section on the manipulative techniques of actual and would-be elites, Lasswell illustrated their use of symbols, controlled violence, material goods (e.g. through rationing or pricing policies) and political techniques (such as centralisation of government or careful dispersion of power). The next section examined the characteristics of the elites which resulted from such manoeuvres. They exhibited a variety of skills including fighting, organising and bargaining, and came from a number of class backgrounds. They represented different personality types including, in conditions of insecurity and crisis, types driven by inhibited (or even uninhibited) rage. A wide range of attitudes was found, including, in Western Europe, a mixture of militancy, parochialism and external orientation, e.g. aggressiveness towards neighbours.

The book just described was complemented by *World Politics and Personal Insecurity* (1965). This was an attempt to come to terms with world-wide shifts in the pattern of elites and the symbols associated with them since the Russian Revolution of 1917. Partial incorporation of the new social pattern had occurred outside Russia in the form of the European fascist movements with their single-party rule, extension of government bureaucracy, reliance on functional rather than territorial representation, and use of plebiscites.

Since 1929 these political movements had flourished in a context of intensified economic parochialism which was undermining the world market. The consequent insecurity could be analysed using a mixture of 'extensive' and 'intensive' procedures. Extensive procedures were typified by the work of Marx and Engels in 'tracing the lineaments of social development'. Intensive procedures included studies of 'the genetic sequence of personality development' (Lasswell 1965: 18), relating to each other the career lines of people living in the same epoch. Using these techniques the analyst could work out how mass tension was likely to be discharged – in response to which social changes and which symbols – and encourage ways of doing this which were less costly than wars and revolutions.

In the body of this work Lasswell applied these extensive and intensive procedures. He examined the role of nations and classes as symbols of identification, the effects of a shifting international balance of power, and the impact of the war crisis, independence movements and imperialism. Economic conditions, migration patterns and the mass media were also considered. One conclusion was that inter-state hostility, increased popular participation in politics, and world depression had produced a dangerous situation by the mid 1930s:

> Diminished material income has provoked efforts to increase psychological income by restoring a new sense of significance to damaged personalities, justifying their existence in relation to the building of a 'Socialist Society' of a 'Third Reich'; new substitutes for bread are supplied by self-selected specialists on the manipulation of symbols, the modern masters of political propaganda.
>
> (Lasswell 1965: 124)

The United States had been relatively isolated from world-wide tendencies. In any case, the slavery issue had inhibited the development of strong class identifications. Lasswell teasingly suggested that socialism might make more headway in America if it called itself 'organized individualism' (166). He offered a prescription for 'an American *Capital*' to inspire collectivist enthusiasm. The book would have to have a slogan-like title and be thick: 'Thickness conveys authoritativeness and discourages reading by the masses who must revere the book as a symbol.' It should have a battery of charts, graphs, tables 'and other impressive impedimenta of exactitude'. The style should be emotive, invidious, ambiguous, obscure, contradictory and, if possible, 'dull, in order to reduce the danger that the work will be extensively read' (167).

More seriously, Lasswell noted that America had fewer 'cultural shock absorbers' than 'more stable civilizations' (174): no confident ruling elite enjoying mass deference, no prestigious bureaucracy, no consensus about action for common goals, no integrated style of living. Increased insecurity was liable to produce rigid centralisation, revolutionary movements and war 'unless the emotional tensions of the nation are handled with skill, luck and persistence' (176).

Personality and power

In *Power and Personality* (1948) Lasswell laid down the main outlines of a policy science designed to serve 'the specific needs of democracy' (109). In this book his treatment of the psychological bases of political careers was approximately the same as in his earlier books, but a change had occurred in his discussion of power. In contrast to his earlier focus upon elites he now stressed that

> it would be a mistake to imagine that . . . we are wholly taken up
> with the few rather than the many . . . . Power is an interpersonal
> situation: those who hold power are empowered. They depend upon
> and continue only so long as there is a continuing stream of
> empowering responses.
>
> (Lasswell 1948: 10)

Earlier he had treated values such as income, deference and safety in
terms of their distribution: 'Those who get the most are *elite*; the rest
are *mass*' (Lasswell 1958: 13; original emphasis). The emphasis had
shifted from the distributional to the relational.

In fact, those at the top of the pyramid were now described in terms
of leadership, rather than exclusive elite membership. The boundary
between elite and mass became very blurred:

> The term 'elite' is used in descriptive political science to describe
> the social formation from which leaders are recruited . . . .
> Democratic leadership is recruited from a broad base and remains
> dependent upon the active support of the entire community. With few
> exceptions every adult is eligible to have as much of a hand in the
> decision-making process as he wants and for which he is successful
> in winning the consent of his fellow citizens. There is no monopoly
> of power in a ruling caste when such conditions prevail, and the whole
> community is a seedbed from which rulers and governors come. The
> elite of democracy ('the ruling class') is society-wide.
>
> (Lasswell 1948: 109)

This set the tone for the rest of the book. Abandoned was the narrow-
eyed realism of *Politics: Who Gets What, When and How?*, which dealt
with the tool-kit of crafty wheezes available to manipulative elites. In
this new post-war approach, the masses were not subject to devious
manoeuvres by elites. Instead, leaders strove to acquire consent from
below. The language changes, investing democracy with positive
vibrations: 'Our conception of democracy is that of a network of
congenial and creative interpersonal relations. Whatever deviates from
this pattern is antidemocratic and destructive' (110). And what had
happened to the politics of prevention, an approach stressing the deliberate
reduction of tension rather than rational discussion to solve social
problems? Lasswell now thought that

> catharsis is not enough. We do not want to protect democracy by
> manipulating the community into a variety of activities deliberately
> encouraged or designed for the purpose of preserving as much of the
> status quo as possible. Any status quo deserves rational, selective,

progressive change. We want a social equilibrium in which men receive the intelligence they need for the making of rational choices, and in which they possess the skill and the will to make decisions in a free society.

(Lasswell 1948: 130–1)

At first sight, Lasswell had beaten a path back to Laski, who also placed great emphasis upon rational discussion and informed judgement. However, Lasswell did not just want a noble-minded democratic leadership capable of encouraging careful discussion of shared values and goals. He also wanted a nation-wide team of political scientists trained to run social observatories. As has been seen, these would monitor the psychic crises and political imaginings of children and young people. Unfortunately for Lasswell, the personnel were not available. Nor did political scientists have as much prestige as their colleagues, the economists who came 'close to providing a symbol that stands for some degree of special competence in describing certain collective features of our common life'. Lasswell observed that

As for the symbol 'political scientist' or 'professional student of government', there is almost no public image. So little, in fact, that Harold J. Laski and other members of the London School of Economics and Political Science find it convenient, on most occasions, to forget the 'political science' and call themselves economists (not always to the satisfaction of the matured-in-wood economists).

(Lasswell 1948: 133)

In fact, as will be seen, the attempt to manage democracy with which Harold Lasswell and his mentor Charles E. Merriam were so closely associated was already under fierce attack from leading economists in the United States.

Conclusion

Three issues focus attention upon the major points of overlap and difference between Laski and Lasswell. They are their treatments of the interplay between rationality and subjectivity, the relationship between the public and private spheres, and relations between political establishments and ordinary citizens.

On the first point, as far as Laski was concerned, individual experience leavened by education was the proper basis of good judgement. A polity should draw upon as wide a range of subjective experiences as possible. It should provide full opportunity for rational discussion among all individuals or groups whose experiences were relevant to specific policy decisions. These discussions should be timed and located within political and economic institutions in such a way as to transmit the distilled wisdom they produced as directly as possible to the effective points of decision-making.

In turn, political and economic institutions should be organised so as to maximise the opportunities for individuals to have experiences in which their intellectual and other functions were expressed to the fullest possible extent. In such a society, the subjective experiences of all citizens would contribute fully to rational policy decisions; and rational policies would establish an occupational structure providing fulfilling experiences for all citizens.

By contrast, Lasswell's interest in the subjective states of individuals was that of a scientist wishing to discover how these states were related to their social performances and to tendencies within social institutions. Subjective experiences had a determinate relationship to individual behaviour which could be uncovered by the scientist on the basis of data about several individuals and the application of psychological and other theories. The subjects of the research were probably ignorant of both the theories and the data.

Rational analysis of the situation was carried out by the external observer, the scientist. As Lasswell wrote (to paraphrase), the discovery of truth was a specialised business. Irrational behaviour swayed by fear, envy and other emotions was extremely commonplace. Indeed, such behaviour could be scientifically produced in wartime using appropriate techniques. In peacetime, the political scientist could advise governments how to minimise tension and even, perhaps, nurture 'congenial and creative' relationships between individuals. Democracy was about the manipulative formation of an appropriate personality type by trained professionals.

Second, as mentioned above, Laski envisaged the setting up of a 'virtuous circle' of mutual support between the state and the private citizen. His scheme of positive liberty assumed that the powers of government would be used to advance the interests of individuals throughout society. A 'vicious circle' was also possible leading to a withdrawal of legitimacy by citizens. This possibility was, unfortunately, being brought closer. Achievement of the desired balance between the public and private spheres was being prevented by the state of relations between property and the people. Capitalist interests inhibited the democratic processes which would enable the necessary reform of institutions and attitudes to take place.

Lasswell's model also focused upon the 'internal dynamics' of the relationship between individual citizens and the realm of government and politics. However, as seen, he introduced a third party – the political scientist – as regulator of the relationship. The possibility of a conflict between capitalism and democracy did not come on to Lasswell's agenda.

He adopted an elite model of politics which treated the possession of income and the manipulation of material goods as just two possibilities within a more complex typology of power resources and political techniques.

Third, both Laski and Lasswell took for granted that political life would be organised 'from above' through the activities of political establishments organised into elites and parties. However, they had radically different attitudes towards individualism and activism on the part of ordinary citizens. Laski was a great supporter of active citizenship and the free expression of opinion at all levels. Such active citizens could all too easily become classified as, to use Lasswell's term, 'agitators'.

Lasswell argued that agitators had failed to resolve certain childhood experiences in a satisfactory manner. They were trying to work out their personality problems in the public arena. When popular participation in politics increased between the wars he suggested it was due to the widespread existence of 'damaged personalities'. In 1835 Tocqueville had treated the high level of active citizenship he found as a sign of considerable maturity and strength. In 1935 Lasswell considered that high levels of participation were an indication of immaturity and weakness. Something had changed.

Chapter eight

Schumpeter and Hayek

The challenge from Vienna

During the early part of the twentieth century the social sciences were beginning to provide new techniques and justifications for intervention by the state in society. Laski's form of political science drew upon Marx and envisaged wholesale social engineering. Lasswell borrowed from Freud and worked on schemes for intervening at the level of the individual. The claims of social science were given credibility by the power of both its major clients, the state and big business.

Justification of intervention had to relate to its contribution to achieving the goals of capitalist democracy. A consensus was beginning to emerge within the American and British capitalist democracies that the crucial test of economic and political arrangements was their capacity to produce decent living standards for the vast majority of the people. 'Decency' in this context meant reasonable availability of material and cultural goods, sufficient leisure and income to enjoy them, and a degree of choice with respect to consumption and use of free time.

The consequences of increased intervention could be judged in terms of a trade-off between individual liberty and social progress in respect of living standards. Joseph Schumpeter and Friedrich A. Hayek both calculated the losses and gains produced by this trade-off. As will be seen, they arrived at conflicting conclusions.

In 1944 Friedrich A. Hayek's book *The Road to Serfdom* (1976a) was published. Harold Lasswell's teacher, Charles E. Merriam, reviewed it in the *American Journal of Sociology*. He did not like its contents:

The author [wrote Merriam] vigorously denounces any and all forms of planning, expresses his reservations about mass democracy, and holds as suspect 'conscious social control.'. . . The author blandly brushes aside all the many forms of city planning, state planning, regional planning, national planning, with one stroke of his pen. Since the socialists have employed the term 'planning' it must be placed on the black list . . . . But this is not argument, academic or nonacademic. It is, indeed, a piece of arrogance . . . . On what meat does this our Caesar feed . . .?

(Merriam 1944: 234)

Merriam objected strongly to an approach so deeply suspicious of administrators: 'The only home of freedom in the Hayek philosophy is the market place . . . . His root error lies, of course, in the assumption that the essence of the political is violence, while that of the economic is freedom of choice' (234).

It would be unfair to both Hayek and Merriam to suggest that this review of *The Road to Serfdom* indicated the considered views of either man on the nature of capitalist democracy. However, it does reveal the intense feelings provoked by Hayek's work. Merriam was upset at planners being lumped together with 'socialists', especially in a book which had made the *New York Times* best seller list and been summarised in the *Reader's Digest*.

When Merriam and Hayek appeared together on a University of Chicago Round Table radio broadcast in April 1945, hostilities broke out once more. Merriam sharply corrected Hayek: 'It must be a disappointment . . . to have a man, an American planner, tell you that we do not use your word in that sense and that we do not like the way you push it on us.' Merriam was referring, indirectly, and not quite pleasantly, to the fact that Hayek was a recent immigrant from Europe, whose style retained some distinctly Germanic features. Hayek was not put down. Shortly afterwards he retorted: 'I am saying that people like you, Merriam, are inclined to burden democracy with tasks which it cannot achieve, and therefore are likely to destroy democracy' (quoted in Karl 1974: 291–2).

Hayek's intervention in the debate on capitalist democracy was one aspect of the highly influential contribution of Viennese intellectuals to Anglo-American scholarship. Joseph Alois Schumpeter, whose pessimistic conclusions about the future of capitalism were set out in *Capitalism, Socialism and Democracy* (1981), first published in 1942, provided no greater comfort to academic experts like Merriam and Lasswell. Many social scientists from Chicago University and elsewhere believed that their political and governmental involvements were a means of promoting true democratic values in an increasingly complex urban industrial society (Smith 1988). Hayek's 'new conservatism' cast serious doubt upon their methods. Schumpeter's 'new realism' undermined belief in the attainability of their goals.

Hayek and Schumpeter were both children of the Austro-Hungarian Empire which perished in the First World War. Schumpeter was born in Moravia (now part of Czechoslovakia) in 1883. After studying law at the University of Vienna he carried out research in economics at the

London School of Economics. Following this he held a number of positions, including professor of political economy at the University of Graz, treasury secretary in Austria's first republican government in 1919, and president of a private bank in Vienna. Following a subsequent period as professor at the University of Bonn, Schumpeter left in 1932 to take up a chair at Harvard, where he remained till his death in 1950.

One of Schumpeter's old Harvard pupils, Paul A. Samuelson, remembered him as 'urbane and cynical' with 'something of the outsider about him. Except that Schumpeter was not Jewish, he shared some of the insecurities and strengths of those other Moravians, Freud and Mahler' (Samuelson 1981: 12). Schumpeter worked very hard, but adopted the pose of a nonchalant denizen of cafe society: 'He always had time for a cup of coffee at the disreputable Merle Cafe across from the Harvard Yard, and a spare hour in which to suffer fools gladly' (1).

Hayek was a different kettle of fish. He was born in Vienna in 1899 to a family of scientists and academics. By 1929 he had the position of *privatdozent* in political economy at the University of Vienna. Two years later he was invited to lecture at the London School of Economics. Lionel Robbins later recalled his arrival: 'I can still see the door of my room opening to admit the tall, powerful, reserved figure which announced itself quietly and firmly as "Hayek" ' (quoted in Craver 1986: 21). Later that same year Hayek was appointed professor of economic science and statistics in Robbins's department. It was from this English base that Hayek launched his critique of current political tendencies in *The Road to Serfdom*. He later moved to Chicago (1950–62) where he published his sequel *The Constitution of Liberty* (1976b). His subsequent appointments were at Freiburg (1962–7) and Salzburg (from 1974). Hayek was awarded the Nobel Prize in Economics in 1974.

Hayek and Schumpeter both perceived a strong drift towards socialism within capitalist societies during the 1930s. In the late 1930s, Schumpeter argued that the very success of capitalism was leading to its self-destruction. Centralist socialism, the socialism of the Russian experiment, was the most likely candidate to succeed capitalism. A few years later, Hayek argued that socialistic tendencies in modern institutions were threatening capitalism with stagnation and failure.

Schumpeter devoted his energies to describing as accurately and rationally as he could the economic, political and social tendencies which he believed were occurring. In an era when fear of economic depression was widespread, he pointed out the enormous material gains that had been achieved and were likely, in his view, to continue to be achieved. By contrast, Hayek concentrated upon identifying as accurately and rationally as he could what had been lost as a result of current political tendencies. In a period when optimism about the potential of planning within national economies was relatively high he pointed out the great losses in personal liberty which had, he believed, occurred and which, he thought, were likely to continue to occur.

Unlike Schumpeter, Hayek lived to see the full flowering of American global economic and political power during the 1950s. He laid his bet not upon socialism but upon 'the unknown civilization that is growing in America' (to quote the dedication in *The Constitution of Liberty*).

Innovation and the entrepreneur

Schumpeter combined the talents of economist and historical sociologist. However, his professional identity was firmly located in economics. Indeed, he believed that the specialised knowledge of the competent professional economist was destined to play a key role as planning acquired increasing importance. Under socialism, the economist would be indispensable (see Perman 1985).

Schumpeter's economic analysis is to be found in his *Theory of Economic Development* (1934), originally published in 1911, and *Business Cycles* (1939). The basic assumptions of his historical sociology are found in *Imperialism and Social Classes* (1951), which contains two essays. The first, on 'the sociology of imperialisms', first appeared in 1919. The second, on 'social classes in an ethnically homogeneous environment', was first published in 1927. The two streams of analysis came together during the Second World War in *Capitalism, Socialism and Democracy*.

Schumpeter criticised his predecessors, Marx being the main exception, for treating business cycles

> as a phenomenon that is superimposed upon the normal course of capitalist life and mostly as a pathological one; it never occurred to the majority to look to business cycles for material with which to build the fundamental theory of capitalist reality.
>
> (Schumpeter 1963: 1135)

To summarise Schumpeter's approach very briefly, he focused upon disruptions of the stationary state or 'circular flow' (Schumpeter 1934: 61) caused by the exploitation of new opportunities for profitable investment. Competition was assumed to be sufficiently imperfect to provide high profits to whoever was first in a new field. These surges of enterprise were closely associated with an expansion of credit, inflation in money supply and rising prices. Overproduction and recession followed, but not before new levels of productivity had been established.

No attempt will be made here to describe in any detail Schumpeter's 'theoretical, historical and statistical analysis of the capitalist process' (to quote the subtitle of *Business Cycles*). However, at its centre was the dynamic part played by the innovating entrepreneur backed up by credit advanced from the banking system. Innovation was more than mere invention. It included not only 'the introduction of new commodities' but also

> Technological change in the production of commodities already in use, the opening up of new markets or of new sources of supply, Taylorization of work, improved handling of material, the setting up of new business organizations such as department stores – in short, any 'doing things differently' in the realm of economic life.
>
> (Schumpeter 1939: 84)

It was evident to Schumpeter that innovation was 'at the center of practically all the phenomena, difficulties and problems of economic life in capitalist society' (87). One reason for this was that innovations did not occur smoothly, continuously and incrementally, but came bunched up together in time and with highly disruptive effects. As a consequence economic evolution ws 'lopsided, discontinuous, disharmonious by nature'. The history of capitalism was 'studded with violent bursts and catastrophes' which disturbed existing structures 'like a series of explosions' (102).

Schumpeter was not referring to the Marxian model of revolutionary class conflict associated with changes in the mode of production. The agent of change was the entrepreneur, who might be the founder of an industrial firm, a salaried employee or an important shareholder. It was 'leadership rather than ownership that matters'. The failure to see this and to recognise 'entrepreneurial activity as a distinct function *sui generis*' (103) was a fault common to the classical economists and Karl Marx. Two points were relevant. First, the entrepreneur did not, strictly speaking, risk his own money. The person who saw the opportunity to innovate had to obtain capital before the opportunity could be seized. If this person was also a capitalist he could invest his own money. This, however, was only one possible case. In many cases, credit was obtained from finance houses or other sources. As for the innovator, '*qua* entrepreneur he loses other people's money'.

Second, entrepreneurs did not form a social class. Those who were successful might succeed in joining the capitalist class, but they came initially from all social classes. Their families might be artisans, aristocrats, professionals, peasants or whatever. Schumpeter added that this was 'a fundamental piece of the sociology of capitalism and of bourgeois society' (104). It derived from his earlier work on capitalism and social class to which we now turn.

The aristocracy and bourgeois society

Schumpeter's two essays on imperialism and social class, respectively, examined the contrasting life styles and life interests of the aristocracy and the bourgeoisie. In 'The sociology of imperialisms' he argued that imperialist movements in late nineteenth- and early twentieth-century Europe and America were not deeply rooted in contemporary capitalism. They were not an emanation of the bourgeoisie. Instead, they were the last fling of a declining aristocracy. Far from being an intrinsic characteristic of the capitalist mode of production and the civilisation that went with it, contemporary imperialism was a mixture of political catch-phrases and vested interests that went against the grain of bourgeois society.

Disraeli had recognised that the British public were not prepared to make sacrifices for the empire. They treated imperialist policy as 'a toy, as a political arabesque'. Foolishly, Joseph Chamberlain took imperialism seriously and marshalled all his resources, including 'a consummate propaganda technique', behind this policy. In response, 'England rejected him' (Schumpeter 1951: 17).

Imperialism had its true place in earlier societies which did not regard making war as a painful disruption of peaceful private pursuits. In ancient empires like Egypt and Persia the nation was organised for war. In such cases the society realised itself in plunder and combat, activities which gave full rein to lust and avarice. As late as the time of Louis XIV, the state was, first and foremost, a war machine. The nobility, confined to 'flirtation, sports and court festivities', yearned for military action: 'Any war would do' (76).

Modern imperialism drew upon this atavistic heritage. At first sight this argument is similar to Veblen's discussion of the predatory instinct. A major difference, however, is that in Schumpeter's scheme of things, the entrepreneur wore a lounge suit rather than a suit of armour. In other words, instead of adopting feudal standards of behaviour, the entrepreneur undermined them. As the leaders of successful economic enterprises increasingly dominated society, so did the guiding principles of their 'actions, desires, needs, and beliefs' (87).

Intellectuals, professionals, industrial workers and rentiers all helped to build a new 'specialized, mechanized world. Thus they were all democratized, individualized and rationalized . . . the marks of this process are engraved on every aspect of modern culture' (88–9). Pure instinct was driven into the background. Business competition absorbed all the energies previously available for war.

Some established entrepreneurs favoured protective tariffs, a concomitant of imperialism, in order to avoid adapting to increased competition from abroad. They typically found allies among non-capitalist groups left over from the old society, especially large landowners. A complementary formation was the alliance between bankers and industrialists within organised or 'trustified' (107) capitalism. In this case, cartelisation of the domestic economy was combined with export of surplus capital.

Although he recognised the existence of imperialist tendencies, Schumpeter argued that beneath 'export-dependent monopoly capitalism' the 'real community of interest among nations' would never disappear: 'Deep down, the normal sense of business and trade usually prevails' (Schumpeter 1951: 111). Imperialism was not a structural imperative but 'the fruit of political action'. Schumpeter concluded that it was *'a basic fallacy to describe imperialism as a necessary phase of capitalism, or even to speak of the development of capitalism into imperialism'* (118; original emphasis).

Class formation processes were tackled more directly in the essay entitled 'Social classes in an ethnically homogeneous environment'. At the base of Schumpeter's approach was the assumption that the family rather than the individual was 'the true unit of class and class theory' (148). Over time, families moved up and down within classes and sometimes crossed class boundaries. Movement into a class or out of one was, paradoxically, both an exceptional event and a normal one. Like a birth or a death within a family it did not happen every day but was far from unexpected.

The position of families within classes and classes within societies very much depended upon the performance of their members. This aspect was crucial to Schumpeter who placed great emphasis upon qualities of management and leadership: 'hard-headed and practical shrewdness in the management of a given position plays a very great part' (151). For example, it mattered *how* profits were used as well as how big they were: 'surplus value *does not invest itself* but must *be invested*' (155; original emphasis). The capacity to innovate was a great help to a family on the make.

A class such as the aristocracy or the bourgeoisie – Schumpeter paid little attention to the proletariat – was constantly being judged by society according to two criteria: the relative significance of the social function it carried out and the degree of success with which it performed that function.

As has been noted, the function of the aristocracy had been to make war. It had provided expert mounted fighters prepared for chivalry. From the late fourteenth century onward, this function had been whittled away. The state had imposed its power through a new administrative machine. The feudal order had been undermined by commerce. Courtly ways corrupted the vigour of the warrior class. By nestling close to the state the aristocracy retained wealth and influence even though it had lost its old function. New functions, especially staffing the state administration and running their estates, cushioned the decline of this class, but at the cost of undermining the knightly ethos. The aristocracy became entangled in the cash nexus and acquired a 'calculating, private-economic' attitude towards property (Schumpeter 1951: 200).

By the early nineteenth century, the bourgeoisie had managed to install itself and its values in a dominant position within society. Unlike the aristocracy, this new class had constantly to repeat the successful performance that enabled it to acquire its position. On the other hand, however, unsuccessful families dropped out of the bourgeoisie so quickly that this class was less damaged by an accumulation of failures than the aristocracy had been. Unfortunately, there was another side to this coin. Unlike its predecessor, the bourgeoisie was denied the prestige that went with having been 'the supreme pinnacle of a uniformly constructed social pyramid', 'lord and master of every sphere of life', and 'physical power incarnate' (201). These assets in the hands of the aristocracy could still be exploited in industrial society since 'The modern industrialist is anything but such a leader' (220). This comment looks forward to *Capitalism, Socialism and Democracy*.

Marxian theory and socialist politics

In *Capitalism, Socialism and Democracy* (1981), Schumpeter was in debate with Karl Marx. He admired the way Marx had been able to combine a great work of positivistic social science with a subtle appeal to extra-rational cravings. As a sociologist he had managed to produce an 'analytical strategy which linked the fate of the class phenomenon with the fate of capitalism in such a way that socialism became . . . by definition, the only possible kind of classless society, excepting primitive groups' (19). In a similar way, he had bound together his economics and his sociology by identifying the economic category of 'labour' with the sociological category of 'proletariat' (45).

As an economist, Marx had made an important contribution to understanding business cycles. His idea that capitalist evolution would catastrophically burst asunder capitalist institutions cleverly combined 'a *non sequitor* with profound vision' (42). However, despite the predictions of violence sometimes made by Marx and his successors, including the theorists of imperialism, Marx himself had been 'much too strongly imbued with a sense of the inherent logic of things social to believe that revolution can replace any part of the work of evolution'. Beneath 'the fantastic glitter of dubious gems', Marx's work carried 'a distinctly conservative implication' (58).

European socialist parties benefited from the serious damage done to the prestige of national ruling classes by the First World War. Many of them entered government faced with the unexpected task of helping to administer not a socialist, but a capitalist society. They had not anticipated 'The bourgeois victim turning to the socialists for shelter' (365). This experience strengthened the practical commitment of socialists to the capitalist invention of democracy.

The Second World War was shifting the balance still further away from the old ruling class towards socialism. After this war, Schumpeter predicted, Anglo-American global rule would take the form of 'Ethical Imperialism'. Europe would be dominated by 'laborite or Social Democratic' (373) governments. The wartime regime of high taxation, inflation and bureaucratic controls would persist. Many contemporary socialists would dislike it. In fact, it was likely 'to present fascist features' (375).

Schumpeter enjoyed shocking his conservative readers by saying capitalism was doomed. At the same time, he told his radical readers that Marx had got it wrong. Nevertheless, socialism seemed inevitable. Schumpeter was well aware that this outcome might be at the expense of certain freedoms. A great deal would depend upon the quality of leadership available and the extent to which people understood the true character of capitalism, socialism and democracy.

Can capitalism survive?

> Can capitalism survive? No, I do not think it can . . . . The thesis I shall endeavour to establish is that the actual and prospective performance of the capitalist system is such as to negative the idea of its breaking down under the weight of economic failure, but that its very success undermines the social institutions which protect it, and 'inevitably' creates conditions in which it will not be able to live and which strongly point to socialism as the heir apparent.
>
> (Schumpeter 1981: 167)

Fifty years of capitalist growth before the late 1920s were likely to be succeeded by another half-century of growth. The relative distribution of income did not vary much over time. However, the standard of living of the poorer sections of the population benefited disproportionately in the course of growth. This was because growth was stimulated by spurts of innovation which produced 'avalanches of consumer goods' (68) for the mass market. Capitalism had succeeded not in 'providing more silk stockings for queens, but in bringing them within the reach of factory girls in return for steadily decreasing amounts of effort' (67).

This brilliant performance was made possible by two factors. First, the efficiency with which capitalism rewarded enterprise and penalised failure. And second, the effects of a remorseless process of 'creative destruction' (83). Innovations in technique, product, supply sources and organisational methods successively created then destroyed institutional forms and economic practices. Price competition was overtaken

by competition between rival commodities, materials and processes.
Monopoly and oligopoly aided this process. They provided protection for the innovating company, allowing it to resist raids by imitators eager to snatch the benefits of inventiveness without bearing the costs. Investment opportunities were unlikely to diminish. Entrepreneurs who scanned their horizons would find plenty of scope for further innovation. The frontier was not closed: 'The conquest of the air may well be more important than the conquest of India was' (Schumpeter 1981: 117).

The civilisation of capitalism was systematic, rationalistic and individualistic. It was also anti-heroic, pacific and devoted to the satisfactions of the private sphere. Business folk were 'inclined to insist on the application of the moral precepts of private life to international relations' (128).

At the heart of capitalism was the bourgeoisie. The dynamism of this class depended upon its successful entrepreneurs. Their function of generating innovation gave meaning and purpose to both the bourgeois class and the capitalist system. Unfortunately, the rationalisation and bureaucratisation which accompanied capitalist growth were having a disastrous effect upon the entrepreneur.

Innovation was becoming routinised. Technological progress was being undertaken by committees, bureaucratic departments and teams of trained specialists. Force of personality was less important now that people were getting used to the idea of change. Innovation was becoming depersonalised. This 'affects the position of the entire bourgeois stratum' since 'the bourgeoisie . . . depends on the entrepreneur and, as a class, lives and dies with him' (134).

Another source of weakness was 'the destruction of the protecting strata' (134) which had provided political shelter for the bourgeoisie. Typically, the bourgeois 'wants to be left alone and to leave politics alone'. Fortunately, the aristocracy carried out the task of political leadership in capitalist societies. They brought to capitalism the mystery and glamour which financiers and industrialists lacked: 'The stock exchange is a poor substitute for the Holy Grail' (137). Ironically, the success of capitalism progressively undermined the social position of the aristocracy. For a while the bourgeoisie even felt sufficiently safe to attack the position of its social betters. However, 'without protection from some non-bourgeois group, the bourgeoisie is politically helpless ... . it needs a master' (138). The final collapse of feudalism would presage the end of capitalism also.

The demise of capitalism was helped along by the steady displacement of small businesses by advancing oligopoly. The old arena of relatively free competition had been inhabited by proprietors with a strong commitment to the values of private property and freedom of contracting. As they went out of business, they became less reliable supporters of the capitalist system. Their passing witnessed 'the evaporation of what we may term the material substance of property – its visible and touchable reality' (Schumpeter 1981: 142).

In these circumstances, the social atmosphere of capitalism was becoming more hostile to the capitalist. Erosion of the final remnants of feudalism loosened the discipline tradition imposed upon the strong residue of popular irrationality.

Unfortunately, capitalism was unable to generate a strong emotional attachment to itself. On the contrary, it had cultivated a spirit of criticism. The intellectual was, in large part, a creature of capitalism. Ironically, the intelligentsia increasingly turned its weapons upon capitalism itself, often adopting the language of socialism.

Finally, the bourgeoisie was losing its faith in the family as a focus of emotional and material investment. Fewer opportunities were available to establish new industrial dynasties. The life of the home was being displaced by the restaurant and the club. Wife and children 'fade out from the moral vision of the businessman' (160). As it lost function and prospects, the inner self confidence of the bourgeoisie was ebbing away. The demise of capitalism might take as long as did the passing away of feudalism – perhaps another century, at least. But, as far as Schumpeter was concerned, the writing was on the wall.

Can socialism work?

> Can socialism work? Of course it can. No doubt is possible about that once we assume, first, that the requisite stage of industrial development has been reached and, second, that transitional problems can be successfully resolved.
>
> (Schumpeter 1981: 167)

By socialism, Schumpeter meant 'an institutional pattern in which the control over means of production and over production itself is vested with a central authority – or, as we may say, in which, as a matter of principle, the economic affairs of society belong to the public and not the private sphere' (167). As will be seen, for Schumpeter the expansion of the public sphere at the expense of the private was a far less ambiguous criterion of socialism than the rule of 'the people'.

In spite of the fears of Hayek and others that socialist bureaucracy would be confronted with an unmanageably complex task (185), Schumpeter accepted that socialism was viable as an economic system. It would be able to make many savings, including the abolition of the leisure class of idle rich. It could dispense with the costs of competition within the national economy. Planning would avoid the costly side effects of manipulating interest rates. Instead of the endemic struggle between the capitalist state which needed taxes and a propertied class defending its profits, socialism would permit a smooth administration of resources. Energies would no longer be lost in defending the sanctity of the private sphere against intrusions from the public realm. The division between the public and private spheres was, in fact, the 'outstanding feature of commercial societies'. With the sole exception of local self-government the two spheres were 'to a great extent manned by different people . . . and organised and run on different and often conflicting principles, productive of different and quite incompatible standards' (Schumpeter 1981: 197).

Relatively little remoulding of the capitalist culture would be required within the successor socialist regime. Farmers, factory workers and office clerks would all be working much as before. The special talents of the bourgeoisie should not be wasted if this was avoidable. Even in a more bureaucratic system it would be possible to satisfy individual egotism by giving marks of personal prestige to high performers. More generally, discipline would be reinforced by the moral authority of the regime. Everyone would be familiar with the economic logic underlying the system. In any case, 'A strike would be mutiny' (215).

Such a programme depended upon a society being mature enough to undertake the transition to socialism with relatively little disruption. England between the wars had given signs of being such a society. Its ruling class were able and adaptable, its people 'state-broken' (229). By contrast, America during the New Deal was decidedly unready.

Socialism was economically viable – under certain conditions. But would it be democratic? Before answering this question, Schumpeter tackled the prior issue: what *is* democracy? The 'classical doctrine' (250) assumed that individual wills might be co-ordinated by rational means so as to arrive at a common will. This common will would specify the most appropriate means to achieve the common good. But public opinion was, in many respects, irrational. Compromise between conflicting wills was not easy to achieve. In any case, while ordinary people were very well informed about their immediate interests at home and at work, when they ventured into public affairs 'the sense of reality is . . . completely lost' (261). The classical doctrine survived for historical and ideological reasons but it did not describe reality.

Schumpeter proposed another model of democracy. The main contribution of the people, he suggested, was to choose their representatives in parliament from the different teams that were presented to them by the political parties. It was the task of the elected representatives to provide support for a government which would do the actual job of governing. In effect, democracy involved competition between politicians for popular votes.

Schumpeter recommended this model on seven counts. First, it emphasised democracy as a method of electing representatives without reference to the content of political goals. The latter aspect of the classical doctrine was confusing since the 'common good' could in theory be achieved by non-democratic means. Second, Schumpeter's model emphasised leadership and accepted the role of the latter in generating a 'Manufactured Will' (Schumpeter 1981: 270). Third, the model took into account the interaction of sectional interests competing to shape opinion. Fourth, the competitive process of selecting political leaders was acknowledged. Fifth, the model gave an important place to freedom of discussion. Sixth, leaders might lose power through the withdrawal of popular support through the ballot box. And seventh, emphasis was placed upon the will of the majority, a more realistic notion than the will of 'the people'.

There was a clear analogy between the market – 'there exists no more democratic institution than a market' (184) – and the democratic political system. The people responded to initiatives taken by competing bands of political salespeople. Parties were liable to change policies in the same way a department store might rearrange its shop windows. They regulated political competition in the manner of a trade association within the market. A lot of energy went into promoting the product. 'The psycho-technics of party management and party advertising, slogans and marching tunes, are not accessories. They are of the essence of politics. So is the political boss' (283). These phenomena which so shocked Ostrogorski were re-invested with legitimacy in the work of Schumpeter.

Returning to the question of whether socialism could be democratic, Schumpeter argued that democratic and non-democratic versions of socialism were both viable. If a democracy were to exist, certain conditions had to be fulfilled. Politicians of high quality were needed, preferably from a stratum used to public life. Democracies should be self-limiting in the sense that they should not try to control too large an area of life. They needed strong and efficient bureaucracies to complement them. There should be a spirit of democratic self-control and moderation.

Capitalist societies were well-equipped to provide some of these conditions, especially in view of the bourgeois preference for a 'parsimonious state' (297). Socialist societies aspiring to be democratic would have to learn to distinguish between bureaucratic management, which would need to extend throughout the social order, and political management which should impose strict limits upon its reach over people's lives. Democracy should not be allowed to interfere with competent administration at the level of the factory. Balancing democracy outside the factory and authoritarian discipline within it would be a delicate task. Indeed, 'As a matter of practical necessity, socialist democracy may eventually turn out to be more of a sham than capitalist democracy ever was' (302). This was a conclusion which would have appealed to Friedrich von Hayek.

The road to serfdom

Hayek shared with Schumpeter an interest in business cycles and a preoccupation with the evolutionary tendencies which lay behind the advance of socialism. For example, he agreed with Schumpeter that 'the working class as a whole benefited from the rise of modern industry' (Hayek 1954: 27). However, unlike Schumpeter, who wove his economics and his historical sociology into the argument of *Capitalism, Socialism and Democracy*, Hayek consciously put aside 'problems of pure economic theory' (1976a: *v*) to write *The Road to Serfdom*. This was to set him on a trail which later led to *The Constitution of Liberty* (1976b) and the three volumes of *Law, Legislation and Liberty* (1973-9).

Hayek perceived a different kind of evolutionary process from the one recognised by Schumpeter. For the latter, evolution was driven by inventive genius, a combination of reason and imagination. For Hayek, the springs of change were unknowable, the limits of reason closely circumscribed. He wanted the learning processes of each individual to be allowed to proceed unhindered so that society as a whole could benefit. Paradoxically, in this last respect Hayek's approach was rather similar to that of one of his opponents, Harold Laski – except that Laski wanted the fruits of individual experience to be harnessed for the benefit of humankind through the state rather than through the market as was Hayek's way.

Murray Forsyth (1988) has pointed out that the metaphysical basis of Hayek's concept of man and the human mind is best understood by an examination of *The Sensory Order* (1952). Briefly, Hayek is shown to be a monist whose

> emphasis . . . is on the fundamental sameness of all kinds of mental activity, conscious and unconscious, and on their reducibility to a physical mechanism. The human being is an animal organism wholly absorbed in adapting to the environment in order to survive. Human thinking is a constantly changing pattern of the nervous system, part reactive and part calculatory, that enables the human being to achieve this end by incessantly grouping and re-grouping indeterminate environmental impulses.
>
> (Forsyth 1988: 24)

At first sight, such a human being hardly seems worth rescuing from serfdom. In fact, the point was not that men and women were too noble to be subjected to dictatorship. It was, rather, that no man or woman was noble enough to exercise that kind of rule over others. This thought, presumably, lay behind the attack on planners which so upset Charles E. Merriam.

Schumpeter and Hayek interpreted the depression of the 1930s in very different ways. Schumpeter stressed the element of continuity. He argued that despite the depression, capitalism would continue to grow, lifting up standards of living for all. Sometime in the future it would transform itself – smoothly, almost unnoticed – into socialism. By contrast, Hayek argued that in Britain, at least, 1931 represented a radical change of direction. Until that date *laissez-faire* had prevailed, even though it had been dispensed with in other European societies such as Germany, Italy and Russia. The individualism of the *laissez-faire* era had produced a flowering of economic enterprise and science. Standards of comfort and security increased to levels previously unimagined. So did expectations.

People acquired a 'new sense of power over their own fate' accompanied by a dangerous delusion: 'With the success grew ambition. . . . What had been an inspiring promise seemed no longer enough, the rate of progress far too slow; and the principles which had made this progress possible in the past came to be regarded more as obstacles to speedier progress, impatiently to be brushed away, than as the conditions for the preservation and development of what had already been achieved' (Hayek 1976a: 13).

Deluded by the achievements of liberalism with its spirit of individual freedom, as early as the 1840s many Europeans had turned towards socialism as a means of supposedly getting something even better. Hayek's definition of the term 'socialism' was broadly the same as Schumpeter's. He meant by it the abolition of private enterprise in favour of a central planned economy. Ironically (again this recalls Schumpeter), 'the very success of liberalism became the cause of its decline' (14). However, the transition from liberal capitalism to centralist planning was interpreted by Hayek in terms quite different from those of Schumpeter.

The latter expected the transition to occur some time in the future within mature capitalist societies as an outcome of monopolistic or oligopolistic tendencies which diminished the function of the heroic entrepreneur. Hayek, by contrast, argued that the transition had been underway since the 1840s, though delayed in Britain until the 1930s. It took the form not of a natural process of evolution but of a deliberate and disruptive process of social engineering. Inappropriate principles were applied by human beings who had a misguided sense of their own abilities. Socialism involved 'a complete reversal of the trend we have sketched, an entire abandonment of the individualist tradition which has created Western civilisation' (15). Attempts at social engineering were based upon a misunderstanding of society. Democratic socialism was unachievable. You could not plan for freedom. The more decisions that were taken by a central planning body, the less freedom you left individuals to plan their own lives. A much better course was to permit competition to flourish within 'a carefully thought-out legal framework' (27). Market prices provided individuals with the information they needed to regulate their actions. Government should have a clear but strictly limited role: to inhibit restrictive practices; maintain health and safety standards; enforce the law on private property, freedom of contract, corporations and patents; and fill in the gaps where markets could not provide necessary or highly desirable services such as road signposting and pollution control.

Technological advance and the development of more complex industrial structures did not make socialist planning – for Hayek all central planning was 'socialist' – inevitable. In fact, centralised planning was developed in Germany from 1878 onward when this industrial society was much 'younger' than Britain, still the flag-bearer of liberalism a half-century later.

The collective frustration of experts and specialists supplied political support for central planning. Unfortunately, they ignored the fact that the many desirable and possible social improvements they envisaged in aggregate could not be achieved all at once. None of them had the knowledge necessary to allow their various schemes to be effectively coordinated. In this respect planning could not match the performance of market competition. The price system allowed entrepreneurs to exploit the benefits of the division of knowledge 'by watching the movement of a comparatively few prices, as an engineer watches the hands of a few dials' (Hayek 1976a: 36).

A comprehensive social plan had to specify a hierarchy of goals. For this purpose a 'complete ethical code' (43) was needed. However, modern western morality completely failed to provide this. There were bound to be fundamental disagreements over planning in a democracy. Hayek had no enthusiasm for Laski's solution to this problem which was, as he understood it, 'that a socialist government must not allow itself to be too much fettered by democratic procedure' (47). Nor was Hayek keen on the implications of leaving matters of detail to the experts. Schumpeter had argued that a clear distinction between (relatively restricted) political control and (more far-reaching) bureaucratic control was desirable in a socialist political order. Hayek thought this gave far too much leeway to the prejudices of professionals and bureaucrats. Democracy was valueless if it sanctioned arbitrary power. The only form of democracy worth preserving was one which brought peace and freedom. 'If "capitalism" means . . . a competitive system based on free disposal over private property, . . . only within this system is democracy possible' (52).

The real choice was between a system where who gets what was decided by a few people (the planners) and one where it was determined by two factors: the distribution of ability and enterprise on the one hand and the play of unforeseeable circumstances on the other. The planned society replaced the influence of property – relatively unoppressive because it was divided among several people – with the unitary authority of an omnipotent state. Planning undermined the widespread habit of fatalistically accepting life's hard knocks. The experts claimed to be in control and could be blamed when things went wrong.

Quoting Lasswell's catchphrase, Hayek argued that under a socialist regime, the planners determined in detail 'who gets what, when, and how' (Hayek 1976a: 81). If they pursued social justice, this boiled down to the imposition upon everybody of a minority view of what was fair and proper. The planners would decide the functions and rewards of specific groups and individuals, discriminating between them according to standards of fairness which, ironically, derived from the old market-based society. Indoctrination and propaganda would be used to persuade the population at large to accept the planners' idea of distributive justice.

Resentment at the way socialist planners favoured the working class had caused a counter-movement among the petit bourgeoisie and service class. This resentment had fed into national socialism and fascism. These movements harboured no illusions about the possibility of combining planning with democracy. They were not inhibited by the liberal inheritance of individual freedom which still influenced the socialist ideal. The tendency towards nastiness within planned societies was encouraged by the need for consensus among their bureaucrats and henchmen. This was cultivated more easily among the less well educated, especially if a simple message was drummed into their heads. Unity was most effectively created by attacking an out-group and cultivating aggressive nationalism. A distinctive morality developed based upon the assumption that the ends of the government justified any effective means. The leader was to be obeyed at all costs. Personal morality should not resist the will of the state.

Hayek suggested that Britain in the mid 1940s, with its socialist tendencies, had a strong resemblance to Germany fifteen years previously, just before the rise of Hitler. Many Nazi supporters had begun as supporters of socialism before discarding its liberal and internationalist aspects. It was essential to restore faith in the Victorian values of Britain, rather than imitate German ideas and methods.

Hayek's prescription for social health included proper respect for the rule of law and a better understanding of the market. The law should not be a means of actively reshaping society. Its rules and penalties should be universal and predictable in their application. However, its effects on specific individuals and groups in particular circumstances should be unknown and unpredictable as far as the lawmakers were concerned. In that sense, justice should be blind. The detailed content of the law was less important than the fact that everyone should know the rules and adapt to them in making their own plans.

Within the market free individuals made choices about their use of scarce resources. Through these choices they decided what to regard as marginal and what to treat as priorities: 'This is really the crux of the matter. Economic control is not merely control of a sector of human life which can be separated from the rest; it is the control of the means of all our ends . . . in short, what men should believe and strive for' (Hayek 1976b: 68–9).

The constitution of liberty

Hayek's positive ideas about how capitalist democracies should be understood were developed further in *The Constitution of Liberty* (1976b). He distinguished between two traditions of freedom. The French tradition made 'flattering assumptions about the unlimited powers of human reason' (Hayek 1976b: 55). It placed high value upon systematic social organisation and the directive powers of the state.

The English tradition placed greater emphasis upon the accumulated wisdom produced through trial and error in the course of social evolution. This approach was 'empirical and unsystematic' (54). It valued the spontaneity of human adherence to moral rules attuned to inherited institutions and unconscious habits. Such rules adapted themselves gradually as society developed. They illustrated the undesigned non-rational substratum in which rational action was grounded.

Hayek favoured a negative view of freedom as the minimisation of coercion upon the individual. Such coercion as there was should, as far as possible, be the province of the judge enforcing the rule of law rather than the state imposing its commands. Individual freedom went with individual responsibility for your actions within the relevant sphere which was, typically, a local and limited one. Individual fulfilment depended upon finding a specific niche which allowed you to use your own special talents. Finding that niche was one of the tasks of a free individual.

The individual's knowledge of the world was very restricted. The aggregate knowledge of society was far from complete. In the absence of information we could not 'plan' an investigation of the unknown. The element of chance and the unexpected was vital to Hayek's model of society. It allowed for discoveries which increased our knowledge. Individual freedom which permitted people to make their own decisions and mistakes maximised the chance that such discoveries would be made.

One of the dangers of despotic rule established by majority vote was that the sphere of experiment in thought and action would be very limited. Hayek cited the career of Joseph Chamberlain (444) as an illustration of the danger of demagoguery. Democracy was of value only as a means to the end of individual freedom. It was vital that opinion formation should be independent of government. In the long run democratic processes of discussion would raise levels of popular understanding and knowledge.

In practice, advanced knowledge was acquired first by a select group and gradually filtered down to the rest of society. The same was true of the material advantages of industrial civilisation. An echelon pattern was typically established in which the rich and highly educated took the foremost position. In Britain, all classes profited from the existence of 'a rich class with old traditions [that] had demanded products of a quality and taste unsurpassed elsewhere' (Hayek 1976b: 47–8). In Hayek's view, the leisure class had a positive role to play in setting high standards and leading the way in experimenting with new things: 'even the successful use of leisure needs pioneering' (129). The rich were an 'advance guard' (130). He opposed egalitarian policies of redistributing wealth.

The ambition of establishing a meritocracy was also based upon a delusion. As consumers, we typically paid for results without enquiring how easily they were achieved. People were rewarded for the value to others of their performance, not the personal merit they deserved as individuals. People did not 'deserve' rewards just for trying hard or being well qualified. In any case, the bureaucracy needed for measuring personal worthiness and matching individual merit to individual reward would be intolerably intrusive. Such a strategy would directly contradict the goal of minimising the coercive powers of the state.

State coercion was to be discouraged since it involved 'the control of the essential data of an individual's action by another'. It could be 'prevented only by enabling the individual to secure for himself some private sphere where he can be protected against such interference' (139). The rights of the individual could be translated into rules about the content of this private sphere. As far as possible, state coercion should be restricted to measures which discouraged coercion by others, prevented avoidance of proper contracts, or established penalties. Such penalties should be either predictable (such as taxation) or contingent and therefore avoidable (such as the sanctions of the criminal law). Hayek had no sympathy with the attacks made by socialist lawyers and political scientists, including Laski, upon this limited concept of the rule of law. The latter supported a positivist doctrine of the law which turned it into an instrument of state administration.

Finally, Hayek identified a new danger. The era of socialism had been from 1848 to 1948. Socialism, he argued, was being replaced by a new enemy: the welfare state. The peril stemmed from the fact that although welfare bureaucracies seemed to be merely performing a social service, in practice they 'constitute an exercise of the coercive powers of government and rest on its claiming rights in certain fields' (258). The planners and bureaucrats were still busily chipping away at individual freedom. Both in terms of its method and its goals, which included the redistribution of wealth through progressive taxation, the welfare state should be resisted strongly.

Conclusion

Hayek's analysis did not pay much attention to two processes which were central to Schumpeter's argument. These were, first, the displacement of the entrepreneur by bureaucratised techniques for managing innovation within large oligopolistic companies, and second, the emergence of a form of democracy based upon competitive promotion of rival political parties. According to Schumpeter, the first change did not diminish the capacity of capitalism to sustain a high rate of growth. The second was a realistic and relatively efficient way of selecting leaders within democracies. By contrast, Hayek was reluctant to concede that the discovery of new things, including industrial inventions, could be planned bureaucratically. He also strongly associated mass appeals to the electorate with the irrational propaganda of national socialism.

Hayek placed his bet upon the strategy of maximising individual liberty. Freedom was not valued for its intrinsic worth to the individual as a noble and rational being. Rather, it was a means of maximising the growth of knowledge for the good of society as a whole. Schumpeter reversed the relationship between individual liberty and social progress. He believed that the price of advancing knowledge and rationality was a diminution of the scope for individual creativity. There is no reason to think that Schumpeter was happy about this. Progress – in terms of innovation, economic growth, increased rationality and greater material comfort – meant a decline in individualism. For Hayek, all these aspects of progress were seriously threatened unless individualism was restored to capitalist democracies.

Chapter nine

Galbraith and Crosland

Demystifying conventional wisdom

This chapter compares the work of two men – both theorists as well as political activists – who each attempted to shape a coherent and practical social-democratic programme during the two decades from the mid 1950s. One of these men is John Kenneth Galbraith, whose best known book is *The Affluent Society* (1979; originally published in 1958). This book was the first of a trilogy which struck three successive blows against neo-classical orthodoxy. The two other volumes were *The New Industrial State* (1974a; originally published in 1967) and *Economics and the Public Purpose* (1974b).

Galbraith will be contrasted with the British Labour politician Anthony Crosland. In a series of books – especially *The Future of Socialism* (1964; originally published in 1956), *The Conservative Enemy* (1962) and *Socialism Now* (1975; originally published in 1974) – Crosland attempted to delineate the theoretical and practical meaning of socialism in postwar Britain.

Galbraith and Crosland both cut their way through dense ideological undergrowth in order to focus upon the interplay between three aspects of contemporary capitalist democracy: the rejection of social inequality, the pursuit of material security and the implications of economic growth. Each presented a model of capitalist democracy which challenged conventional wisdom. Both men set out programmes of radical social reform based upon the need for a proper balance between the public and private sectors. Galbraith thought the latter was underdeveloped in the United States. Crosland thought that British socialism was fixated upon public ownership and paid too little attention to the social benefits flowing from widespread personal prosperity.

Worldliness and wit added force to the moral critique contained in these works by Galbraith and Crosland. In fact, both had a puritan streak in their backgrounds. Galbraith, born in 1908, came from a rural community of Scotch-Canadians in Ontario. On the basis of a strict

Calvinist upbringing, he made his way from Ontario Agricultural College to the University of California at Berkeley in the 1930s, where he carried out research in agricultural economics.

Tony Crosland, born ten years later, was the child of Exclusive Brethren. His background was more prosperous than Galbraith's since his father was a senior civil servant who could afford to send his son to public school. However, the fact that Crosland's father and his uncle both refused the offer of knighthoods shows that it was not a conventional English upper middle class family. Crosland studied Classics at Oxford, a course interrupted by the Second World War. Following active war service he returned to Oxford and switched to Philosophy, Politics and Economics. He became president of the Oxford Union.

Both men could draw upon practical experience of public business. During the Second World War Galbraith was, in turn, economic adviser to the National Defense Advisory Committee and deputy head of the Office of Price Administration. He later spent time in Germany studying the effects of Allied bombing. In 1948 he became professor of economics at Harvard University. He was American Ambassador to India (1961–3) during President Kennedy's period of office.

Beween 1940 and 1945 Crosland served in the Royal Welch Fusiliers and the 2nd Parachute Brigade, becoming a Captain. He served in North Africa, Italy, France and Austria. After the war he spent a few years as a fellow of Trinity College, Oxford and entered Parliament in 1950 as MP for South Gloucestershire. *The Future of Socialism* appeared soon after he lost this seat in 1955. Between 1959 and his death in 1977 Crosland was MP for Grimsby. This coincided with two periods of Labour government, 1964–70 and 1974–9. Crosland held several major offices, including responsibility for economic affairs, education and science, and the environment. In 1976 he became foreign secretary.

Unlike Galbraith, who wrote his major books after a lengthy career in public administration, Crosland produced his major work, *The Future of Socialism*, before becoming directly involved with government. His last major book, the collection of essays entitled *Socialism Now*, gives some clues to the way his ideas were altering in the light of his experience of the bruising business of being a minister. He did not live long enough to set down his mature reflections at length. Nevertheless, Crosland came nearer than either Joseph Chamberlain or Charles E. Merriam (two earlier examples of would-be philosopher–statesmen) to combining the roles of powerful politician and innovative political theorist.

Although Crosland disagreed with Galbraith on some matters, reviewing *The Affluent Society* he declared 'I am . . . wholeheartedly a Galbraith man' (Crosland 1962:103). It is therefore a good idea to begin with Galbraith.

The affluent society

Following the Second World War in the United States, there was what could have been called the free enterprise, possibly the market revival. It deeply engaged the conservative mind. Our conservatism is normally thought to depend on self-interest, moral indignation, violent expression and something approximating religious revelation. This is unjust. The influence of ideas is ubiquitous and cannot be excluded anywhere.

This quotation is from Galbraith's introduction to the third edition of *The Affluent Society* (1979). The passage continued with the comment that post-war conservatism had rediscovered the Benthamite world of the nineteenth century and

derived a new scholarly sanction from F. A. von Hayek's *The Road to Serfdom*, an alarming tract against socialism and the state, which, as the name implies, it identified extensively with servitude. And in the years following, it achieved considerably more academic reputability from an energetic group of evangelists who gathered, along with von Hayek, at the University of Chicago with intellectual outriders in other academic centres.

(Galbraith 1979: 7)

Ironically, the appearance of the third edition of *The Affluent Society* was quickly followed in 1979 by the election of Margaret Thatcher at the head of a Conservative government in the United Kingdom, and the success of Ronald Reagan, the Republican candidate in the 1980 American presidential election. Hayek's work was much admired in Thatcherite circles. Meanwhile, the Reaganite message stressed the need to return to old verities through a programme of cutting taxes and 'getting government off the backs of the people'. Following a relatively brief 'liberal hour' (to quote the title of another Galbraith text), the conservative mind had made a spectacular come-back. However, during the 1960s and 1970s Galbraith had outlined with increasing precision an alternative model of social, economic and political reality.

His central message of *The Affluent Society* was contained in the following passage:

The family which takes its mauve and cerise, air-conditioned, power-steered and power-braked automobile out for a tour passes through cities that are badly paved, made hideous by litter, blighted buildings, billboards and posts for wires that should long since have been put underground. They pass into a countryside that has been rendered largely invisible by commercial art. (The goods which the latter advertise have an absolute priority in our value system. Such aesthetic considerations as a view of the countryside around accordingly come

153

Capitalism and the Rise of Big Government

second. On such matters, we are consistent.) They picnic on exquis-
itely packaged food from a portable icebox by a polluted stream and
go on to spend the night at a park which is a menace to public health
and morals. Just before dozing off on an air mattress, beneath a nylon
tent, amid the stench of decaying refuse, they may reflect vaguely
on the curious unevenness of their blessings. Is this, indeed the
American genius?

(Galbraith 1979: 203–4)

The well-upholstered life-style just depicted lay beyond the ken of
traditional economics. From Adam Smith to Alfred Marshall it had been
assumed that privation was just around the corner for ordinary folk.
Ceaseless effort to increase economic efficiency was necessary to stave
off material disaster. Matters were made worse by the inequality endemic
to capitalist society and the insecurity produced by episodic bouts of
unemployment.

By the 1950s, inequality and insecurity had been taken off the political
agenda. The power of the rich became less obvious. Government and
the trade unions rivalled the plutocracy in influence. Company
bureaucrats took practical control out of the hands of shareholders. The
New Deal made farmers, industrial workers, the poor and the
unemployed feel more secure. Surprisingly, there was apparently no fall-
off in hard work and enterprise. This was fortunate because the banishing
of inequality and insecurity depended on making the economy as
productive as possible. Growth would solve social problems without
threatening the assets of the rich.

Keynes provided a rationale for the new approach. The idea was to
manipulate the level of aggregate demand through adjustments in government spending. In this way production could be maintained at a level
which would reduce unemployment, aid farmers, help investors, and
give a boost to local and state governments: 'Scarcely a social problem
was left untouched . . . . Most important of all for its influence on the
liberal mind, to promise to maintain production and reduce unemployment won elections' (155).

However, growth was pursued in a very haphazard way. Capital
formation was neglected. Technological innovation in basic industries
was skimped. Since the state was supposed to be an agent of tyranny,
production of public goods – schools, roads, parks and so on – was
relegated to 'second-class citizenship'. Above all, the production system
depended upon synthetic desires. Wants were socially manufactured: 'We
do not manufacture wants for goods we do not produce' (133). Advertising helped to produce these wants, creating what Galbraith called 'the
Dependence Effect' (148).

Two problems were endemic. One was the growing mountain of

154

consumer debt. The other was inflation. This was caused in part by a wage-price spiral in which unions and corporate management were both implicated. Despite experiments with monetary and fiscal policies, inflation had not been tamed. Direct controls were hardly used since they supposedly interfered with the market allocation of resources.

Even more fundamental, the public sphere was neglected in favour of the private sphere. This suited the vested interests of business people. The conventional excuse for the structural imbalance was that the people had brought it about by making a democratic choice. Galbraith claimed that this was a dishonest argument. In fact, wants were artificially stimulated by private business which then proceeded to satisfy them – at a price: 'No similar process operates on behalf of the nonmerchantable services of the state' (209). In fact, attempts to increase taxation levels for public spending ran into difficulties. First, the question of who should pay how much tax resurrected the thorny issue of social inequality. Second, a popular device for fighting inflation was to cut public spending.

There was an overemphasis on production and an underemphasis on the potential satisfactions afforded by the public sphere. Although Galbraith's principal object was to expose the myth that the production of goods for private consumption was the main business of society, he also had a number of positive proposals. For example, society could afford to maintain the unemployed at a comfortable income level. Government should automatically receive a *pro rata* share of society's increasing income to distribute in accordance with relative need. More public investment was needed to deal with the remnants of poverty. Efforts should be made to increase the relative size of the 'New Class' (266) of white-collar professionals who had comfortable and enjoyable work lives. This class was the true successor to the wasteful leisure class. Not least, people should be taught that happiness could not be equated with the possession of goods.

The new industrial state

In *The New Industrial State* (1974a), Galbraith presented his model of the working of modern capitalism. He focused upon the 'industrial system' (21) of large bureaucratic companies dominated by the networks of predominantly salaried, mainly white-collar experts and specialists collectively labelled by him as the 'technostructure' (86). This is a world Schumpeter would have recognised. The individualistic entrepreneur had little or no place within it. In the light of his own views as set out in the last chapter, Schumpeter might well have sympathised with Galbraith's comment, in connection with capitalist and Soviet economic arrangements, that 'convergence between the two ostensibly different industrial systems occurs at all fundamental points' (384).

Galbraith's object in this book was to explain the relationships between a number of changes in American society. For example, massive industrial corporations had achieved a dominating position in the economy even though their leading executives were largely unknown to the public. There were no modern Carnegies. Also, government spending had increased so that it accounted for about one quarter of all economic activity by the late 1960s. In the wake of the Keynesian revolution the state engaged in the management of aggregate demand in the economy. It also tried to stop wages and prices from forcing each other upwards. The business cycle of boom and slump had been ironed out to a great extent.

Three other changes had occurred. There had been a considerable growth in 'the apparatus of persuasion and exhortation' (Galbraith 1974a: 23). Union membership had grown to a peak of about a quarter of the labour force in the mid 1950s. Finally, a large expansion had occurred in enrolment for higher education.

An important factor in explaining the interrelatedness of these changes was the growing sophistication of industrial technology. New machinery and products required substantial investments in capital and the services of large teams of experts. The processes of research and design took much longer than they used to do in the case of less sophisticated industrial processes and products. This meant a longer period of time would pass between initial conception and entry into the market with something you could sell. The large corporation had an advantage in this situation because it could recruit the large number of skilled people needed and also summon up the capital.

Such large commitments of capital and organisational capacity required detailed planning and forecasting. Great corporations such as General Motors had the advantage of being able to influence the markets in which they operated and this gave an added degree of predictability with respect to wages, prices, supply sources and so on. A further source of power over the environment was the capacity of advertisers to manage consumer demand for products being developed. The element of risk associated with technological innovation was reduced further to the extent that the state paid for some of the background costs of technical development or guaranteed a market for the product: 'Suitable justification – national defence, national prestige, deeply-felt public needs such as for supersonic travel – can readily be found. Modern technology thus defines a growing function for the modern state' (24).

The state also made a contribution by its efforts to stabilise overall demand within the economy. This was desirable in view of the savings, both personal and corporate, generated in an age of affluence. There was no certainty about the pattern of future changes in the balance between saving, spending and investment. Government monitoring and regulation of overall demand could help avoid new products such as motor cars appearing on the market at a time when people had no money to spend.

Historically, the rise of the industrial system had witnessed a shift in social power and motivation. At one time, this power had devolved upon land and had been enforced through physical compulsion. Subsequently, power had passed to industrial capital and the main motivation for obedience to its wishes had been the desire for money. During the next phase the inheritor of power was not the working class, as Marx had predicted, but the technostructure, an 'association of men of diverse technical knowledge . . . [that] extends from the leadership of the modern industrial enterprise down to just short of the labour force' (Galbraith 1974a: 74). The technostructure effectively excluded mere shareholders from day-to-day power but it included more than just top management in its ranks.

Conventional wisdom assumed that management would seek to maximise profits (as opposed to, say, their own salaries) on behalf of unknown and relatively powerless shareholders. According to such a notion, 'Those in charge forgo personal reward to enhance it for others' (127). In fact, the 'mature corporation' was not forced to maximise its profits. By not doing so, the technostructure was able to pursue other goals. Above all the technostructure valued the autonomy that flowed from security. This was achieved by ensuring that corporation earnings regularly reached a comfortable minimum level even though that was significantly below the maximum possible.

Such was the influence of the corporations within American society that autonomy and security had become major national goals also. In turn, however, the technostructure accepted and implemented the goals of the society at large, especially society's desire for 'technological virtuosity' (170). Consistency was sought between the goals and values of the individual, the corporation and society. A complex process of adaptation occurred between these three levels. The individual identified closely with the goals of the corporation because they were positively related to broader social goals. Pecuniary motivation was not enough. Moral commitment required more than this. It was helpful to believe, however falsely, that by increasing production one was adding to the sum of happiness in society.

The technostructure was able to shape its own market, raise its own capital from retained earnings, undertake effective manpower planning through liaison with highly organised trade unions, and impose its requirements for macroeconomic management on the state. It was a very powerful force. Too powerful, in Galbraith's view.

An important sector of the economy – the market sphere – was not represented in its councils. Small retailers, local firms, independent craftspeople, farmers and so on had less contact and less influence with unions and government, a smaller capacity to influence the market, and a greater dependence upon external sources of capital. Unfortunately, they did not receive the benefits of planning which bolstered the industrial system.

More generally, the technostructure placed a low reckoning upon important values such as civilised leisure and non-industrial educational pursuits, including those in the arts. In fact, under the baleful influence of the technostructure with its narrow horizons, standards in higher education had declined. Although he is less vitriolic than Veblen in *The Higher Learning in America*, Galbraith's fundamental criticism was similar. However, he saw more hope of reform than did his predecessor. Galbraith noted that

> one of the problems of the industrial system may be in reproducing the technostructure. And there may already be signs of difficulty. Once the schools of business, the most general training grounds for the technostructure, were among the most prestigious branches of American higher education. They are so no longer. Some, with the caution of those who do not wish admission of a fact to reinforce a trend, report a serious decline in the quality of their applicants. The best schools have ceased to expect to recruit the best students. And good students, when asked about business, are increasingly adverse. They hold it to be excessively disciplined, damaging to individuality, not worth the high pay, or dull. We reach an interesting if speculative result. Emancipation could be the salvation of the industrial system. Its discipline will be worse but only thus will it attract people who are sufficiently good.
>
> (Galbraith 1974a: 262–3)

By 'emancipation' Galbraith meant the liberation of education (and the state) from domination by the industrial system. The political lead in this process of emancipation could be taken, in his view, by the 'educational and scientific estate, with its allies in the larger intellectual community' (375). This is, roughly speaking, the modern counterpart of the 'learned class' or 'clerisy' whose potential for civilising society was so evident to John Stuart Mill. Through emancipation, the economic system could be made to serve 'man's physical needs' in a way which was 'consistent with his liberty' (388). And by liberty Galbraith did not just mean 'the freedom of the businessman' (390). The industrial system had to be kept in its proper place. What this proper place was and how to make sure it stayed there were problems he dealt with in the third book in this trilogy: *Economics and the Public Purpose*.

Economics and the public purpose

In Galbraith's view, one of the tasks of economics was to demonstrate that the interests of the industrial system (which he re-labelled in this book 'the planning system') were very different from the public interest. This disjunction was disguised by ideological insistence upon neo-classical models of the market and democracy which claimed that the consumer and citizen, respectively, were sovereign. In fact, the planning system looked after the wants of the technostructure. Its power was reinforced by the authority derived from group decision and consensus.

The rhetoric of individualism disguised the excessive character of collective power. The subordination of two other groups – small business people in the competitive or 'market system' and females providing household services – was glossed over with references to their virtuous character. The ideology praised their hard work, willingness to please and readiness to accept relatively small returns for their labour. These examples of 'Convenient Social Virtue' (Galbraith 1974b: 30) disguised the unfair way they were treated.

The planning system was closely related both to the state and the market system. Neo-classical economics persisted in basing its model only upon the competitive sector, that is the market system. The Keynesian model recognised a role for the state but the extent to which Keynesian demand management operated in favour of the planning system was not widely recognised. Nor was the tendency for the penalties of macroeconomic policies such as the restriction of borrowing to impact most harshly upon the market system. Galbraith set out to remedy these misperceptions.

The market system was the natural home for firms engaged in tasks which were unstandardised, involved geographical dispersion of workers, entailed personal service or required individual creativity. A significant aspect of the market system was the high degree of exploitation entailed, both of the entrepreneur and the workforce. Contractual arrangements to provide materials, goods or services for large corporations usually ensured that the small partner's profit was cut to the bone. Generally, the relationship of the market system to the planning system was one of great inequality.

The planning system was, as has been seen, guided by the protective and affirmative goals of the ruling technostructure. These goals were not entirely conflict-free. For example, growth was generally a good idea since it meant more job opportunities and greater capacity to generate a satisfactory minimum level of earnings – but some kinds of growth, especially if they involved acquiring other companies, meant taking on a dangerous degree of indebtedness. Nor was technological investment always risk free.

However, the technostructure was able to control its environment to a high degree. This was achieved both at home and, through multinational companies, in foreign markets. Some corporations closely involved with government, for example in the field of nuclear energy, were able to achieve a state of 'Bureaucratic Symbiosis' (Galbraith 1974b: 143), in other words the relevant private and public bureaucracies were able to serve each other's interests on a wide front. Such arrangements could easily work against the public interest. The public might also have legitimate doubts as to the usefulness of all the new products and processes being developed, not least with regard to their effects on employment and the environment.

Furthermore, unlike the market system, the planning system was inherently unstable. 'Downward instability' (180) was due to a tendency to recession caused by the lack of coordination between decisions with respect to savings and investment. Keynesian remedies involved a large commitment to defence spending, easily justifiable in terms of national defence although its hidden purpose was to stabilise the planning sector. Upward instability, in other words, the systematic tendency to inflation, was less widely recognised and less easily dealt with. Direct wage- and price-fixing by government was generally resisted on ideological grounds although exceptions occurred.

The indictment against the planning system and its relations with the market system and the state was a considerable one: 'Unequal development, inequality, frivolous and erratic innovation, environmental assault, indifference to personality, power over the state, inflation . . . [and] failure in inter-industry coordination' (211). The Galbraithian reform package envisaged three phases: 'emancipation of belief' (222), emancipation of the state, and the mobilisation of the state as the leading edge of reform.

Emancipation of belief meant unpicking the bonds of ideology. Women should acquire practical equality with men both within the household and within the male-dominated technostructure. The education system, including the teaching of economics, should be released from assumptions serving the interests of the planning system. Resistance to the blandishments of corporate advertising should be encouraged. A much more critical attitude to public life should flourish. In sum, there was a need for 'Public Cognizance' (229), a refusal to be taken in.

The state would have to be emancipated by way of the electoral process. Members of Congress had to be detached from their cosy links with vested interests. Once the state was recaptured for the public interest, public cognizance should be applied in a strategy of strengthening the market system, taming the planning system and establishing a proper balance between them. More specifically, action was required in seven areas.

First, the relative influence of the two systems should be equalised.

This meant positive action upon the market system. Small businesses should be allowed to combine to stabilise prices and output. There should be government regulation of prices and production reinforced by international agreements, support for trade-union organisation, minimum wage legislation, and state backing for the educational, capital and technological requirements of the market system.

Second, the state should bolster the competence of the market system by socialistic measures, especially in the spheres of housing, transport, health services, and the arts. Public planning was essential in these areas:

> The new socialism allows of no acceptable alternatives; it cannot be escaped except at the price of grave discomfort, considerable social disorder and, on occasion, lethal damage to health and well-being. The new socialism is not ideological; it is compelled by circumstance.

> (Galbraith 1974b: 277)

Third, equality of return as between the two systems and also within the planning system should be encouraged. The scope of tax policy and collective bargaining should be widened to include these objectives. Fourth, the public interest in a healthy environment should be actively pursued through the legislature. Fifth, the public interest should be built into the management of public expenditure. Galbraith criticised the close association between federal tax raising and the demands of the planning system. Federal taxes tended to expand with the economy. The public interest largely depended upon local and state taxes which did not expand in the same way.

Sixth, the inflationary and deflationary tendencies of the planning system had to be eliminated. Galbraith favoured fiscal rather than monetary measures. Taxes should be set to raise the spending power required by the public interest rather than the needs of the large corporations. Beyond that, excessive demand should be dealt with by increasing taxes at the expense of private consumption. Deficient demand should trigger an increase in public expenditure. Finally, inter-industry co-ordination – something the planning system could not manage – had to be undertaken by government. Ideally, planning should extend to the co-ordination of different national systems.

It is evident that, like Schumpeter, Galbraith was able to envisage plenty of work for his disciples in the emerging social order. They would be key functionaries in the newly reformed world for which Galbraith was arguing. The industrial capitalist had succeeded the landlord. The technostructure had seized power from the latter. Was the hoped-for heir of the technostructure to be the professional economist, doyen of the educational and scientific estate?

Left of centre

Galbraith's *The Affluent Society* and Crosland's *The Future of Socialism* appeared within two years of each other in the second half of the 1950s. Both were examples of progressive left-of-centre thought. However, they reflected two very different social and political contexts.

In *The Affluent Society* Galbraith responded to the evident material success of post-war American capitalism. He asked Americans to step back from their material achievement. He wanted them to be less hectic in pursuit of growth within the existing system. Galbraith also proposed a more active role for government in strengthening the public sector. By contrast, in *The Future of Socialism*, Crosland was responding to the fulfilment, as he saw it, of the major objectives of the traditional socialist programme as a result of the 1945–51 Labour government. Socialism had achieved a major political success and carried out a process of social engineering that seemed likely to be permanent.

Crosland also asked his compatriots, especially in the Labour party, to step back a little. It was possible, he suggested, to achieve major socialist objectives through forms of planning which did not involve wholesale nationalisation. Like Galbraith, Crosland believed many people around him were guided by an out-of-date ideology which failed to describe accurately the character and needs of contemporary society.

The dragon faced by Crosland was not neo-classical economics, Galbraith's foe, but 'pre-war socialist assumptions' (Crosland 1964: 1). In this connection, Crosland cited in particular two prominent Marxist intellectuals, John Strachey and Harold Laski. The writings of the latter had been 'In the political field . . . the outstanding influence' (2).

Crosland wanted the British Labour party to go for growth in a very determined way. This prescription was obviously very different from Galbraith's. In a review of *The Affluent Society*, Crosland pointed out that Britain's level of affluence was much lower than it was in America. Consequently, he argued, there was 'still an overwhelming case in Britain for treating growth and efficiency as being urgent, at least for some decades ahead' (Crosland 1962: 100).

However, Crosland was quite prepared to accept Galbraith's view of contemporary America as a true picture of what lay ahead for Britain. The latter's work would enable the British to 'make some mild preparations for our destiny' (103). Crosland noted some overlap in theme with his own work. *The Affluent Society* included, for example, 'a brilliant exposition of a point to which I have long attached importance in the context of the British scene: namely, that the higher the average level of real income, whatever its distribution, the greater the subjective sense of social equality' (97).

In fact, the coincidence of themes was even closer than this. As has been noted, at the centre of both men's work was a preoccupation with the interplay between equality, security and growth.

The future of socialism

Crosland acknowledged Marx as a 'towering giant' (Crosland 1964: 2), on the scale of a Freud or a Keynes, but insisted that his concepts and prophecies were irrelevant to contemporary Britain. Contrary to the expectations of socialists caught up in the inter-war enthusiasm for Marxism, capitalism was not collapsing. However, it was changing in three ways.

First, the business class was losing power to the state. Crosland rejected Laski's assertion that 'Whatever the forms of state, political power will, in fact, belong to the owners of economic power' (Laski 1930: 52). It was wrong and oversimplified. In fact it would be nearer the truth to 'turn Laski's statement on its head' (Crosland 1964: 10). Second, aided by full employment, the trade unions had gained in power at the expense of industrial management: 'Here one can speak, without exaggeration, of a peaceful revolution' (13).

Third, the social character of management had changed. It had become less exploitative, more sensitive to public opinion. The invisible hand had been replaced by 'the glad hand' (18). Crosland borrowed this phrase from David Riesman whose book *The Lonely Crowd* (Riesman *et al.* 1953) had appeared in 1950. Riesman had been guided by Freud rather than Marx in his argument that modern American society was increasingly conformist. Crosland agreed with Riesman that co-operation, team work, sensitivity in personal relations and a desire for the approval of others had become widespread. He found this tendency in Britain also. Old-style, naked, self-seeking ambition was quite out of fashion.

Within society at large, a substantial measure of basic welfare provision and income redistribution had also been achieved in spite of the low expectations of the Marxists. The latter had tended 'absurdly to under-rate the socio-economic consequences of political democracy' (Crosland 1964: 24). Once more, Laski was wrong. He had expected capitalist forces to respond to Labour's democratic challenge to their interests by saying 'If democracy stands in the way, so much the worse for democracy'. In the 1950s this sounded 'like an echo from another world' (33).

The old socialism was irrelevant because the economic and political framework of British society had been profoundly altered. In Schumpeterian vein, Galbraith commented: 'And to the question "Is this still Capitalism?", I would answer "No" ' (42). His next chapter began: 'If this is not still capitalism, then what is socialism all about?' (431). His first answer was that it meant more than 'Keynes-plus-modified-capitalism-plus-Welfare-State' (79). The latter was, in fact, more or less the formula elaborated by Galbraith two years later.

In her biography of Tony Crosland, Susan Crosland mentioned that at the age of twenty-two her husband had written to a friend: 'I am revising Marxism & will emerge as the modern Bernstein' (Crosland 1982: 13). A decade and a half later, in *The Future of Socialism*, Crosland wryly acknowledged 'the anger with which criticisms of militancy or class-struggle are often greeted. [Eduard] Bernstein, the great socialist "revisionist" discovered this more than 50 years ago' (Crosland 1964: 62). In view of this, Crosland prepared his ground carefully, reviewing at length the great variety of doctrines, often mutually contradictory, passing under the name of 'socialism'. He concluded that three traditional objectives remained relevant.

The first – a desire to substitute co-operation for competition – was the most ambiguous. In Britain competition was relatively unaggressive. In few countries was 'individual exertion more suspect' (70). Having made this Veblenesque point, Crosland added that although competition advanced at the expense of co-operation (in some respects, a pity), it also made inroads into caste privilege (a highly desirable result). In any case, group co-operation could easily turn into group exclusiveness.

The other two goals were more clear-cut. There was a need for more social welfare to increase security and relieve distress. And it was important to achieve an equal and classless society. The first of these goals could be attained by strengthening the welfare system's performance in four areas: the sphere of secondary poverty (including the disabled), family disintegration due to changing social attitudes, the maldistribution of income relative to need, and special situations needing therapy, casework and preventive treatment. Providing universal free services was less important than bringing standards in public sector health, education, housing and so on up to those in the private sector. This was closely related to the long-term socialist goal closest to Crosland's heart, which was to achieve equality and create a class-free society.

Paradoxically, despite the large amount of redistribution that had occurred, Britain remained ridden with class feeling. Collective discontent manifested itself in unofficial strikes, bloody-mindedness and a general spirit of antagonism in industry. Crosland believed this lowering discontent was partly due to the frustration felt by well-paid workers who were denied genuine participation on the shop-floor. Industrial antagonism was matched by political resentment caused by the fact that world power had obviously passed from London to Washington.

Income redistribution had done little to alter power hierarchies within Britain. Inheritance of wealth helped perpetuate sharp class distinctions. However, Veblenesque conspicuous consumption was less of a problem than the cultural gulf between classes perpetuated by a divisive education system which separated public school children from grammar school children, and the latter from the rest.

Much to Hayek's disgust, Crosland argued that 'every child had a natural "right" as citizen, not merely to "life, liberty, and the pursuit of happiness", but to that position in the social scale to which his natural talents entitle him' (Crosland 1964: 140; see Hayek 1976b: 82). Crosland certainly did not want to suppress competition but it should occur within a context of democratic social mixing. He was able to pursue this policy later in his role as education minister by encouraging the spread of comprehensive schools. More generally, the objective was to work for a degree of social equality which reduced social waste without threatening economic efficiency, the survival of high culture or the liberty of the individual (as feared by Hayek).

A much more democratic social atmosphere existed in America. This seemed to Crosland to be due to social mixing in school, more widely shared consumption norms, a higher standard of living for all and the fact that bitter conflict between unions and management did not spill over into other areas of life. Progress towards greater equality could be made in Britain by attacks on four spheres of power and privilege: education, consumption, inherited wealth and industry.

With respect to education, Crosland's approach was very straightforward. He proposed the gradual integration of the private and public sectors and the introduction of a comprehensive system of secondary schools. On the second front, that of consumption, his thinking owed a great deal to Schumpeter. He expected that growth would raise living standards all round. Luxuries would come within reach of the masses. There would be progressively fewer opportunities for invidious conspicuous consumption by a gilded elite. However, affluence should not be treated with disdain by puritanical socialists. Brotherly love was fine but 'why should not the brothers be affluent?' (217). He dismissed Tocquevillean fears that a consumer society would be condemned to perpetual frustration.

Absolute equalisation of wealth was not on Crosland's agenda, but extreme private opulence had to be cut back. Death-duty commissioners would rake off a healthy slice of personal wealth. This would supply a convenient source of risk capital for industry. Taxes on capital gains and gifts would also be part of the government's armoury. At the same time, wider working-class share-ownership would be encouraged. The changed social climate created by such measures would help to lower the level of antagonism within industry, the final area of attack.

Four measures would help here. They were: a fairer and more imaginative system of wage bargaining, preferably including productivity deals; an increase in consultation with the work force; forms of worker participation which did not compromise the unions' proper oppositional stance as bargainers with management (specifically, workers' representatives on company boards should be elected directly by employees and not chosen from the local union hierarchy); and, finally, consultation by trade union organisations with top industrial management at the national level. Success in the fields just mentioned depended on the achievement of growth. Crosland accepted that in the United States, affluence was so widespread that problems secondary to growth – such as concern over waste and frivolity in the consumption sphere – had come to the fore. Despite the optimistic hopes of pre-war socialists, Britain was not in the same happy state. Without higher growth it would be impossible to relieve hardship at home and abroad, increase social and manufacturing investment, raise living standards and export more goods.

Crosland was reasonably optimistic. Keynesian demand-management techniques seemed to be 'both practicable and broadly effective' (Crosland 1964: 290). Full employment had lowered resistance to technological innovation. Managers had learned to accept the rate of company growth as a measure of prestige. Lurking dangers included slackness in cost efficiency when demand was high, a reluctance by firms to export when home demand was buoyant, and wage pressure from labour. Another challenge was the need to ensure that a substantial proportion of profits became available for socially-valuable investment rather than managerial salaries and dividend payments. A flat-rate profit tax was the device preferred by Crosland.

Apart from growth, planning presented another set of problems. Nationalisation of major industries such as electricity and coal had achieved neither redistribution of wealth nor effective planning. Future Labour governments should consider investing in 'competitive public enterprises' (333), allowing management to get on with the job but giving the public a direct stake in growth through its investment. Ideally, the economy as a whole should have a 'diverse, diffused, pluralist and heterogenous pattern of ownership' (340).

Planning had its place in such an economy since 'no one of any standing now believes the once-popular Hayek thesis that any interference with the market mechanism must take us down the slippery slope that leads to totalitarianism' (343). On the one hand, industry had lost its old ideological attachment to *laissez-faire*. On the other hand, planners had become less ambitious. Crosland, for instance, accepted that

> The price-mechanism is now a reasonably satisfactory method of distributing the great bulk of consumer-goods and industrial capital-goods, given the total amount of resources available for consumption and national investment. The consumer is the best judge of how to spend his money; and even if he were not, the principle of individual liberty would still require that he should be left free to spend it, subject only to . . . social service considerations.
>
> (Crosland 1964: 346)

Crosland also argued that production for use and production for profit could be taken as broadly coinciding in view of the growth of working-class purchasing power. As Samuel Brittan pointed out, Crosland left plenty of scope for Adam Smith's invisible hand (Brittan 1988e: 240).

Going for growth

By the early 1970s, Crosland was less optimistic than he had been in the mid 1950s. It was true that part of his programme had been achieved. Public expenditure was maintained at a reasonable level, despite pressure for cuts. There had been some redistribution of income through the social services. Comprehensive education reform had been set in train. More houses had been built. Against this, balance of payments difficulties and an inflexible exchange rate had held back economic growth.

In the absence of high growth it had been almost impossible to carry out an egalitarian policy and increase exports at the same time. Of particular significance, during the late 1960s many manual workers found themselves caught up in the net of progressive direct taxation for the first time. This contributed to a vicious circle of inflation, strikes and unrest.

In 1956 Crosland had been optimistic about the socialistic tendency of working-class voters. By 1974 he was forced to write that 'the pressure of democracy has exerted much less beneficial influence than I anticipated' (Crosland 1974: 23). He had described the besetting sins of the British in 1962 as being 'conservatism' and 'parochialism' (Crosland 1962: 7). By 1974 British society appeared 'slow-moving, rigid, class-ridden' (Crosland 1974: 44). In the same essay, he commented: 'We retain an amazing sense of class and little sense of community' (23). Going for growth meant a short-term strategy of high public spending and a medium-term policy of equalising the distribution of wealth. Neither was politically popular. Both would require a recovery of 'practical radical will-power' (53).

This radical will-power re-entered British politics five years later in the shape of Margaret Thatcher. The Thatcherite government espoused two of Crosland's goals: higher levels of personal consumption and an increase in the rate of growth. However, it adopted means that were the reverse of Crosland's: immediate deflationary cut-backs in public expenditure leading, in the medium term at least, to increases in social inequality. To some extent the 'peaceful revolution' which empowered the British trade union movement was also reversed.

In Britain since the late 1970s Hayek's critique of socialism has delivered arguments justifying a reduction of direct taxation, the sale of public assets and the privatisation of many services previously delivered directly by the state. On each side of the Atlantic the democratic system had by 1988 delivered power three times in a row to national politicians hostile to the social-democratic or liberal strategies of Crosland and Galbraith.

Conclusion

Finally, the comparison of Crosland and Galbraith may be drawn together. Although Crosland once called himself 'a Galbraith man' he differed from the latter on at least four counts. First, partly because of the dissimilar states of the American and British economies, Crosland gave growth a higher priority than did Galbraith. The British politician was very suspicious of the anti-growth conservationist lobby which grew strong during the 1960s and 1970s. He thought it had a clear middle- and upper-class bias: 'Its champions are often kindly and dedicated people, but they are affluent, and fundamentally, though not of course consciously, they want to kick the ladder down behind them' (Crosland 1974: 78).

Second, Crosland wanted positive action to reduce class inequalities, whereas Galbraith merely noted that the issue of inequality had been taken off the agenda in the United States by an overall increase in consumption levels. The imbalance that bothered Galbraith was not between classes but between the public and private sectors. This leads to the next point.

Third, Crosland was not persuaded that private industry grew at the expense of, or more quickly than, the public sector. In *The Conservative Enemy* (1962: 20) he suggested that the proportion of public spending would tend to rise with increasing affluence – partly because of democratic political pressure, partly because progressive taxation produced a higher overall yield as people became more prosperous and entered higher tax brackets.

Fourth, unlike Galbraith, Crosland had little sympathy with the view that people were deluded by advertising. On the contrary, advertising encouraged the introduction of new products and was, more generally, 'the price we pay for a high and varied standard of consumption' (Crosland 1962: 63). Perhaps Crosland suspected a lurking puritanism behind academic complaints about the advertising profession. Personally, he gave full recognition to the values of private enjoyment. People should find the leisure to cultivate grace and gaiety in their lives. As far as he was concerned you could definitely have too much of the New England town-meeting style of life: 'one does not necessarily want a busy, bustling society in which everyone is politically active, and spends his evenings in group discussions, and feels responsible for all the burdens of the world' (Crosland 1964: 255).

Chapter ten

Friedman, Brittan, Miliband, Piven, and Cloward

Capitalism versus democracy

The two theorists considered in the previous chapter – John Kenneth Galbraith and Tony Crosland – both assumed that the interests served by democracy and industrial capitalism were compatible. In other words, through intelligent Keynesian management a level of growth and a pattern of wealth and income distribution could be achieved which would satisfy the demands of the people. However, during the past two decades considerable doubt has arisen about the capacity of governments to contain inflationary pressures by Keynesian means.

This chapter examines four analyses which considered the origins and implications of failures of economic management during the 1960s and 1970s. Although each approach is unique, they divide into two pairs with respect to redistributive policies. Two of the analyses – those by Milton and Rose Friedman (1980) and Samuel Brittan (1988e) – were frankly unsympathetic to political programmes which attempted to implement egalitarian measures. By contrast, Ralph Miliband (1982) and co-authors Frances Fox Piven and Richard A. Cloward (1982) were in favour of such programmes.

Two of the analyses – by Brittan and Miliband – argued that considerable erosion of democratic freedoms was a likely outcome of the overloading of government with economic demands by special interests. Two were more optimistic, though from radically different perspectives. Friedman suggested that if his policies were followed, democracy and capitalism would both emerge unscathed. Piven and Cloward took the view that the likely outcome of the economic and political difficulties of the American government in the 1970s was a victory of democracy over capitalism.

Free to choose

Milton Friedman belongs to the network of economists based at the

169

University of Chicago who are strongly sympathetic to the intellectual approach of Hayek. Apart from his specialised work on inflation, unemployment and monetary policy, Friedman has also published more general works on capitalism and democracy including *Capitalism and Freedom* 1962) and (with Rose Friedman) *Free to Choose* (1980). The last-named book is particularly accessible, presenting his approach in a very clear and concrete way.

In *Free to Choose* it was argued that the history of the United States was the story of 'an economic miracle and a political miracle' (Friedman and Friedman 1980: 19). They were made possible by putting into practice the principles of freedom set out in Adam Smith's *The Wealth of Nations* (1979) and Thomas Jefferson's Declaration of Independence. John Stuart Mill was cited as providing an even more unqualified assertion of individual freedom. In fact, both the United States and Britain had enjoyed 'a golden age' in the nineteenth century, especially the former since it had several advantages: 'fewer vestiges of class and status; fewer governmental restraints; a more fertile field for energy, drive and innovation; and an empty continent to conquer' (Friedman and Friedman 1980: 21). Unfortunately, during the twentieth century an accumulation of political controls had diminished economic freedom. An increasing proportion of our income was being taken in taxes and spent on our behalf. When you voted for a government you had to take as a job lot all the policies they spent your money on. You were not able to pick and choose among specific items the way you could if you went into a supermarket. In the market specialised exchanges took place which benefited all participants without making them all buy the same things. However, obtaining services via the ballot box meant you had to accept a package that was a compromise between the wishes of several different interests: 'The ballot box produces conformity without unanimity; the marketplace, unanimity without conformity' (90).

The expenditure of government bureaucracy was much more wasteful than spending your own money on yourself. The bureaucrat was spending someone else's money to solve someone else's problem. There was little incentive to economise or maximise efficiency. Just as counter-productive were efforts to increase social equality by government action. The ideal of fair shares was inimical to personal freedom. The element of chance certainly made life fundamentally unfair but at least we had the choice of using our talents or opportunities well or badly.

The willingness to take risks – choosing to increase the element of chance – was important if society was to advance. The main beneficiaries of technological progress produced by risk-takers were ordinary people, not plutocrats and lords. (The argument runs close to Schumpeter at this point.) In this respect, the poorer element of society benefited from economic and political freedom. Freedom indirectly promoted equality.

To attack equality directly would injure freedom and so be self-defeating. Societies faced a fundamental choice between two methods of organising the division of labour and social cooperation. One was a command system based upon the transmission of orders downwards through a centralised administration. This worked best in small collectivities where the commander could obtain a very high proportion of the information relevant to decision-making. The command system was much less efficient in a large society like Russia. In fact, the private profit motive and the black market operated in the interstices of socialist society.

By contrast, the market system enabled exchanges to occur with relative ease across barriers of language, culture and politics. The efficiency of the market hinged upon the price system. Market prices transmitted information to potential buyers and sellers. They also provided incentives for economy in production and marketing. Finally, they provided a mechanism for determining the distribution of income between buyers and sellers.

Any attempt to interfere with the second and third of these functions, for example by creating a monopoly or restricting the labour supply, would also disrupt the first function. In other words it would prevent the price system from transmitting information accurately. Governments and trade unions were the worst offenders. Their interventions in the markets produced inefficiency. The role of government in large societies should be restricted to national defence, internal law and order, some (very limited) public works and care for a minority who were unfit to undertake the responsibilities of citizenship.

The argument was illustrated by contrasting the success of market economies such as West Germany since the Second World War and nineteenth-century Japan with the failure of command economies such as East Germany and twentieth-century India which 'adopted the policies of Harold Laski' (Friedman and Friedman 1980: 333). Also relevant was the comparison between the United States before and after the New Deal.

New Deal and after

The depression of the 1930s, the argument goes, was the result not of a failure of private enterprise, but of a faulty response by government – more specifically, the Federal Reserve Board – to events within the market. The monetary supply was mishandled in a botched attempt to intervene to counteract 'the alleged instability of the free market' (115). Despite this fact, which was not sufficiently understood at the time, government intervention over a wide range of economic and social relationships increased in the course of the New Deal. The welfare state appeared. Unfortunately, its consequences were oppressive.

For example, the social security programme added to the costs of employing labour and imposed a huge burden on the tax payer. It redistributed money from the young to the old and, ironically, from the less well-off to the better-off. Public assistance justified a huge paper-shuffling bureaucracy. Its practices were inconsistent between different parts of the country, generating discontent, resentment and accusations of cheating. Urban renewal projects mainly helped the owners of property purchased for public housing.

These programmes were ideologically justified in terms of a mixture of 'Fabian socialism and New Deal liberalism' (Friedman and Friedman 1980: 331–2). However, people were beginning to realise that socialistic programmes claiming to be promoting the general interest were actually led 'by the invisible political hand' (340) to promote a number of special interests instead. Majority government was, in fact, a government answerable to a large coalition of minorities all feverishly lobbying away in Washington.

However, the tide was turning in the 1970s. Opinion was moving against high taxation and interventionist government. A number of states had adopted constitutional amendments limiting the amount of taxes that could be imposed. A National Tax Limitation Committee had been set up. The National Taxpayers Union was working for a national convention to be called by Congress. This would propose an amendment to balance the budget. A campaign was also underway to limit federal spending. In fact, an economic Bill of Rights was needed to complement the original Bill of Rights.

Milton and Rose Friedman included in *Free to Choose* a series of other proposed constitutional provisions. They were intended to encourage international free trade, abolish restrictive practices and wage and price controls, abolish corporation tax, restrict the expansion of the monetary base by government and prevent government benefiting from inflation. They concluded: 'Fortunately, . . . we are as a people still free to choose which way we should go – whether to continue along the road we have been following to ever bigger government, or to call a halt and change direction' (359).

There is little doubt that a change of direction did occur during the Reagan years. However, in 1988 the outgoing presidential regime left a large budgetary deficit for its successor. And the commitment of the Bush administration to international free trade has yet to be demonstrated. Nevertheless, the Friedman approach conveys effectively the enthusiastic optimism of the political culture from which it stems. This optimism was matched, on the other side of the political fence, by Piven and Cloward as will be seen. However, at this point a more pessimistic British perspective will be introduced.

Economic consequences of democracy

Samuel Brittan is a leading financial journalist with strong government and academic connections, including Nuffield College, Oxford and the Chicago Law School. In the mid 1970s, he conjectured that 'liberal representative democracy suffers from internal tensions, which are likely to increase in time, and that, on present indications, the system is likely to pass away within the lifetime of people now adult' (Brittan 1988a: 247). The system had developed serious defects which it would be difficult to remedy through mere force of argument and moral persuasion.

There were two problems: people were encouraged to expect too much from the political system; and self-interested groups were disrupting the market. Too great a burden was being placed upon 'the "sharing out" function of government' (248). In his analysis of these phenomena, Brittan was very influenced by Schumpeter's model of democracy. In his discussion of a possible solution, some of Hayek's ideas, especially regarding the rule of law, were drawn upon.

Schumpeter correctly noted that most voters had very little direct involvement with the details of politics. They registered only a few general impressions of the most highly publicised issues. Instead of making fine distinctions between competing parties with respect to ideology or policy, their judgements were 'more performance-related than issue-related' (250). For example, which side was doing best at keeping unemployment or prices down? Competing political merchandisers had learnt the techniques of mass advertising. Pushing the brand tended to take precedence over quality control.

In everyday life, voters could check advertising claims against practical experience (for example, of a new washing powder). Politics did not get such close interest or attention. The implications and consequences of specific demands or measures were not considered in detail. Although voters knew the importance of compromise and establishing priorities in their own economic affairs, budgetary constraint went out of the window in the political sphere. As a consequence

> The temptation to encourage false expectations among the electorate becomes overwhelming to politicians. The opposition parties are bound by promises to do better and the government party must join in the auction – explaining away the past and outbidding its rivals for the future whether by general hints or detailed promises. Voters may indeed be cynical about promises. Yet citizens' demands for government action and their attribution to it of responsibility for their own or the nation's past performance are altogether excessive.
>
> (Brittan 1988a: 255)

Excess money creation and a budget deficit were tempting means by which governments could satisfy some of the demands of pressure groups. Elections and economic trends could even be co-ordinated to some extent in a 'political trade cycle' (Brittan 1988b: 285). Trade unions and other groups had learned to compensate for the effects of inflation by pitching their demands even higher. Restraint by special interests would have had benefits for the whole economy in terms of stable prices, less unemployment or faster growth. However these were public goods shared by all. The extra benefits won for an interest group by using its economic muscle far outweighed its share of the society's loss in terms of public goods. Many groups thought in these terms. This posed a fundamental threat. Their demands were likely to add up to far more than the economy was able to produce.

Schumpeter had argued that a workable democracy required a well-trained bureaucracy, limitations upon the range of matters that were subject to political decision-making, and the exercise of tolerance and self-restraint by pressure groups. In the British case, the second and third conditions were ceasing to apply. For example, the electorate was learning the extent of its power and consequently extending the range of its demands. The 'moral heritage of the feudal system', which imposed a sense of hierarchy and duty, was being destroyed by 'secular and rationalistic inquiry' (Brittan 1988a: 264–5). Borrowing heavily from Schumpeter, Brittan pointed out that modern politicians and business leaders lacked aristocratic glamour or the trappings of a heroic tradition. They did not invite deference.

The scale of political ambition had increased. Governments were now trying to 'transfer from the private to the public sphere the determination of who gets how much' (265), applying some notion of the just wage. Since there was no rational or political basis for consensus on what was 'fair' this was a doomed enterprise. The destructive pressure of coercive demands and excessive expectations would not be curbed in that way. In fact, society was heading in a Hobbesian direction: via extreme individualism to extreme authoritarianism.

Britain already had a degree of political centralisation greater than any other major Western democracy. Matters were arranged more conveniently in the United States with its greater separation of powers. Instead of one major 'adversary contest' (Brittan 1988b: 311) between the national parties, there were several at local, state and national levels. Voter alignments could vary between different contests and issues without threatening the integrity of parties and governments.

New rules

Brittan argued that a solution to the problems of British democracy could not, unfortunately, be found through schemes to establish a social order based on social justice. The difficulty was not the worthiness of the idea but making it work. If social resources were like a 'pie', when you divided it up how did you evaluate the different contributions made by those who helped to produce it? If property was held by individuals who were at liberty to enter into voluntary exchanges, how did you determine the content of property rights and the rules of contract? How did you decide how much inequality between rewards was acceptable? (see Nozick 1974; Rawls 1973; Jouvenel 1957).

If things went on as they were doing, it was quite possible that nothing would remain of liberal democracy beyond its rhetoric. The regime which succeeded it might be of the left or the right. It might be authoritarian without being efficient. One possibility was a society with 'pockets of anarchy combined with petty despotism, in which many of the amenities of life and the rule of law are absent, but in which there are many things which we will be prevented from doing or saying' (272).

Defensive measures against these possible futures should work upon social attitudes. Opinion counted a great deal. For example, 'Many of our present tensions would be much less important in the unlikely event of a genuine revulsion against materialism or the "consumer society"' (274–5). One helpful move would be a loosening up of the highly focused status system so that a much wider range of occupations than at present was accorded high prestige. It would be an improvement if all workers could regard themselves as 'true aristocrats' (274). Second, attention should be shifted away from current income differentials and directed towards the improvement shared by all as compared with previous generations. If this were done it would increase our sense of satisfaction and dissipate the current climate of envy and resentment: 'The idea of equality has had a noble role in history . . . . But it has now turned sour' (277).

Positive progress might also be made towards 'a new political settlement' (1988d: 303) which could even take the form of a written constitution. It is at this point that the influence of Hayek's idea of the rule of law is felt. Brittan suggested that a new constitution would embody the idea that citizens' rights were protected from interference even at the hands of a democratic parliament. In effect, several aspects of social organisation would be taken out of politics and made inviolable.

The exact content of this constitutional settlement would have to be negotiated – and periodically renegotiated as society changed. A bargain might be reached,

> in which the affluent agree to a reduction in their property rights . . . in return for a limit on state redistribution. The better-off make a sacrifice in previously held wealth in return for more certain enjoyment of the remainder . . . . The worse-off . . . would be secure of the redistribution they already have against a right-wing victory

at the polls or against back-sliding by a government of the Left'.
(Brittan 1988d: 308)

The constitution would also set out new rules for electing governments. As Brittan put it,

> The current model of elective dictatorship needs to give way to the principle of more general consent. Majority rule is no longer, if it ever was, a sufficient guarantee of a tolerably stable, let alone free, or efficient, society.
(Brittan 1988d: 313)

Instead of first-past-the-post or winner-takes-all, Brittan suggested that a government should be required to have at least 51 per cent of the total vote. A strong incentive would be given to the development of understandings between different parties who might be coalition partners at some time in the future. This would prevent radical changes being imposed by a party which achieved a majority of parliamentary seats on the basis of a minority vote in the country.

In the absence of a written constitution along the lines envisaged by Brittan, the political possibility just outlined has in fact occurred in the United Kingdom in the period since 1979. With the support of well under half the electorate, the Thatcher government has carried out a radical policy designed to undermine many of the coercive groups whose demands had helped produce high levels of inflation. For some years the inflation level fell to a much lower level than previously. Although Brittan's 'new political settlement' would have prevented the policy from being enacted on the basis of a minority vote, Thatcherism has apparently weakened some of the pressures identified by Brittan as being a threat to democracy. Ironically, it has also moved British society in the direction of the Hobbesian condition of individualism and authoritarianism which, by Brittan's reasoning, signals the end of democracy. Tocqueville and Mill would have appreciated the point.

Having examined two non-egalitarian views of Keynesian and post-Keynesian capitalist democracy, the rest of this chapter deals with two accounts of the same phenomena from Marxian perspectives. Both appeared in 1982. Again, the first was American and optimistic, the second British and pessimistic. The first was *The New Class War. Reagan's Attack on the Welfare State and its Consequences*. Its authors were Frances Fox Piven, professor of political science at Boston University, and Richard A. Cloward, professor of social work at Columbia University. The second was *Capitalist Democracy in Britain* by Ralph Miliband who had taught at the London School of Economics, the University of Leeds and Brandeis University.

The two books provided overviews of the past, the present and possible futures in British and American society respectively. The authors all agreed that capitalism and democracy were in conflict. However, very different outcomes were predicted for the two societies.

The new class war

Piven and Cloward have written a number of books on poverty and social movements including *Regulating the Poor* (1971) and *Poor People's Movements* (1977). In *The New Class War* (1982) they argued that income-maintenance programmes for the poor were being drastically cut back under President Reagan in order to redress the balance of power between capital and labour. Big business was in trouble because the postwar boom was over and America was facing severe competition from Japan and Western Europe.

Income-maintenance programmes – such as housing assistance, unemployment insurance and food stamps – were important because they prevented working-class families from being too badly hurt by high unemployment. In these circumstances, employers could not keep wages as low as they would like. They were not able to rely upon their workers' fear of unemployment and the existence of a reserve army of idle and starving men and women to moderate wage demands.

This was one of the reasons why Keynesian economic management had run into difficulties during the late 1960s. Normally, the economy was steered between too much inflation on the one hand and too much unemployment on the other. Employers had a preference for unemployment over inflation. However, by the end of the 1960s they were getting both. Wages did not fall with higher unemployment.

This development had to be understood in its historical and institutional context. Since the beginning of capitalism, property rights and subsistence rights had been in conflict. Even in democratic America the rights of property had won out over the right of ordinary people to food, shelter and basic comforts. Americans had been 'party to the spellbinding idea that the state belonged to the people, and to the vaulting promise of a better life inherent in that idea. But the idea and the promise were thwarted' (Piven and Cloward 1982: 41).

The doctrine of *laissez-faire* separated economic rights from political rights. The market and politics were held to be distinct spheres. Democracy gave citizens protection against coercion by the state but the state did not protect them against the predations of property owners. As a consequence, the people lost the customary rights to subsistence embedded in a 'moral economy'. The rich and powerful forced upon them a new regime of exclusive private property. Property was, in fact, 'not . . . a natural condition that antedates the political process . . . [but] . . . a political artefact, created by state law and maintained by state force' (Piven and Cloward 1982: 53). The people protested but they were put down. By the end of the century the American poor had lost all claims on poor relief. The industrial bourgeoisie were victorious.

This had occurred in spite of universal suffrage, because the people had been exposed to a subtle mixture of ideology, experience and structural pressures. Property rights had been secured against the opposition of kings and feudal lords. They were regarded as the bedrock of freedom. The sanctity of property was reinforced by the American Constitution. Furthermore, property and the people did not confront each other directly within the political system.

Most ordinary men and women encountered politics at the neighbourhood level. It was a matter of local taxes, school management and petty patronage. Business people targeted their political efforts at higher levels within the system. When they failed to reform the municipalities in the late nineteenth and early twentieth centuries, they turned their attention to the state capitals. When state legislatures threatened to hurt business corporations in the progressive period, company bosses shifted their attention to the federal government. The mobility of capital gave it an advantage over government at all levels. Large corporations could play cities off against each other, a game multinational corporations later learned to play when dealing with national governments.

Within this structure, business managed to obtain a great deal of support from the state while maintaining the fiction that politics and the economy were separate spheres. This fiction began to lose its credibility from the 1880s onward as central government was forced to take token action against giant trusts and business combinations. By the 1930s, big business was relying wholeheartedly upon its connection with the state in order to increase stability and predictability in the economy.

The people strike back

However, by the time of the New Deal ordinary voters were also demanding economic help from the government. They were backing these demands with insurgency. The unemployed sometimes took to the streets to back up their demand for subsistence as a political right. Their private suffering was recognised as a public issue. City machines failed to cope with the overwhelming demand for help. Increasingly, popular demands were directed at the national level. Federal relief programmes were enacted. Trade unions won new rights. Social security provision was greatly expanded. The framework of the welfare state was established.

During the 1960s, the Southern civil rights movement and the Northern black movement were, once more, too much for city governments to handle. Federal action was required, greatly expanding the welfare state. The consequences were profound:

popular victories . . . created new institutional arrangements that helped expose the state to democratic influence in a continuing way. The new programs of the 1930s and the 1960s produced pervasive new linkages between the state and democratic publics that paralleled older linkages between the state and business.

(Piven and Cloward 1982: 119)

The poor, the unemployed, women, blacks, the elderly, the disabled, the unions and environmental groups were all involved: 'By incorporating so wide a range of an enfranchised population, the state itself has become partially democratized' (119). The bureaucrats staffing the new regulatory and benefit agencies were closely linked to the constituencies they served. They articulated and focused the demands upon government made by these constituencies.

By the early 1970s big business was complaining hard about the 'rising tide of entitlement' (123). America was getting too democratic for comfort. Social commentators began to write about the system being 'overloaded' with demands. The organised power of working people was making it difficult to apply tight money/high unemployment policies. The counterattack by big business and its friends in government was strongly pressed after President Reagan took office. It included at least four measures.

First, stringent tax cuts which reduced the number of welfare programmes and the level at which they were funded. Second, appointment of industrial representatives to regulatory agencies such as the Environmental Protection Agency, rather than experts from within the sector to be regulated. Third, resurrection of the *laissez-faire* doctrine which decreed that government should not interfere with the working of the market. And finally, decentralisation of control over programmes such as Medicaid and Aid to Families with Dependent Children (AFDC).

By moving responsibility for these programmes to the state or local level, the energy of political activists would be diverted into competition for resources between local areas. Below the federal level, government agencies were much weaker in confronting big business. National minimum standards would be much more difficult to enforce.

Piven and Cloward did not believe the old *laissez-faire* ideology with its emphasis upon the separation between the state and the market could be made credible again. The intricate pattern of interdependency between capital and the state had become highly visible. Furthermore, popular consciousness had changed. There was a new 'moral economy of the welfare state' (137). Governments were blamed for the state of the economy. Elections were fought on that issue. In attacking income-maintenance programmes and the agencies associated with them, the Reagan administration had begun a war on several fronts simultaneously.

It was likely to escalate, bringing in all the groups previously mentioned: the poor, the unemployed, women, blacks, the unions and so on. The welfare programme agencies, staffed with discontented officials, were a potential focus of popular mobilisation.

If the benefit cuts were successfully resisted, the freedom for manoeuvre of big business in coping with its economic difficulties would be greatly reduced. In fact, 'If democracy can no longer be contained, and if it cannot be stamped out either, then we are at a historic turning point in the development of American institutions' (Piven and Cloward 1982: 146).

It would be facile to point out that two years after this book appeared Ronald Reagan was re-elected by a landslide. The present purpose is to contrast the analysis of the United States by Piven and Cloward with Miliband's analysis of British society which appeared in the same year.

Capitalist democracy in Britain

In *Capitalist Democracy in Britain* (1982) Ralph Miliband drew upon analyses he had previously developed in his *Parliamentary Socialism* (1972) and *The State in Capitalist Society* (1973). Miliband's argument was based upon two propositions. The first was that British society is very unequal and class divided. The second was that there is 'a fundamental contradiction or tension, in a capitalist society such as Britain, between the promise of popular power, enshrined in universal suffrage, and the curbing or denial of that promise in practice' (Miliband 1982: 1). Both historically and in the early 1980s the resulting tensions had to be managed: 'capitalism . . . now more than ever requires the containment of pressure from below' (2). Ironically, democratic forms could be used to channel and reduce those very pressures.

Containment was made easier by the relative homogeneity of the dominant class and divisions within the working class. The dominant class included not only the owners and controllers of capital but also top politicians, professionals and bureaucrats. The working class was divided by occupation, skill, gender, race, religion and political orientation. The Labour movement, its political expression, was also divided: between radical and 'sensible' leaders, grass-roots activists and ordinary followers, and between its industrial and political wings.

Labour's entry into parliamentary politics passed through several phases. In the wake of the 1867 Act which gave many skilled workers the franchise, the established political parties began to use democratic phraseology in their rhetoric. Working-class activists were welcomed into subordinate positions within the Conservative and Liberal parties, a strategy which delayed the formation of an independent working-class party. Between 1900 and 1945 the Labour party, now independent of other parties, gradually increased its strength in the House of Commons.

It was motivated by a wish to serve the interests of the trade unions, not by any serious ambition to bring about socialism.

The party readily accepted the existing institutional framework, designed to serve the interests of the dominant class. The moderation of the Labour leadership made them useful agents of containment. When real parliamentary power was achieved for the first time in 1945, the Labour party made sure it curbed the expectations of its more zealous socialist elements.

Parliament provided a means whereby those in charge of government could get on with their business without being interfered with too much by the people. Enough participation was allowed to provide democratic legitimisation for the state. Local government gave more scope for non-capitalist interests to be forcefully expressed. Some town councils, such as those at Poplar in the 1920s and at Clay Cross in the 1970s had directly challenged central government by the high levels of services and resources they had illegally devoted to local working-class communities. However, such cases were rare. Professionalised council officials generally nipped such moves in the bud. Local government was restricted to minor matters of improvement. Ambitious schemes of municipal socialism were curbed.

Miliband had been taught by Harold Laski at the London School of Economics. He quoted with approval Laski's view that British society would have been transformed if the Labour party had been genuinely socialist. Miliband thought the ambition unrealistic but 'the argument itself is right' (Miliband 1982: 16). In fact, the Labour party was little more than an electoral machine. This fact generated considerable tension between the parliamentary leadership and the grass roots activists upon whom they relied for local organisation and getting the vote out. During the 1960s and 1970s the parliamentary party had also come into conflict with its trade union counterpart.

The trade unions had become deeply involved in a network of cooperation with government and employers, especially during the Second World War. They derived little influence from this although they were drawn into the process of containment as a result. In any case, the unions were resolutely constitutionalist. Tension with the Labour party developed at the point when they began to move to the left in the 1960s. The power of the unions was criticised by people from all parties and they became a scapegoat for Britain's poor economic performance.

Hegemony and force

The dominant class maintained its position partly by constantly re-inforcing its ideological message and partly by controlling key positions of influence within state and society. Their hegemonic influence was exercised through radio and television, which indoctrinated the public in subtle ways such as 'agenda-setting' and the preservation of 'balance'. The press covered a narrow range of issues from a narrow perspective as determined by its wealthy owners. Most intellectuals were either defenders of the status quo or interested only in moderate reforms, usually with an eye to making the containment of the working class more effective. Miliband cited J.S. Mill as an example of a cautious intellectual who had wanted to buttress the interests of the propertied and wealthy in the face of democracy.

There was some resistance to the dominant capitalist ideology, for example in the education system and in the churches, but there was very little support for developing an alternative radical value system which could challenge the established order. Hegemony was most effective when accompanied by economic growth and affluence. Miliband mentioned both Galbraith and Crosland as 'Fabian' voices whose ideas were hostile to the socialist left.

During the 1960s and 1970s the state was drawn more directly into the task of containment. It had several arms of which the elected government was only one. Government in a democracy had to appear responsive to the people's wishes. It needed the votes of trade unionists and other working-class people. It had to pay attention to the message being conveyed from below by events such as the urban riots which occurred in 1981. Flexibility was needed, which meant relative autonomy from capitalist interests – if only to serve those interests more effectively and less obviously.

Many agencies of the state were well insulated from democratic pressure. The civil service imposed secrecy, conformity and caution on its members. The judiciary were typically ready to restrain the disruptive actions of agents of change such as local councils and trade unions. They were backed up by the military and the police and, less directly, by the monarchy and the House of Lords. All contributed to the task of containment.

In the 1970s and 1980s the pressures from below had built up considerably. They showed in racial tensions, mass unemployment and 'a generalized sense of uncertainty, insecurity and resentment' (Miliband 1982: 146). Could the political system continue to protect the capitalist social order in these circumstances? Miliband envisaged three possible futures for British society. First, a continuation of the existing arrangements with some slight modifications. Unless there was a catastrophic military defeat or a major disaster in Ulster, he thought the present capitalist regime was probably quite secure. Urban riots and disparate protests were little threat. More serious for the regime would be a combination of unrelieved economic decline and an effective opposition from organised labour.

The actual effect of the increase in unemployment levels was widespread 'desubordination' (151), a spirit of disaffection and resistance among working-class people and some intellectuals. As it fed into the increasingly bitter fight for diminishing resources, 'desubordination' contributed to the 'dangerous "overload"' on the governmental system' (Miliband 1982: 153). In these circumstances, the forms of democracy which permitted this kind of pressure to be exercised might be threatened. This led Miliband to the second possible future for British society which was an increase in authoritarianism and a consequent reduction in individual freedom.

The third possibility was the election of a majority government pledged to radical reform. This was unlikely to occur through the present Labour party which was not only opposed to a social revolution but also out of favour with the public. In fact, 'there is no major political force which can at present be said to offer the promise of an effective change to the existing structures of power in Britain' (160).

Ironically, although the point could not be made so clearly in 1982, the Thatcher government has subsequently undermined many of the structures – especially the trade unions and local government – which provided power bases for resistance to central government. Power structures have indeed changed, but in a very different way from that envisaged, with little expectation, by Miliband.

Conclusion

Although they were dealing with different societies, the arguments made by Piven and Cloward and by Miliband had some important similarities. First, in both cases it was pointed out that the promise of democracy was contradicted by the exploitative and repressive character of capitalism. The nastiness of capitalism was to some extent hidden by ideological sleight of hand. Second, the working class, though internally differentiated, had organised to improve its situation within the economic and political spheres. Third, the organisation of working people to pursue their sectional interests had become sufficiently effective by the 1970s and 1980s to threaten the government with 'overload'.

At this point the arguments divided. Piven and Cloward were confident that in the American case the interests of working people were firmly enough embedded in the state apparatus to resist suppression. The wide variety of minorities fighting to resist cut-backs in benefits would unite and successfully challenge the power of capitalism to get its way. They did not look beyond the moment when capitalism threw in the towel although, by implication, a more decent and humane order would prevail.

By contrast, Miliband was quite confident of the continuing capacity of the dominant ruling class and the capitalist interests at its centre to contain the working class. Unlike Piven and Cloward he seriously considered the possibility that the state might become more authoritarian and repressive. He also gave far more significance than did Piven and

Cloward to the political weakness flowing from organisational disunity and ideological vacuity within the working class.

Piven and Cloward were able to represent the values of big business as alien to the democratic philosophy which lay behind the demands of the insurgent poor. Miliband could not rely upon any such implication. He had to accept that there was a close alignment between capitalism and the dominant values of British culture. By contrast, socialism was a misunderstood stranger at the gate.

Turning for a moment to Brittan and Friedman, they also have agreements and differences. Both believed the implementation of egalitarian policies by government was impracticable and, according to Friedman at least, wrong in principle. Both considered that increased stability and efficiency could be injected into capitalist democracy through constitutional reforms which changed the rules of the game. And both believed that success in enacting and implementing reform depended very largely upon the state of public opinion. A major difference between them was that Brittan was concerned about increased individualism being accompanied by a drift towards Hobbesian authoritarianism whereas for Friedman individualism was as American as apple pie. Cutting back government was like cleaning the rust off an old machine and getting it to work properly again.

The visions of the future embodied in the four approaches reflect not only varying ideological dispositions but also differences of national experience and political culture. From their two different perspectives, Friedman, Piven and Cloward all put their trust in the capacity of the people for political action. They focused upon different elements within the people – tax payers on the one hand and benefit recipients on the other. Nevertheless, the message was, in each case, that the people would arise and find the pathway to economic abundance. By contrast, neither Brittan nor Miliband displayed such confidence in the regenerative powers of the people. From their different viewpoints, they both saw before them the road to serfdom.

Chapter eleven

Who benefits?

Two concepts of property

Three great intellectual systems – those of Marx, Freud and Keynes –
have dominated capitalist democracies during the period since the First
World War. Popular versions of Marxism made everyone familiar with
the idea that the struggle for economic advantage was the stuff of politics;
in fact, of all life. It provided a warning, apparently exemplified in Russia,
of what might happen if the people were not made satisfied. Freudianism
– as developed by, for example, Lasswell or Riesman – undermined the
model of the rational economic actor or citizen. However, it also raised
hopes that with the help of psychology and the social sciences
considerable possibilities for organised mass persuasion were open to
business and government. The population could be 'managed'.

Keynesianism responded to the state of mind induced by Marxianism
and Freudianism. Keynes provided intellectual tools which could
apparently be applied by government to shape the economic behaviour
of the population. Properly applied Keynesian techniques would avoid
the kind of disastrous economic failure which makes capitalists fear
bankruptcy and governments worry about social unrest.

Since the First World War – but especially since the 1940s – there
has been enough economic growth in both Britain and the United States
for property ownership to be extended to a high proportion of the working
population. By the 1950s an affluent working class was edging its way
into private home ownership. Since then, enough overlap has developed
between the interests of property and those of the people to take the
political sting out of the issue. Or, more accurately, the venom has been
transferred to complaints against 'social security scroungers' who spend
the money earned by 'hard-working tax-payers'. The propertyless are
becoming marginalised. They provide scant material for a 'new class
war'. The capitalist system has become a less attractive target for the
organised working-class; hence the disappointment of Laski and Miliband
with the performance of British and American labour. Egalitarian

policies of the kind proposed in Britain by Crosland were actually felt as threatening by many working people.

Two concepts of property have been in competition with each other during the past seven or eight decades. One is that property is justified by the contribution it permits the owner to make to the goals of the society. For example, Laski argued that property rights should be justified according to their contribution to the performance of legitimate functions within the state. Ironically, his ideological opponent, Hayek, has justified individual property rights on similar grounds. The rich, even the idle rich, make a contribution to technical and cultural innovation within a society since they have resources available for experimentation.

Another view of property is that it is a prize to be fought for and exploited by the individual concerned for his or her own purposes. Schumpeter believed that the property rights of the industrialist in the business enterprise were ceasing to have this character. The decline of the entrepreneur was, in part, related to the increasingly intangible and impersonal character of this property. Carrying this analysis further, Galbraith suggested that the regime of the industrial capitalist had been succeeded by a new age of anonymous technocrats driven not by pecuniary motives but by their desire to advance the interests of the organisation. However, these same affluent technocrats enjoyed the possession of material things at home in their own private sphere. It is property in this latter sense which is becoming more widespread within capitalist democracy.

The idea of a fundamental conflict between the people and property – the skeleton Chamberlain rattled to frighten the House of Lords – has been undermined in two ways. First, the employment relation is typically regulated not by the direct commands of specific owners but by impersonal rules which are the object of constant negotiation. Second, a large proportion of the electorate are enjoying or expect to enjoy the satisfactions of property as a 'prize' – the house, the car and so on. There are national differences. In the United States cultural support for the feeling of being obliged to perform a socially useful function with your capital, or, as a surrogate, to stress the social worthiness of your gainful occupation, is stronger than in Britain. Sustained propaganda in the latter society about the virtues of enterprise during the 1980s have not produced any noticeable cultural change in this respect.

The shift of ideological focus away from the property/people relationship has been accompanied by increased attention to relations between the public and private spheres. The debate has concentrated on consumption patterns and the organisation of economic production. Deficiencies of investment in public goods (parks, schools, hospitals) have been blamed upon the undue influence of big business over government (Galbraith). By contrast, deficiencies of investment in private industry have been blamed on the undue influence of government over big business (Friedman, following Hayek). Failure in both respects is measured in terms of the incapacity of the capitalist democracy to provide voters and consumers with the rewards they 'have a right' to expect. Taken together, the assumptions which lie behind these debates are worth exploring further because they derive from a model of capitalist democracy which would have appeared strange or perverted to the people discussed in part one.

Nostalgia and idealism

The argument can be taken in three stages. First, it is worth juxtaposing once more Laski and Hayek, contemporaries on the teaching staff at the London School of Economics but at first sight a long way apart in terms of ideas. In fact, they both stand apart from the other writers considered by virtue of their utter intellectual devotion to specific ideal schemes of the social order. In both cases, the ideal of liberty is central:

> Tyranny flows easily from the accumulation of petty restrictions. It is important that each should have to prove its undeniable social necessity before it is admitted within the fabric of the law. We ought . . . to be critical of every proposal that asks for a surrender of liberty. Its enemies, we must remember, never admit that they are concerned to attack it; they always base their defence of their purpose upon other grounds.

The sentiments sound Hayekian. They actually come from Laski's *Liberty in the Modern State* (1930: 175).

Laski and Hayek both disliked the way the world was moving in the 1930s. Both looked back to a simpler, clearer world and explored ways of approximating it in the present. Laski wanted to recapture the amalgam of fulfilling individual activity and deep public involvement that Tocqueville had found in Jacksonian America. He designed a charter of principles and a constitution for such a society under conditions of urban industrial life in *The Grammar of Politics*. Like Tocqueville, he understood that the barrier standing in the way of his goal was the power of industrial capitalism.

Hayek performed an intellectual feat just as daring and just as not-quite-believable in his *The Constitution of Liberty* which managed to portray a vision of modern society without directly discussing the modern business corporation as a distinctive institution. Hayek's ideal was the kind of free and experimental civilisation, running on entrepreneurship and co-ordinated through the market, that had supposedly existed in the early American Republic. The value of learning through experience was as central to his schema as it was to Laski's. However, Hayek's bugbear was not the modern form of capitalism but the modern form of political democracy, the 'socialist' (or centralising, planning) state. He had no confidence whatsoever in the capacity of planners to achieve civilised purposes. They could only destroy.

From manipulation to regulation

The second stage of the argument brings in Lasswell and Schumpeter. Compared to Laski and Hayek, these two were gritty realists. Schumpeter saw the drift of things was shutting down the world of the independent entrepreneur. Lasswell and he both realised power within democracies lay with powerful minorities. Participatory democracy was a sham. The voters were not controlling things from below. They were being manipulated from above. Schumpeter and Lasswell both thought in terms of an elitist model of capitalist democracy, as defined below:

> The *elitist* model of capitalist democracy assumes that the public sphere is legitimately and quite overtly dominated by influential minorities – including organised political parties and pressure groups representing vested interests – who seek to advance their interests by applying persuasion to the government and/or the citizenry.

In fact, the elitist model is the manipulatory model made respectable and decked out in its Sunday suit. Two factors helped it come in from the cold. First, the increasingly effective organisation of trade unions as national pressure groups in both Britain and the United States which gave working people a feeling of having a place at the bargaining table. And second, the existence of fascist and communist polities which could be villified in order to heighten the sense of contrast with the system at home. Hayek was shrewd enough to point out the element of trickery in all this.

Lasswell and Schumpeter offered the professional services of their colleagues – political scientists and economists respectively – to help political leaders manage capitalist democracy now it had become legitimate to admit that effective guidance did not come from the people or the market. The adoption of Keynesian demand management within the elitist model helped to bring about another, closely related, ideological reversal.

In the early part of the century Hobson and Veblen had helped to lay the foundations for a model of hegemonic capitalist democracy which, to oversimplify, claimed that big business had achieved considerable political influence and was deluding and exploiting the people with the state's help (see p. 102). The model was taken up in the 1930s but the relationships between its component parts – big business, the state and the people – were altered. In the new, officially acceptable version of this model, the state regulated big business and with its cooperation was able to produce economic rewards for the people. This was backed up by an extensive system of official propaganda. The model of regulatory capitalist democracy was born, although, as has been seen, it had been anticipated, in part, by Bryce:

> The *regulatory* model of capitalist democracy assumes that the task of government is to use expert knowledge in order to minimise social tension and optimise economic growth. The object is to generate feelings of economic security (preferably prosperity) and psychological contentment among the population at large, especially those sections who are most closely connected to the current political establishment and those most capable of threatening the position of that establishment.

This is the point where we came in. In other words, it is with reference to this regulatory model that Galbraith and Friedman criticised the failure of governments to give voters and consumers the rewards they 'have a right' to expect.

Vice becomes virtue

In the third stage of the argument, Galbraith plays a role rather similar to Mill a century before. Mill had complained that the commercial middle class was acquiring too much influence in government and too much power over the people, imposing their narrow dogmas and infecting the population with a passion for trivia. He hoped to combat this trend by mobilising the intelligentsia in allegiance with the state bureaucracy. Galbraith, faced with the challenge of the large corporations and the affluent society, called upon the educational and scientific estate to redress the balance, armed with the techniques of modern economic management. Big business would be properly subordinated to the state. Like Mill, Galbraith was happy to slow down the pace of economic growth and was not averse to a little bit of socialism.

Crosland and Friedman wanted to tinker with the triad of state, business, people at different points. Crosland wished to use the state to create more equality among the British people. Friedman hoped by populist campaigning to persuade the American people to force the state to unhitch itself from big business.

Two contrasting developments of the model of regulatory capitalist democracy are implied by the ambitions of the writers just mentioned. Galbraith and Crosland favoured the compensatory model of capitalist democracy. Friedman (along with Hayek) wants a minimalist model to be implemented:

> The *compensatory* model of capitalist democracy assumes that the

state will restructure the public sphere, intervene in the private sphere and rectify any imbalance between the two. As necessary, it will also reduce the relative degree of advantage enjoyed by the minority benefiting most from the unequal distribution of private property. In both respects, the state's actions are intended to provide rights and rewards which compensate for market failures and unjust patterns of economic distribution through the market.

The *minimalist* form of capitalist democracy assumes that the regulatory function of government will not involve compensatory activity (which is regarded as counter-productive for all involved) but will be restricted almost entirely to enforcing a body of law. The laws enforced by the state will maximise the freedom of private individuals within a stable environment thus optimising the chance for achieving the goals of minimum social tension and optimum growth as predicated in the regulatory model.

Piven and Cloward anticipated that the people (or at least the poor) would engage in conflict with big business through the medium of the state. In this way the state could be stopped from drifting towards a minimalist model and pushed back towards a compensatory model. Miliband believed that the model of hegemonic capitalist democracy continued to apply beneath the surface of the regulatory model whether in its simple form or in its compensatory and minimalist variants. The repressive potential of hegemonic capitalist democracy might, he thought, get worse as the capacity of the state to keep its promises or meet demands upon it was stretched beyond its limit. Brittan also bore witness to the authoritarian potential inherent in the regulatory model.

The distinctive models of mid twentieth-century capitalist democracy are built upon a legitimisation of the acknowledged vices of the nineteenth-century and early twentieth-century system. Acknowledged as vices, that is, by commentators at the time such as Tocqueville, Mill, Carnegie, Chamberlain, Bryce, Ostrogorski, Veblen and Hobson. The emphasis upon private affluence, the encouragement of passivity in the public sphere except for making an occasional choice between two or more sets of packaged policies, the wholesale organisation of political life through a party system, the systematic management of public opinion, and political appeals to the lowest pecuniary motives: that these values and practices should now be regarded as the essence of capitalist democracy rather than its perversion would presumably have horrified our predecessors.

Chapter twelve

Three phases of capitalist democracy

Ten types of capitalist democracy

In conclusion, it may be helpful to summarise in a relatively formal way the book's conclusions regarding the logic expressed in the sequence of models of capitalist democracy which have been encountered.

The nine models so far introduced are listed here with the addition of a further model whose significance will be explained later (see Diagram A, p. 194):

1. The *participatory* model of capitalist democracy assumes that individuals will invest their time and energy as fully in the public as in the private sphere and that private property will not provide the basis for domination by a powerful minority.

2. The *mediatory* model of capitalist democracy assumes that an educated and propertied minority will complement its dominance in the market with intelligent and humane leadership in the public sphere.

3. The *paternalistic* model of capitalist democracy assumes the priority of the private over the public sphere but recommends that the most successful business people should use their superior judgement and wealth to provide services to the community.

4. The *manipulatory* model assumes the improper and generally covert dominance of private interests, especially business people, within the public sphere. This influence is exercised partly through the promise of jobs and favours.

5. The model of *hegemonic* capitalist democracy assumes that the public sphere is managed by agents who use their relative autonomy to advance, directly or indirectly, the interests of capital at the expense of the interests of the people as a whole, especially the working class.

6. The *elitist* model of capitalist democracy assumes that the public sphere is legitimately and quite overtly dominated by influential minorities – including organised political parties and pressure

groups representing vested interests – who seek to advance their interests by applying persuasion to the government and/or the citizenry.

7   The *regulatory* model of capitalist democracy assumes that the task of government is to use expert knowledge in order to minimise social tension and optimise economic growth. The object is to generate feelings of economic security (preferably prosperity) and psychological contentment among the population at large, especially those sections who are most closely connected to the current political establishment and those most capable of threatening the position of that establishment.

8   The *compensatory* model of capitalist democracy assumes that the state will restructure the public sphere, intervene in the private sphere and rectify any imbalance between the two. As necessary, it will also reduce the relative degree of advantage enjoyed by the minority benefiting most from the unequal distribution of private property. In both respects, the state's actions are intended to provide rights and rewards which compensate for market failures and unjust patterns of economic distribution through the market.

9   The *minimalist* form of capitalist democracy assumes that the regulatory function of government will not involve compensatory activity (which is regarded as counter-productive for all involved) but will be restricted almost entirely to enforcing a body of law. The laws enforced by the state will maximise the freedom of private individuals within a stable environment thus optimising the chance for achieving the goals of minimum social tension and optimum growth as predicated in the regulatory model.

10 The *conservatory* model of capitalist democracy assumes that strategies with respect to economic growth and individual or group behaviour within the market should be made compatible with the acceptance of a shared responsibility for proper management of ecological resources. This includes the task of maintaining or improving the environment's capacity to sustain a healthy and civilised lifestyle for citizens.

Before discussing the dynamic interplay between the various models the particular meanings of four terms to be used – elaboration, delegitimisation, relegitimisation, and transformation – will be briefly indicated. A preliminary point is that a distinction may be made between two aspects of a model: the interconnected structures, processes and strategies to which a model refers (the 'facts' asserted by the model) and the attitude towards them expressed in the model (the 'values' it asserts). With respect to their incorporation of facts and values, the different models may be related to each other in one or more of three ways:

First, the facts and values specific to model X may be incorporated within the more complex intellectual structure of model Y. In this case, model Y involves an *elaboration* of model X.

Second, model Y may emphasise the same facts as model X but embody a negative critique of model X's values. As a consequence, facts (structures, processes, strategies) that were regarded as legitimate in model X are regarded as illegitimate in model Y (or *vice versa*). In this case, model Y has either *delegitimised* or *relegitimised* the facts of model X.

Third, model Y may accept the special significance of the structures, processes and strategies incorporated in model X but assert that these facts are related to each other in a different way. In this case, model Y entails a *transformation* of model X.

Three sequences of ideological development

Diagram A represents the models of capitalist democracy encountered in this book in terms of their participation in three successive sequences of ideological development. During the *first* sequence, from approximately the 1830s to the early 1900s, a spiralling process of delegitimisation occurred. A series of models were produced, each one challenging the claims of its predecessor and being in turn challenged. The participatory model was unreservedly accepted by none of the writers or politicians studied. Even Tocqueville wanted it to be combined with the mediation of the judiciary. No one supported complete political and social equality. Apart from the judiciary, the strategic groups in the different versions of the mediatory model included industrialists and successful professionals (Chamberlain), bureaucrats and intellectuals (Mill) and strong-minded 'independent citizens' (Bryce).

The participatory and mediatory models were both undermined by the two assumptions of the paternalistic model as set out by Carnegie: that the public sphere was of low worth; and that a high proportion of the population were unfitted to share in the management of society's business. It should be added that 'softer' forms of paternalism, more respectful of the public sphere, existed, especially in Britain, where they complemented rather than contradicted the mediatory model. The work of the Quaker manufacturer George Cadbury, especially at Bournville to the south west of Birmingham, is a well-known example.

Both the mediatory and paternalistic forms were, in turn, delegitimised at the hands of the manipulatory model of capitalist democracy developed by Ostrogorski and Bryce. The manipulatory model accepted the facts as represented in the mediatory and paternalist models – especially the great influence over British and American government and politics enjoyed by wealthy business people – and declared them evil.

During the *second* sequence, from about the First World War to the

Diagram A Three sequences of ideological development

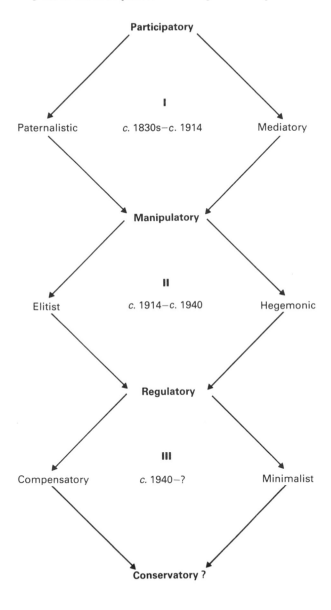

1940s, two cycles of transformation, elaboration and relegitimisation occurred, both leading from the manipulatory model to the regulatory model.

One route led by way of the elitist model. Theorists such as Lasswell and Schumpeter acknowledged the special significance of the political domination exercised by powerful minorities but did not condemn the situation. On the contrary, the facts were relegitimised. The point was to accept the reality and find out how it worked. In pursuing their enquiries, the exponents of the elitist model subjected the facts of the manipulatory model to a transformation which demoted business people to just one elite among a number. Business people were no longer the omnipotent wirepullers of politicians, bureaucrats, labour leaders and so on. Instead, controllers of different resources – capital, votes, organisational capacity, charisma and so on – competed with each other for advantage.

Turning for a moment to the other route from the manipulatory model, the hegemonic model (Veblen, Hobson) accepted both the facts and evaluation of this earlier model. However, Veblen and Hobson both elaborated the manipulatory model by locating it within a more comprehensive system. This was based on the assumption that business interests were relatively successful in imposing policies upon the state which served the needs of capitalism at the expense of the people. The hegemonic model incorporated a function for advertising as a means of shaping the motivation and behaviour of the population.

The two routes subsequently converged upon the regulatory model. The elitist model was elaborated and made part of a more dynamic system. This system was the hegemonic model transformed and relegitimised. The central triad of big business, government and the people remained in place. So did the role of propaganda. However, the initiative switched from capital to government. Its tasks were three: to shape the behaviour of business in ways which generated rewards for the population; to shape the behaviour of the population in ways which maintained economic growth; and to monitor points of tension and conflict in order to minimise their consequences for the system as a whole.

The incorporation of the elitist model into the regulatory model made government the focal point for a bargaining process over the distribution of rewards and penalties. The trade unions found a place in this model which they were denied in the hegemonic model. Schumpeter and Lasswell had made a start at writing the job descriptions for professional economists and political scientists as government advisers under the regulatory scheme of things. The techniques of economic management recommended by Keynes or used in his name were also available.

The *third* sequence was under way as soon as the regulatory model was established and has not yet been resolved. Two contrary pressures were exerted from the 1940s onward. One was towards elaboration of the regulatory model to permit a much greater degree of intervention in the affairs of business and the people at large. This compensatory model was designed to achieve an optimum combination of economic growth, social justice and civilised decency. Galbraith and Crosland have been prominent exponents of variations of this approach.

Minimalism, the competing approach, denies legitimacy to the compensatory model, objecting both to the values implanted within it and the factual understandings upon which it is based. Minimalists accept the aims of the original regulatory model but believe that the compensatory approach makes it more difficult to achieve these. Instead, they propose a regulatory model transformed in two ways. First, as far as possible regulation is restricted to the enactment and supervision of a legal framework providing stability and guaranteeing individual freedom. Second, the sharp distinction between big business and the people which is central to the regulatory model becomes much less clearcut. The business corporation tends to disappear from view. The foreground is occupied by [to use Galbraith's term] the market sector. The latent image is of a free market populated by active entrepreneurial individuals.

After nearly a decade of minimalist rule in both Britain and the United States there is some justification for believing that another downward spiral of delegitimisation is under way. There has been a sustained attack upon the compensatory model in both societies. Memories of inflation, high taxation and unsuccessful policies of income restraint have been battered into the public mind and associated, however unfairly, with the past performances of the British Labour party and the American Democratic party. It will be difficult to go back down this road.

Ironically, the implementation of minimalist policies has involved a considerable amount of governmental intervention, especially in Britain, in order to dismantle or restructure institutions in accordance with the ruling idea. In Britain, this high-profile activity has helped maintain the authority of central government; it is seen to be doing things. In the United States, the personal popularity of Ronald Reagan, studiously achieved through a masterly performance, sustained the prestige of the White House in spite of numerous accusations of incompetence and even worse.

There has been unemployment, higher than for decades and, in some localities, of horrifying proportions. The drug problem, one index of social despair, has got much worse in both societies. Britain had very serious urban riots in 1981. However, a large proportion of the people have been rewarded for their political support by a consumer boom which has induced a feeling of prosperity.

The minimalist regimes have apparently destroyed their ideological rival, the compensatory model, and left themselves alone in the field. The central theme of the Reagan years was that America had found itself again and re-established contact with a vital spirit. This spirit had made it great in the past and would do so in the future. Minimalism in America claimed the authority of national tradition.

National culture re-examined

However, American national culture also supplied a powerful critique of the individualist pursuit of material wealth at the expense of other values. A wave of self-criticism swept across America in the later Reagan years, perhaps encouraged by the dramatic changes in international relations – the impact of *glasnost* and *perestroika* on the Cold War and the resurgence of South-East Asia – discussed at the beginning of this book. Two widely-read critiques of contemporary American culture from the latter part of the 1980s both drew inspiration from a much earlier commentator. In *The Closing of the American Mind*, subtitled 'How higher education has failed democracy and impoverished the souls of today's students', Allan Bloom acknowledged that 'Tocqueville taught me the importance of the university to democratic society' (Bloom 1987: 246).

In a nutshell, Bloom believes that American universities have imbibed the moral and cultural relativism (or indifference) of the wider society. The opposing ideal asserted by Bloom is represented by Plato's *Republic* with its evocation of 'The real community of man [which] . . . is the community of those who seek the truth' (281). The universities had, unfortunately, forgotten their duty to teach students to inquire into the nature of the true and the good. Such a failure heralded great danger for 'when there are no shared goals or visions of the public good, is the social contract any longer possible?' (27).

Robert Bellah and his colleagues took the very title of their book – *Habits of the Heart* (subtitled 'Middle America observed') – from Tocqueville's *Democracy in America*. They strongly opposed the contemporary tendency to think about American society solely in terms of political economy. As a result of their inquiries into love and marriage, therapeutic practices, voluntary associations and campaign organisations Bellah's team concluded that there was both a need and a desire to revive 'civic virtue in order to mitigate the tension [between private interest and public good] and render it manageable' (Bellah 1988: 270). Public virtue had to be revived for the good of the survival of the American nation as 'a free people'. The big question was: 'Is it possible that we could become citizens again and together seek the common good in the post-industrial, post-modern age?' (271).

The issue of post-modernism will be taken up shortly after noticing that in Britain also the 1980s were a time of reflection upon national identity. The focus was upon the interplay between tradition, political ideas and institutions, geography and ethnicity: specifically Englishness – and, of course, Scottishness, Welshness and Irishness. Some aspects of these themes had been broached decades earlier by, for example, Raymond Williams in *Culture and Society* (1963). In his *The Break-Up of Britain* (1981), originally published in 1977, Tom Nairn carried forward 'a gathering movement of historical revisionism' (1981: 303). During the mid 1980s the flood tide broke with the appearance of works such as *The Invention of Tradition* (Hobsbawm and Ranger 1983), *The Great Arch. English State Formation as Cultural Revolution* (Corrigan and Sayer 1985), *On Living in an Old Country. The National Past in Contemporary Britain* (Wright 1985), *Englishness, Politics and Culture 1880–1920* (Colls and Dodd 1986) and, with an Anglo-American focus, *Class and Space. The Making of Urban Society* (Thrift and Williams 1987).

The new debate on Englishness is still in its early stages, but one tentative conclusion is that, unlike being an American, being English does not embody an ideological commitment to some version of the high ideals of citizenship to which Bloom and Bellah refer. American-ness embodies a programme, both individual and collective. For the sake of legitimacy, this programme has to retain visible links with the founding principles of the American Republic. Within those limits battle rages. To be American is to belong to what Louis Hartz has called 'the liberal tradition' (Hartz 1955).

Englishness is equally a historical product but its ideological content is more flexible. For a few generations – during the half-century following the act which gave the vote to all Englishmen (1918) – liberalism was a constituent element in Englishness. In *Modern Democracies* Bryce wrote:

> Abiding foundations of policy glide . . . into principles which have come to so inhere in national consciousness as to seem parts of national character. Such, for the English, are the respect for law, the feeling that every citizen is bound to come forward in its support . . . . The traditional love of liberty, the traditional sense of duty to the community, be it great or small, the traditional . . . wish to secure reforms by constitutional rather than violent means – these were the habits ingrained in the mind and will of Englishmen.
> (Bryce 1921a: 156–60)

This view – shaped by the moral interests of middle-class Christianity and upper-class paternalism – became the stock in trade of both the Conservative party and the infant Labour party (Smith 1987). Indeed, the very success of the Liberal party in establishing its central principles in national political life may have been partly responsible for its inter-war decline.

During the past two decades the main institutional supports for this liberal version of Englishness – the British Broadcasting Corporation, the Church of England, the universities and the Chamberlainite tradition of local government – have been seriously undermined. It is by no means dead. However, a more atavistic form of Englishness has emerged, expressed at its worst in football hooliganism and the more extreme manifestations of chauvinism evident during the Falklands War of 1982.

The balance between the two forms of Englishness might shift back in favour of the former – or a quite different type of Englishness might eventually emerge. However, most likely is that the Americanisation of British culture which is under way will reinforce the selfish and parochial element in Englishness. If this is correct it would be an ironic counterpart to the reverse process – the export to America of English middle-class materialism and individualism – which John Stuart Mill observed during the mid nineteenth century.

To summarise: capitalist democratic ideology is currently subject to a process of delegitimisation. Some indications of a moral revolt against minimalism in the United States have been indicated. Englishness does not supply equivalent tools for critique. However, despite its evident cultural power, minimalism does not yet dominate the British national psyche to the same extent.

Post-modernism and its antecedents

Some clues to the cultural character of minimalism may emerge from a brief consideration of post-modernism. Post-modernism, as analysed by Jean Braudillard, is consumer capitalism dominated by signs, messages and images (Poster 1988). For Frederic Jameson it is the abandonment of narratives and the loss of our historical sense, for example in architecture and film (Jameson 1979; Jameson 1981; Jameson 1984). For Daniel Bell it is the loss of old anchorages in time and space (Bell 1978). For Lasch its essence is narcissism (Lasch 1980). For Lash and Urry, post-modernist sensibility includes the denial of the separation of art from life and of high from low culture; culture is to be consumed in a state of 'distraction' for the purpose of immediate enjoyment (Lash and Urry 1987: 287).

These analyses lead back, yet one more time, to Tocqueville and his fascination with the contrast between aristocratic, class-ridden Europe and democratic, individualistic America. He found in the 1830s that Americans were, in cultural matters, devoted to 'the hypocrisy of luxury[;] . . . the arts [he added] have recourse to every kind of imposture' (1968: 600). The image or representation of a precious stone was as well valued as the real thing. Instead of a taste for the lofty and enduring,

They like facile forms of beauty, self-explanatory and immediately enjoyable; above all, they like things unexpected and new . . . lively emotions, sudden revelations, brilliant truths, or errors able to rouse them up and plunge them, almost by violence, into the middle of the subject.

(Tocqueville 1968: 608)

In their theatres, 'Democratic peoples have but little reverence for learning and scarcely bother at all what happened in Rome or Athens. They want the talk to be about themselves and to see the present world mirrored' (630).

Immediacy, enjoyment, narcissism and a preoccupation with signifiers (e.g. paste diamonds) rather than with things of real and lasting value: Tocqueville was describing a bourgeois culture released from aristocratic supports or restraints. Veblen analysed a later version of this culture around the turn of the century. Conspicuous consumption had become a complex charade signifying social aspirations. Architectural styles, whether at world fairs such as the Columbia Exposition of 1893 or in the mansions of Chicago plutocrats, showed scant regard for history or geography, happily juxtaposing ancient Egypt with absolutist France.

Insofar as post-modernist culture recalls these earlier manifestations, the reason may be that it expresses a new release of capitalism – iconoclastic, subversive, disrespectful and individualistic – from social restraints. If that is the case then minimalism and post-modernism are well matched. However, the latter is less a source of moral support for minimalism than a cultural emanation, a sort of glow around it.

As Schumpeter predicted, in the 1980s a larger proportion of the population is able to share the material fruits of capitalism than was the case in the 1890s. The property-owning, property-enjoying part of society now includes a large number of white- and blue-collar employees and their families. As tax-payers they are likely to resist a shift back to compensatory capitalist democracy but their support for minimalism is, it may be suggested, dependent upon its practical success. Specifically, minimalist regimes must maintain low inflation, sustain high rates of economic growth and compete effectively in the global economy if they are to survive in their present form. Their credit, both political and financial, depends upon this.

The conservatory model

Two dragons stand in the path of minimalist regimes. One is the possibility of a widespread recession, perhaps triggered by a repetition on an even larger scale of the stock market crash of late 1987. It was the great crash of 1929 which brought to an end the glittering era described and condemned by Veblen. Another very sudden and massive collapse might presage a revival of sentiment in favour of compensatory strategies. However, governments might be able to control the impact of such a recession so that it hit certain groups unequally and at different times. In such circumstances, a minimalist regime might continue, coexisting with a more authoritarian strategy with respect to law and order.

Ironically, a recession would put back the evil day when the second dragon might have to be faced. This is the threat to the environment posed by continuing industrial development. Even with present rates of economic growth in the advanced industrial societies, there appears to be a serious threat to the ecological system. Anxieties about the 'greenhouse effect' and damage to the ozone layer are only two aspects of the impact environmental issues are having on the mainstream politics of capitalist democracy. A systemic ecological crisis would put all stakes at risk.

It is unrealistic to expect 'green' parties to achieve majority positions within the British or American legislatures in the near future. However, in the medium term campaigners upon ecological issues are likely to achieve strategic positions within major parties or multi-party coalitions. The sensitivity of the public to this issue was dramatically shown late in 1988 when Edwina Curry, junior health minister in the British government, suggested that egg production was widely infected with salmonella. Within a short period of time sales of eggs in Britain dropped by 50 per cent. Mrs Curry was forced to resign but, whatever the facts of the case, she clearly hit a very sensitive spot.

People feel very threatened in their relationship with nature: water pollution, nuclear leaks, acid rain, food irradiation, skin cancer, Aids – and so on. Concern is growing that the industrial economy is beginning to burst out of its ecological container. The concern of the 1970s was that occupational and consumer interests were 'overloading' the political system. By contrast, during the 1990s the talk will probably be of 'growth machines' (Molotch 1976) 'overloading' the environment. At worst we could be in for a period of deep anxiety reminiscent of the millenarian 990s when bishops and abbots prophesied the imminent demise of mankind.

A time might come when ordinary people are persuaded that it is in their interests to forsake the prospect of further material gains in order to protect the value of what they already have. They would have to be shown a practical strategy for doing this. Whatever the content of such a strategy, it would probably have to be legitimised in terms of what might be labelled a 'conservatory' model of capitalist democracy:

> The *conservatory* model of capitalist democracy assumes that strategies with respect to economic growth and individual or group behaviour

within the market should be made compatible with the acceptance of a shared responsibility for proper management of ecological resources. This includes the task of maintaining or improving the environment's capacity to sustain a healthy and civilised lifestyle for citizens.

Were such a model to be seriously implemented it would pose severe difficulties for existing patterns of capitalist democracy. Would capitalism be able to find sufficient investment opportunities in the context of such constraints? Would a conservatory strategy be able to avoid 'overload' on government due to well-organised pressure from below for immediate material rewards? No definite answers can be given to those questions but at the very least major tensions would be generated by a serious attempt to implement a conservatory model.

Despite the innovative thinking of some socialists (e.g. Cook 1984), the shift to a conservatory ideology would create immediate problems for politicians previously committed to a compensatory ideology. The search for justice and the pursuit of growth appear inseparable within this approach. The skepticism of Tony Crosland towards conservationists has already been noticed.

Minimalism also pushes for growth but politicians of this school are tactically better placed, in the short run at least. While the compensatory strategy boils down to 'growth as a precondition of justice', the minimalist approach can be summarised as 'freedom and stability leading to growth'. If a minimalist regime runs into very serious trouble either due to a failure to achieve balanced growth (overheating in the economy?) or due to severe environmental dysfunctions (overheating in the ecology?), it has at hand the beginnings of an alternative line of action and propaganda.

The earlier phases of the minimalist programme – liberty and stability – could be retained, though probably with a more authoritarian cast. The virtues of lowering the rate of growth could then be preached. This might be increasingly acceptable to an electorate learning the hard way that when the environment is overburdened dirt and disease are no longer the prerogative of the poor and weak. The 'good housekeeping' rhetoric of minimalism – with which the British, at least, have become familiar – could in such circumstances be adapted smoothly to the world ecology: humankind as a whole must learn to 'keep its global house in order', we all have a responsibility to leave the world in as good a condition as when we found it, and so on.

The international dimension of a conservatory approach would be crucial. Its objectives would be well served if the United States, Britain and other potential conservatory regimes increased the practical support they gave to bodies such as the United Nations. The Western powers might even take the opportunity, for highly 'moral' reasons, to focus international disapproval and diplomatic pressure upon the fast-growing economies of South-East Asia. In a world edging towards ecological overload too much industrial vigour would not be a good thing.

The advantage enjoyed by minimalist politicians would be short term only. Their claim to office ultimately depends upon making people – enough people – feel prosperous and secure. The bedrock of minimalism is the responsibility of the individual to look after him or herself combined with the individual's right to enjoy the fruits of private property. The security offered by minimalism is based upon individual possession within a stable environment. However, the environment is becoming radically destabilised. Individual property rights will have no more sway over the course of global ecological deterioration than did King Canute over the waves. The rules of the game are changing very quickly.

In conclusion, these speculations will be given a more formal character. A shift from compensatory and minimalist models towards a conservatory model of capitalist democracy would involve further processes of delegitimisation, transformation, and elaboration.

First, legitimacy would be denied to the unrestrained pursuit of economic growth and to interpretations of freedom which allow individual selfishness to damage our shared interest in a habitable world.

Second, the framework in terms of which justice is sought within the compensatory model would be transformed. To be specific, the compensatory model assumes that increased exploitation of nature, through economic growth, will facilitate social engineering in favour of the less privileged and thus make a decent standard of living available to more people. The conservatory model also assumes that a readjustment of the relationship between society and nature will optimise the possibility for decent human lives. However, not only does it assume that the pressure for growth should be put into reverse gear, but it also requires that material demands should be restrained by rich and poor alike.

Third, the search for stability characteristic of minimalism would be elaborated and given a much broader character. Specifically, it would extend beyond the need to guarantee the rule of law within society, encompassing the far greater task of preserving, as far as possible, the global ecological balance.

The conservatory model would pose serious problems for politicians and citizens attached to its compensatory and minimalist antecedents. Would the pursuit of survival wipe out all hope of improving the relative position of the worst-off within society? Would a commitment to ecological concerns be at the expense of individual freedom? Capitalist democracy remains on trial.

Bibliography

The bibliography includes all the work referred to in the text plus a few which, although not mentioned in the text, are relevant to the book's theme.

Alford, R. and Friedland, R. (1985) *Powers of Theory: Capitalism, the State and Democracy*, Cambridge: Cambridge University Press.

Allett, J. (1981) *New Liberalism. The Political Economy of J.A. Hobson*, Toronto: University of Toronto Press.

Amis, M. (1984) *Money. A Suicide Note*, London: Jonathan Cape.

Andrain, C.F. (1984) 'Capitalism and Democracy Revisited: A Review Essay', *Western Political Quarterly* 37 (4): 652–64.

Arblaster, A. (1984) *The Rise and Decline of Western Liberalism*, Oxford: Basil Blackwell.

Arnold, M. (1888) 'Civilisation in the United States', *Nineteenth Century* 23 (134): 481–96.

Aron, R. (1968) *Main Currents in Sociological Thought: 1*, translated by Richard Howard and Helen Weaver, Harmondsworth: Penguin.

Bell, D. (1973) *The Coming of Post-Industrial Society: A Venture in Social Forecasting*, New York: Basic Books.

Bell, D. (1975) 'The end of American exceptionalism', *Public Interest*, 41: 193–224.

Bell, D. (1976) *The Coming of Post-Industrial Society. A Venture in Social Forecasting*, Harmondsworth: Penguin.

Bell, D. (1978) *The Cultural Contradictions of Capitalism*, second edition, London: Heinemann.

Bellah, R., Madsen, R., Sullivan, W.M., Swidler, A., and Tipton, S.M. (1988) *Habits of the Heart. Middle America Observed*, London: Hutchinson.

Berger, P.L. (1987) *The Capitalist Revolution. Fifty Propositions about Prosperity, Equality and Liberty*, Aldershot: Wildwood House.

Berman, M. (1983) *All That Is Solid Melts Into Air. The Experience of Modernity*, London: Verso.

Blackbourn, D. and Eley, G. (1984) *The Peculiarities of German History: Historical and Contemporary Perspectives*, Oxford: Oxford University Press.

Bloom, A. (1987) *The Closing of the American Mind*, Harmondsworth: Penguin.

Bobbio, N. (1987) *The Future of Democracy*, Cambridge: Polity Press.

Boorstin, D.J. (1981) *The Lost World of Thomas Jefferson*, Chicago:

University of Chicago Press (originally published in 1948).

Bosanquet, B. (1899) *The Philosophical Theory of the State*, London: Macmillan.

Bowles, S. and Gintis, H. (1987) *Democracy and Capitalism. Property, Community and the Contradictions of Modern Social Thought*, London: Routledge & Kegan Paul.

Brailsford, N. (1948) 'The Life-Work of J.A. Hobson', *L. T. Hobhouse Memorial Trust Lecture, No. 17*.

Brittan, S. (1973) *Capitalism and the Permissive Society*, London: Macmillan.

Brittan, S. (1988a) 'The politics of excessive expectations', in Brittan 1988e: 247–78 (originally published in 1974).

Brittan, S. (1988b) 'Inflation and democracy', in Brittan 1988e: 279–302 (originally published in 1977).

Brittan, S. (1988c) 'Invest in failure – a bipartisan style', in Brittan 1988e: 142–61 (originally published in 1971).

Brittan, S. (1988d) 'Towards a new political settlement', in Brittan 1988e: 303–14.

Brittan, S. (1988e) *Economic Consequences of Democracy*, Aldershot: Wildwood House.

Brookeman, C. (1984) *American Culture and Society since the 1930s*, London: Macmillan.

Brown, L. (1981) *Building a Sustainable Society*, New York: W.W. Norton.

Bryce, J. (1894a) *The American Commonwealth, Vol. I*, London: Macmillan (originally published in 1888).

Bryce, J. (1894b) *The American Commonwealth, Vol. II*, London: Macmillan (originally published in 1888).

Bryce, J. (1902) 'Preface' in Ostrogorski 1902a: *xxxix–xlvii*.

Bryce, J. (1921a) *Modern Democracies. Vol. I*, London: Macmillan.

Bryce, J. (1921b) *Modern Democracies. Vol. II*, London: Macmillan.

Bulmer, M. (1984) *The Chicago School of Sociology: Institutionalization, Diversity, and the Rise of Sociological Research*, Chicago: University of Chicago Press.

Burawoy, M. (1985) *The Politics of Production. Factory Regimes under Capitalism and Socialism*, London: Verso.

Burnheim, J. (1985) *Is Democracy Possible?*, Cambridge: Polity Press.

Burritt, E. (1868) *Walks in the Black Country and its Green Border-Land* London: Sampson, Low, Son, and Marston.

Caesar, J. (1985) 'Alexis de Tocqueville on political science, political culture, and the rôle of the intellectual', *American Political Science Review* 79(3): 656–72.

Campbell, C. (1987) *The Romantic Ethic and the Spirit of Modern Consumerism*, Oxford: Blackwell.

Cannadine, D. (1980) 'Urban development in England and America in the nineteenth century: some comparisons and contrasts', *Economic History Review* 33 (3): 309–25.

Carnegie, A. (1886) *Triumphant Democracy or Fifty Years March of the Republic*, London: Sampson, Low, Marston, Searle, and Rivington.

Carnegie, A. (1891) 'The advantages of poverty', *Nineteenth Century* 31 (169): 367–84.

Carnegie, A. (1900) *The Gospel of Wealth and Other Timely Essays*, New

York: The Century Company.

Carnegie, A. (1902) *The Empire of Business*, New York: Doubleday, Page & Company.

Carnegie, A. (1905) *James Watt*, New York: Doubleday, Page & Company.

Carnoy, M. and Shearer, D. (1980) *Economic Democracy. The Challenge of the 1980s*, White Plains, NY: M.E. Sharpe.

Chamberlain, J. (1866) 'Manufacture of iron wood-screws', in Timmins 1866: 604–9.

Chamberlain, J. (1914) *Mr Chamberlain's Speeches*, Volume One, edited by Charles W. Boyd with an introduction by Austen Chamberlain, London: Constable and Company.

Collini, S. (1979) *Liberalism and Sociology. L.T. Hobhouse and Political Argument in England 1880–1914*, Cambridge: Cambridge University Press.

Colls, R. and Dodd, P. (eds) (1986) *Englishness. Politics and Culture 1880–1920*, London: Croom Helm.

Cook, R. (1984) 'Towards an alternative ecological strategy', *New Ground Magazine* 2.

Cooke, A.B. and Vincent, J. (1974) *The Governing Passion. Cabinet Government and Party Politics in Britain 1885–86*, Brighton: Harvester Press.

Corrigan, P. and Sayer, D. (1985) *The Great Arch. English State Formation as Cultural Revolution*, Oxford: Basil Blackwell.

Craver, E. (1986) 'The emigration of the Austrian economists', *History of Political Economy* 18 (1): 1–32.

Creswicke, L. (1904) *The Life of the Right Honourable Joseph Chamberlain*, Volume One, London: Caxton Publishing Company.

Crosland, C.A.R. (1962) *The Conservative Enemy. A Programme of Radical Reform for the 1960s*, London: Jonathan Cape.

Crosland, C.A.R. (1964) *The Future of Socialism*, London: Jonathan Cape (originally published in 1956).

Crosland, C.A.R. (1974) *Socialism Now*, London: Jonathan Cape.

Crosland, S. (1982) *Tony Crosland*, London: Jonathan Cape.

Crozier, M. (1987) *État Modeste. État Moderne. Strategies pour un autre changement*, Paris: Éditions Fayard.

Dahl, R.A. (1985) *A Preface to Economic Democracy*, Cambridge: Polity Press.

Dahrendorf, R. (1982) *On Britain*, London: British Broadcasting Corporation.

Dale, A.W.W. (1898) *The Life of R.W. Dale*, London: Hodder & Stoughton.

Dedmon, E. (1953) *Fabulous Chicago*, New York: Random House.

Dicey, A.V. (1893) 'Alexis de Tocqueville', *The National Review* 21: 771ff.

Diggins, J.P. (1978) *The Bard of Savagery. Thorstein Veblen and Modern Social Theory*, Brighton: Harvester Press.

Dore, R.P. (1987a) *Taking Japan Seriously. A Confucian Perspective on Leading Economic Issues*, London: Athlone Press.

Dore, R.P. (1987b) 'Citizenship and employment in an age of high technology', *British Journal of Industrial Relations* 25 (2): 201–25.

Dorfman, J. (1970) *Thorstein Veblen and His America*, London: Gollancz.

Dos Passos, J. (1933) *The Big Money*, New York: Harcourt, Brace and Company.

Drescher, S. (1964a) 'Tocqueville's Two Democracies', *Journal of the History of Ideas* 25 (2): 201–16.

Drescher, S. (1964b) *Tocqueville and England*, Cambridge, Mass.: Harvard University Press.

Duncan, D. (1911) *Life and Letters of Herbert Spencer*, London: Williams and Norgate.

Dunn, J. (1979) *Western Political Theory in the Face of the Future*, Cambridge: Cambridge University Press.

Durkheim, E. (1957) *Professional Ethics and Civic Morals*, translated by C. Brookfield, London: Routledge & Kegan Paul.

Ellis, A. and Kumar, K. (1983) *Dilemmas of Liberal Democracies. Studies in Fred Hirsch's 'Social Limits to Growth'*, London: Tavistock.

Faher, F. and Heller, A. (1983) 'Class, democracy, modernity', *Theory and Society* 12 (2): 211–44.

Fisher, H.A.L. (1927) *James Bryce*, London: Macmillan.

Foner, E. (1984) 'Why is there no socialism in the United States?' *History Workshop Journal* 17: 57–80.

Forsyth, M. (1988) 'Hayek's bizarre liberalism: a critique', *Political Studies* 36 (2): 235–50.

Foster, H. (ed.) (1984) *Postmodern Culture*, London: Pluto.

Friedman, M. (1962) *Capitalism and Freedom*, Chicago: University of Chicago Press.

Friedman, M. and Friedman R. (1980) *Free To Choose*, Harmondsworth: Penguin.

Furet, F. (1984) 'Naissance d'un paradigm: Tocqueville et le voyage en Amérique (1825–31)', *Annales: Économies, Sociétés, Civilisations* 39 (2): 225–39.

Galbraith, J.K. (1963a) *The Liberal Hour*, Harmondsworth: Penguin (originally published in 1960).

Galbraith, J.K. (1963b) *American Capitalism. The Concept of Countervailing Power*, Harmondsworth: Penguin (originally published in 1952).

Galbraith, J.K. (1974a) *The New Industrial State*, Harmondsworth: Penguin (originally published in 1967).

Galbraith, J.K. (1974b) *Economics and the Public Purpose*, London: André Deutsch (originally published in 1973).

Galbraith, J.K. (1976) *Money: Whence It Came, Where It Went*, Harmondsworth: Penguin (originally published in 1975).

Galbraith, J.K. (1979) *The Affluent Society*, Harmondsworth: Penguin (originally published in 1958).

Galbraith, J.K. (1981) *The Galbraith Reader*, Harmondsworth: Penguin (originally published in 1977).

Garvin, J.L. (1932) *Life of Joseph Chamberlain: I, Chamberlain and Democracy 1836–1885*, London: Macmillan.

Garvin, J.L. (1934) *Life of Joseph Chamberlain: III, Empire and World Policy 1895–1900*, London: Macmillan.

Gershuny, J. (1978) *After Industrial Society. The Emerging Self-Service Economy*, London: Macmillan.

Gladstone, W. (1890) 'Mr Carnegie's "Gospel of Wealth"', *Nineteenth*

Century 28 (165), 677–93.

Goldman, E.F. (1956) *Rendezvous with Destiny. A History of Modern American Reform*, New York: Random House.

Goodell, G. (1985) 'The importance of political participation for sustained capitalist development', *European Journal of Sociology* 26 (1): 93–127.

Gould, K.M (1928) 'Cinepatriotism', *Social Forces* 7 (1): 120–9.

Gray, J. (1986) *Liberalism*, Milton Keynes: Open University Press.

Green, C. (1973) 'Birmingham's politics, 1873–1891: the local basis of change', *Midland History* 2 (2): 84–98.

Green, T.H. (1883) *Prologemena to Ethics*, Oxford: Clarendon Press.

Habermas, J. (1976) *Legitimation Crisis*, London: Heinemann.

Hall, J.A. (1988) *Liberalism, Politics, Ideology and the Market*, London: Paladin.

Halliday, R.J. (1976) *John Stuart Mill*, London: George Allen & Unwin.

Hart, V. (1978) *Distrust and Democracy. Political Distrust in Britain and America*, Cambridge: Cambridge University Press.

Hartz, L. (1955) *The Liberal Tradition in America*, San Diego: Harcourt Brace Jovanovich.

Harvie, C. (1976) *The Lights of Liberalism. University Liberals and the Challenge of Democracy 1860–86*, London: Allen Lane.

Haydl, J. (1985) 'Factory politics in Britain and the United States: engineers and machinists, 1914–1919', *Comparative Studies in Society and History* 27 (1): 57–85.

Hayek, F.A. (ed.) (1935) *Collectivist Economic Planning. Critical Studies on the Possibilities of Socialism*, London: Routledge & Kegan Paul.

Hayek, F.A. (1952) *The Sensory Order*, London: Routledge & Kegan Paul.

Hayek, F.A. (ed.) (1954) *Capitalism and the Historians*, London: Routledge & Kegan Paul.

Hayek, F.A. (1973) *Law, Legislation and Liberty, Vol. 1: Rules and Order*, London: Routledge & Kegan Paul.

Hayek, F.A. (1976a) *The Road to Serfdom*, London: Routledge & Kegan Paul (originally published in 1944).

Hayek, F.A. (1976b) *The Constitution of Liberty*, London: Routledge & Kegan Paul (originally published in 1960).

Hayek, F.A. (1976c) *Law, Legislation and Liberty, Vol. 2: The Mirage of Social Justice*, London: Routledge & Kegan Paul.

Hayek, F.A. (1978) *New Studies in Philosophy, Politics, Economics and the History of Ideas*, London: Routledge & Kegan Paul.

Hayek, F.A. (1979a), *Law, Legislation and Liberty, Vol. 3: The Political Order of a Free People*, London: Routledge & Kegan Paul.

Hayek, F.A. (1979b) *The Counter-Revolution of Science. Studies on the Abuse of Reason*, Indianapolis: Liberty Press (originally published in 1952).

Heertje, A. (ed.) (1981) *Schumpeter's Vision. Capitalism, Socialism and Democracy after 40 Years*, New York: Praeger.

Heilbroner, R.L. (1983) *The Worldly Philosophers. The Lives, Times and Ideas of the Great Economic Thinkers*, Harmondsworth: Penguin.

Heilbroner, R.L. (1985) *The Nature and Logic of Capitalism*, New York: W.W. Norton.

Heilbroner, R.L. (ed.) (1986) *The Essential Adam Smith*, Oxford: Oxford University Press.

Held, D. (1987) *Models of Democracy*, Cambridge: Polity Press.

Hendrick, B.J. (1932) *The Life of Andrew Carnegie*, Volume One, New York: Doubleday, Doran & Company.

Hirsch, F. (1977) *Social Limits to Growth*, London: Routledge & Kegan Paul.

Hirschman, A.O. (1977) *The Passions and the Interests. Political Arguments for Capitalism before Its Triumph*, Princeton: Princeton University Press.

Hirschman, A.O. (1982) *Shifting Involvements. Private Interest and Public Action*, Princeton: Princeton University Press.

Hobsbawm, E. and Ranger, T. (eds) (1983) *The Invention of Tradition*, Cambridge: Cambridge University Press.

Hobson, J.A. (1901) *The Psychology of Jingoism*, London: Grant Richards.

Hobson, J.A. (1914) *Work and Wealth. A Human Valuation*, London: Macmillan.

Hobson, J.A. (1915) *Towards International Government*, London: Macmillan.

Hobson, J.A. (1917) *Democracy After the War*, London: Allen & Unwin.

Hobson, J.A. (1930) *Wealth and Life*, London: Macmillan.

Hobson, J.A. (1936) *Veblen*, London: Chapman and Hall.

Hobson, J.A. (1938a) *Confessions of an Economic Heretic*, London: Allen & Unwin.

Hobson, J.A. (1938b) *Imperialism. A Study*, London: Nisbet (originally published in 1902).

Hoffman, J. (1988) *State, Power and Democracy. Contentious Concepts in Practical Political Theory*, New York: St Martin's Press.

Holyoake, G.J. (1893) *Sixty Years of an Agitator's Life*, London: T. Fisher Unwin.

Holyoake, G.J. (1905) *Bygones Worth Remembering*, Volume One, London: T. Fisher Unwin.

Horn, D. (1986) *The Public Culture. The Triumph of Industrialism*, London: Pluto Press.

Institute of Economic Affairs (1984) *Hayek's 'Serfdom' Revisited*, London: Institute of Economic Affairs.

Ions, E. (1968) *James Bryce and American Democracy 1870-1922*, London: Macmillan.

Jameson, F. (1979) 'Reification and utopia in mass culture', *Social Text* 1: 130–48.

Jameson, F. (1981) *The Political Unconscious*, London: Methuen.

Jameson, F. (1984) 'Postmodernism and consumer society', in Foster (1984).

Jessop, B. (1978) 'Capitalism and democracy: the best possible political shell', in Littlejohn *et al.* (1978).

Jessop, B. (1982) *The Capitalist state. Marxist Theories and Methods*, Oxford: Martin Robertson.

Jouvenel, B. de (1957) *Sovereignty*, Chicago: Chicago University Press

Kammen, M. (1980) *People of Paradox. An Inquiry Concerning the Origins of American Civilization*, New York: Oxford University Press (originally published in 1972).

Karl, B.D. (1974) *Charles E. Merriam and the Study of Politics*, Chicago: University of Chicago Press.

Katznelson, I. (1981) *City Trenches. Urban Politics and the Patterning of Class in the United States*, Chicago: University of Chicago Press.

Katznelson, I. (1986) 'Working-class formation: constructing cases and comparisons', in Katznelson and Zolberg 1987, 3–41.

Katznelson, I. and Zolberg, A.R. (eds) (1986) *Working-Class Formation Nineteenth-Century Patterns in Western Europe and the United States*, Princeton: Princeton University Press.

Keane, J. (1984) *Public Life and Late Capitalism*, Cambridge: Cambridge University Press.

Keating, P. (ed.) (1981) *The Victorian Prophets. A Reader from Carlyle to Wells*, London: Fontana.

Kennedy, P. (1987) *The Rise and Fall of the Great Powers*, London: Allen & Unwin.

Keynes, J.M. (1973) *The Collected Writings of John Maynard Keynes Vol. VII The General Theory of Employment, Interest and Money*, London: Macmillan.

Kidd, B. (1984) *Social Evolution*, London: Macmillan.

Kitamura, H. *et al.* (1985) *Between Friends: Japanese Diplomats Look At Japan–US Relations*, translated by D.R. Zoll, Tokyo: Weatherhill.

Klass, G.M. (1985) 'Explaining America and the welfare state: an alternative theory', *British Journal of Political Science* 15 (4): 427–50.

Koerner, K.F. (1985) *Liberalism and Its Critics*, London: Croom Helm.

Kumar, K. (1978) *Prophecy and Progress. The Sociology of Industrial and Post-Industrial Society*, Harmondsworth: Penguin.

Lasch, C. (1980) *The Culture of Narcissism*, London: Sphere.

Lash, S. and Urry, J. (1987) *The End of Organized Capitalism*, Cambridge: Polity Press.

Laski, H.J. (1930) *Liberty in the Modern State*, London: Faber & Faber.

Laski, H.J. (1932) *The Crisis and the Constitution: 1931 and After*, London: Fabian Society.

Laski, H.J. (1933) *Democracy in Crisis*, London: Allen & Unwin.

Laski, H.J. (1935) *The State in Theory and Practice*, London: Allen & Unwin.

Laski, H.J. (1936) *The Rise of European Liberalism*, London: Allen & Unwin.

Laski, H.J. (1943) *Reflections on the Revolutions of Our Time*, London: Allen & Unwin.

Laski, H.J. (1948) *The American Democracy*, New York: The Viking Press.

Laski, H.J. (1952) *The Dilemma of Our Times. An Historical Essay*, London: Allen & Unwin.

Laski, H.J. (1980) *The Grammar of Politics*, London: Allen & Unwin (originally published in 1925).

Lasswell, H.D. (1948) *Power and Personality*, New York: W.W. Norton & Co.

Lasswell, H.D. (1949a) 'The language of power', in H.D. Lasswell, N. Leites *et al.* (1949): 3–19.

Lasswell, H.D. (1949b) 'Style in the language of politics', in H.D.

Lasswell, N. Leites *et al.* (1949): 20–39.

Lasswell, H.D. (1951a) *Psychopathology and Politics* in Lasswell 1951d (originally published in 1930).

Lasswell, H.D. (1951b) *Politics: Who Gets What, When and How?* in Lasswell 1951d (originally published in 1936).

Lasswell, H.D. (1951c) 'Democratic character' in Lasswell 1951d: 465–525.

Lasswell, H.D. (1951d) *The Political Writings of Harold D. Lasswell*, Glencoe, Illinois: Free Press.

Lasswell, H.D. (1958) 'Postscript', in *Politics: Who Gets What, When and How?*, New York: World Publishing Co.

Lasswell, H.D. (1963) *The Future of Political Science*, London: Prentice-Hall.

Lasswell, H.D. (1965) *World Politics and Personal Insecurity*, New York: Free Press (originally published in 1935).

Lasswell, H.D. (1971) *Propaganda Technique in World War I*, Cambridge, Mass.: The MIT Press (originally published in 1927).

Lasswell, H.D. and Kaplan, A. (1950) *Power and Society. A Framework for Political Inquiry*, New Haven: Yale University Press.

Lasswell, H.D., Leites, N. *et al.* (1949) *Language of Politics. Studies in Quantitative Semantics*, Cambridge, Mass.: The MIT Press.

Lehmann, J.-P. (1982) *The Roots of Modern Japan*, London: Macmillan.

Lenin, V.I. (1964a) *Imperialism. The Highest Stage of Capitalism*, in Lenin 1964b: 185–304 (originally published in 1917).

Lenin, V.I. (1964b) *Collected Works, Vol. 22*, London: Lawrence & Wishart.

Lerner, M. (1968) 'Introduction' in Tocqueville 1968: *xxxvii–cxvii.*

Lindert, P.H. and Williamson, J.G. (1985) 'Growth, equality and history', *Explorations in Economic History*, 22 (4): 341–77.

Lippman, W. (1965) *Public Opinion*, New York: Free Press (originally published in 1922).

Lipset, S.M. (1964) *The First New Nation. The United States in Historical and Comparative Perspective*, London: Heinemann.

Lipset, S.M. (1981) *Political Man. The Social Bases of Politics*, Expanded Edition, Baltimore: Johns Hopkins University Press.

Littlejohn, G., Smart, B., Wakeford, J., and Yuval-Davis, N. (1978) *Power and the State*, London: Croom Helm.

Lustig, R.J. (1982) *Corporate Liberalism: The Origins of American Political Theory*, Berkeley: University of California Press.

McCarthy, J. (1904) *British Political Leaders*, London: Fisher Unwin.

McCloskey, H.J. (1971) *John Stuart Mill: A Critical Study*, London: Macmillan.

McCloskey, R.G. (1951) *American Conservatism in the Age of Enterprise 1865–1910. A Study of William Graham Sumner, Stephen J. Field and Andrew Carnegie*, Cambridge, Mass.: Harvard University Press.

Machlup, F. (ed.) (1977) *Essays on Hayek*, London: Routledge & Kegan Paul.

MacIntyre, A. (1982) *After Virtue. A Study in Moral Theory*, London: Duckworth.

Macpherson, C.B. (1972) *The Real World of Democracy*, Oxford: Oxford University Press.

Macpherson, C.B. (1980) *The Life and Times of Liberal Democracy*, Oxford: Oxford University Press.

Mann, M. (1987) 'Ruling class strategies and citizenship', *Sociology* 21

(3): 339–54.

Marshall, G., Rose, D.Vogler, C., and Newby, H. (1985) 'Class, citizenship, and distributional conflict in modern Britain', *British Journal of Sociology* 36 (2): 259–84.

Marshall, G., Vogler, C., and Newby, H. (1987) 'Distributional struggle and moral order in a market society', *Sociology* 21 (1): 55–73.

Martin, K. (1953) *Harold Laski, 1893–1950. A Biographical Memoir*, New York: Viking.

Massey, D.S. (1985) 'Ethnic residential segregation: a theoretical synthesis and empirical review', *Sociology and Social Research* 69 (3): 315–50.

Matthew, H.G.C., McKibbin, R.T., and Kay, J.A. (1976) 'The franchise factor in the rise of the Labour Party', *English Historical Review* 91.

Mayer, J.P. (1954) *Alexis de Tocqueville. Oeuvres Complètes. Tome VI. Correspondance Anglaise*, Paris: Gallimard.

Mayer, J.P. (1968) 'Introduction' in Tocqueville 1968: *xi–xxi*.

Merriam, C.E. (1925) *New Aspects of Politics*, Chicago: Chicago University Press.

Merriam, C.E. (1944) 'Review of Hayek's *Road to Serfdom*', *American Journal of Sociology* 50 (3): 234–5.

Merriam, C.E. (1945) *Systematic Politics*, Chicago: University of Chicago Press.

Miliband, R. (1972) *Parliamentary Socialism. A Study in the Politics of Labour*, second edition, London: Merlin Press (first edition published in 1961).

Miliband, R. (1973) *The State in Capitalist Society*, London: Quartet Books (originally published in 1969).

Miliband, R. (1977) *Marxism and Politics*, Oxford: Oxford University Press.

Miliband, R. (1982) *Capitalist Democracy in Britain*, Oxford: Oxford University Press.

Miliband, R. and Saville, J. (eds) (1965) *The Socialist Register*, London: Merlin Press.

Mill, J.S. (1833) 'Municipal institutions', *The Examiner*, 11 August: 496–7.

Mill, J.S. (1835) 'De Tocqueville on America', *London Review* 2 (3): 85–129.

Mill, J.S. (1871) *The Principles of Political Economy with Some of Their Applications to Social Philosophy*, 7th edn, London: Longman & Co. (originally published in 1848).

Mill, J.S. (1873) *Autobiography*, London: Longmans, Green, Reader and Dyer.

Mill, J.S. (1844) *A System of Logic. Ratiocinative and Inductive'*, London: Longman & Co.

Mill, J.S. (1964a) 'On liberty', in Mill 1964d: 65–170 (originally published in 1859).

Mill, J.S. (1964b) 'Considerations on representative government', in Mill 1964d: 175–393 (originally published in 1861).

Mill, J.S. (1964c) 'Utilitarianism', in Mill 1964d: 1–60 (originally published in 1861).

Mill, J.S. (1964d) *Utilitarianism, Liberty, Representative Government*, with an introduction by A.D. Lindsay, London: Dent.

Mill, J.S. (1976a) 'M. de Tocqueville on Democracy in America', in Mill 1976b: 186–247 (originally published in 1840).

Mill, J.S. (1976b) *John Stuart Mill on Politics and Society*, selected and edited by Geraint L. Williams, London: Fontana/Collins.

Mill, J.S. (1981) 'Civilization', in Keating 1981: 70–103 (originally published in 1836).

Miller, J.M. (1984) 'Ronald Reagan and the techniques of deception', *Atlantic Monthly* 253 (2): 62–8.

Molotch, H. (1976) 'The city as a growth machine', *American Journal of Sociology* 82: 309–32.

Moore, B. (1969) *Social Origins of Dictatorship and Democracy*, Harmondsworth: Penguin.

Moore, G.E. (1962) *Principia Ethica*, Cambridge: Cambridge University Press.

Moorhouse, H.F. (1973) 'The political incorporation of the British working class: an interpretation', *Sociology* 7 (3): 341–59.

Mulhall, S. (1987) 'The theoretical foundations of liberalism', *European Journal of Sociology* 28 (2): 269–95.

Mummery, A.F. and Hobson, J.A. (1889) *The Physiology of Industry*, London: Murray.

Munslow, A. (1988) 'Andrew Carnegie and the discourse of cultural hegemony', *Journal of American Studies* 21 (2): 213–24.

Nairn, T. (1981) *The Break-Up of Britain*, second expanded edition, London: Verso (originally published in 1977).

Nozick, R. (1974) *Anarchy, State and Utopia*, Oxford: Blackwell.

O'Connor, J. (1973) *The Fiscal Crisis of the State*, New York: St Martin's Press.

Oestreicher, R. (1988) 'Urban working-class political behavior and theories of American electoral politics, 1870–1940', *Journal of American History* 74 (4): 1257–86.

Offe, C. (1984) *Contradictions of the Welfare State*, London: Hutchinson.

Offe, C. (1985) *Disorganized Capitalism*, Cambridge: Polity Press.

Olsen, E.A. (1985) *US-Japan Strategic Reciprocity: A Neo-Institutionalist View*, Stanford, Cal.: Hoover Institution Press.

Olson, M. (1982) *The Rise and Decline of Nations, Economic Growth, Stagflation, and Social Rigidities*, New Haven: Yale University Press.

Orloff, A.S. and Skocpol, T. (1984) 'Why not equal protection? Explaining the politics of public social spending in Britain, 1900–1911, and the United States, 1880s–1920', *American Sociological Review* 49 (6): 726–50.

Ostrogorski, M. (1902a) *Democracy and the Organization of Political Parties Vol. I*, translated by Frederick Clarke with an introduction by James Bryce, London: Macmillan.

Ostrogorski, M. (1902b) *Democracy and the Organization of Political Parties Vol. II*, translated by Frederick Clarke with an introduction by James Bryce, London: Macmillan.

Ouchi, W. (1981) *Theory Z: How American Business Can Meet the Japanese Challenge*, Wokingham: Addison Wesley.

Packe, M. St J. (1954) *The Life of John Stuart Mill*, London: Secker & Warburg.

Paine, T. (1969) *Rights of Man*, Harmondsworth: Penguin.

Paine, T. (1976) *Common Sense*, edited with an Introduction by I.
    Kramnick, Harmondsworth: Penguin (originally published 1776).
Pappe, H.O. (1964) 'Mill and Tocqueville', *Journal of the History of Ideas*
    25 (2): 217–34.
Pascale, R.T. and Athos, A.G. (1982) *The Art of Japanese Management*,
    Harmondsworth: Penguin.
Paul, E.F., Miller, F.D., Paul, J., and Ahrens, J. (eds) (1986) *Marxism
    and Liberalism*, Oxford: Basil Blackwell.
Pearson, C.H. (1893) *National Life and Character: A Forecast*, London:
    Macmillan.
Peel, J.D.Y. (1971) *Herbert Spencer. The Evolution of a Sociologist*,
    London: Heinemann.
Perman, D. (1985) 'Schumpeter's sociology of economics: the role of the
    "competent economist" ', *Economy and Society* 14 (4): 429–49.
Peterson, M.D. (ed.) (1977) *The Portable Thomas Jefferson*,
    Harmondsworth: Penguin.
Piven, F.F. and Cloward, R.A. (1971) *Regulating the Poor*, New York:
    Pantheon Books.
Piven, F.F. and Cloward, R.A. (1977) *Poor People's Movements*, New
    York: Pantheon Books.
Piven, F.F. and Cloward, R.A. (1982) *The New Class War. Reagan's Attack
    on the Welfare State and its Consequences*, New York: Pantheon Books.
Pocock, J.G.A. (1975) *The Machiavellian Moment*, Princeton: Princeton
    University Press.
Pope, W. (1986) *Alexis de Tocqueville. His Social and Political Theory* (in
    collaboration with Lucetta Pope), Beverley Hills: Sage.
Poster, M. (ed.) (1988) *Jean Baudrillard. Selected Writings*, Cambridge:
    Polity Press.
Przeworski, A. (1986) *Capitalism and Social Democracy*, Cambridge:
    Cambridge University Press.
Ralph, J. (1890) 'The best governed city in the world', *Harper's Monthly
    Magazine* 81: 99–110.
Raphael, R.R. (1985) *Adam Smith*, Oxford: Oxford University Press.
Rawls, J. (1973) *A Theory of Justice*, Oxford: Oxford University Press.
Reddy, W.M. (1987) *Money and Liberty in Modern Europe. A Critique of
    Historical Understanding*, Cambridge: Cambridge University Press.
Riesman, D., Denney, R., and Glazer, N. (1950) *The Lonely Crowd. A
    Study of the Changing American Character*, New York: Doubleday.
Riley, J. (1985) 'On the possibility of liberal democracy', *American
    Political Science Review* 79 (4): 1135–51.
Rogers, J.G. (1903) *An Autobiography*, London: James Clarke.
Roper, J. (1989) *Democracy and its Critics. Anglo-American Democratic
    Thought in the Nineteenth Century*, London: Unwin Hyman.
Rosenberg, B. (ed.) (1963) *Thorstein Veblen*, New York: Thomas Y.
    Cromwell.
Roszak, T. (1979) *Person/Planet: The Creative Disintegration of Industrial
    Society*, New York: Anchor Books.
Ryan, A. (1984) *Property and Political Theory*, Oxford: Basil Blackwell.

Samuelson, P. (1981) 'Schumpeter's *Capitalism, Socialism and Democracy*', in A. Heertje (ed.) *Schumpeter's Vision*. Capitalism, Socialism and Democracy *after 40 Years*, New York: Praeger.

Sandel, M. (1982) *Liberalism and the Limits of Justice*, Cambridge: Cambridge University Press.

Schumacher, E.F. (1974) *Small is Beautiful*, London: Abacus.

Schumpeter, J.A. (1934) *Theory of Economic Development*, Cambridge, Mass.: Harvard University Press

Schumpeter, J.A. (1939) *Business Cycles. A Theoretical, Historical, and Statistical Analysis of the Capitalist Process*, two volumes, New York: McGraw-Hill.

Schumpeter, J.A. (1951) *Imperialism and Social Classes*, Oxford: Oxford University Press.

Schumpeter, J.A. (1963) *History of Economic Analysis*, edited from manuscript by E.B. Schumpeter, London: Allen & Unwin.

Schumpeter, J.A. (1981) *Capitalism, Socialism and Democracy* with an introduction by Tom Bottomore, London: Allen & Unwin (originally published in 1942).

Schwartz, P. (1968) *The New Political Economy of John Stuart Mill*, London: Weidenfeld & Nicolson.

Seidl, C. (ed.) (1984) *Lectures on Schumpeterian Economics*, New York: Springer Verlag.

Seidman, S. (1983) *Liberalism and the Origins of European Social Theory'*, Berkeley: University of California Press.

Sennett, R. (1986) *The Fall of Public Man*, London: Faber & Faber (originally published in 1977).

Skidelsky, R. (1983) *John Maynard Keynes Vol I: Hopes Betrayed 1883–1920*, London: Macmillan.

Skidelsky, R. (ed.) (1988) *Thatcherism*, London: Chatto.

Skocpol, T. and Finegold, K. (1982) 'State capacity and economic intervention in the early New Deal', *Political Science Quarterly* 97 (2): 255–78.

Skocpol, T. and Ikeberry, J. (1983) 'The political formation of the American welfare state in historical and comparative perspective', *Comparative Social Research* 6: 87–148.

Smith, A. (1979) *The Wealth of Nations Books I–III*, with an Introduction by Andrew Skinner, Harmondsworth: Penguin (originally published 1776).

Smith, D. (1977) 'Social development, the state and education: a structural analysis of Francis Adams's *History of the Elementary School Contest in England'*, *Prose Studies* 1 (1): 19–36.

Smith, D. (1982) *Conflict and Compromise: Class Formation in English Society 1830–1914. A Comparative Study of Birmingham and Sheffield*, London: Routledge & Kegan Paul.

Smith, D. (1983) *Barrington Moore Jr: A Critical Appraisal*, London: M.E. Sharpe.

Smith, D. (1986) 'Englishness and the Liberal inheritance after 1886', in Colls and Dodd 1986: 254–82.

Smith, D. (1987) 'Knowing your place: class, politics and ethnicity in

Chicago and Birmingham, 1890–1983', in Thrift and Williams 1987: 276–305.

Smith, D. (1988) *The Chicago School. A Liberal Critique of Capitalism*, New York: St Martin's Press.

Smith, E.B. (1896) *The Municipal Outlook*, Chicago: Chicago Municipal Voters' League.

Smith, P. (1986) 'Anglo-American religion and hegemonic change in the world system, *c.* 1870–1980', *British Journal of Sociology* 37 (1): 88–105.

Spencer, H. (1850) *Social Statics*, London: Williams & Norgate.

Spender, J.A. (1925) *The Public Life*, London: Cassell.

Stead, W.H. (1894) *If Christ Came to Chicago! A Plea for the Union of All Who Love in the Name of All Who Suffer*, London: Review of Reviews.

Talmon, J.L. (1970) *The Origins of Totalitarian Democracy*, London: Sphere (originally published in 1952).

Thomas, W. (1985) *Mill*, Oxford: Oxford University Press.

Thompson, E.P. (1965) 'The peculiarities of the English', in Miliband and Saville 1965: 311–62.

Thorne, C. (1978) *Allies of a Kind: The United States, Britain and the War Against Japan 1941–45*, New York: Oxford University Press.

Thorne, C. (1986) *The Far Eastern War. States and Societies 1941–45*, London: Unwin.

Thrift, N. and Williams, P. (eds) (1987) *Class and Space. The Making of Urban Society*, London: Routledge.

Timmins, S. (ed.) (1866) *Birmingham and the Midland Hardware District* London: Robert Hardwicke.

Tocqueville, A. de (1954) *Oeuvres Complètes, 6: Correspondance Anglaise. Correspondance d'Alexis de Tocqueville avec Henry Reeve et John Stuart Mill*, with an introduction by J.-P. Mayer, Paris: Gallimard.

Tocqueville, A. de (1955) *The Old Regime and the Revolution*, translated by S. Gilbert, Garden City, NY: Doubleday (originally published in 1856).

Tocqueville, A. de (1958) *Journeys to England and Ireland*, translated by George Lawrence and K.P. Mayer, edited by J.-P. Mayer, New Haven: Yale University Press.

Tocqueville, A. de (1959) *Journey to America*, translated by George Lawrence, edited by J.-P. Mayer, London: Faber & Faber.

Tocqueville, A. de (1968) *Democracy in America*, two volumes, translated by George Lawrence, edited by J.-P. Mayer and Max Lerner, New York: Collins.

Tocqueville, A. de (1970) *Recollections*, translated by George Lawrence and edited by J.-P. Mayer and A.P. Kerr with an introduction by J.-P. Mayer, London: Macdonald (originally published in 1893).

Tocqueville, A. de (1985) *Alexis de Tocqueville. Selected Letters on Politics and Society*, translated by James Toupin and Roger Boesche, edited by Roger Boesche, Berkeley: University of California Press.

Turner, B.S. (1986) *Citizenship and Capitalism: The Debate over Reformism* London: Allen & Unwin.

Veblen, F. (1931) 'Thorstein Veblen: Reminiscences of his brother Orson' *Social Forces* 10 (2): 187–95.

Veblen, T. (1919) *On the Nature and Uses of Sabotage*, New York: Dial Publishing Co.

Veblen, T. (1923) *Absentee Ownership and Business Enterprise in Recent Times. The Case of America*, London: George Allen & Unwin.

Veblen, T. (1963) 'Why is economics not an evolutionary science?', in Rosenberg 1963: 39–57 (originally published in 1898).

Veblen, T. (1964) *Imperial Germany and the Industrial Revolution*, New York: Augustus M. Kelley (originally published in 1915).

Veblen, T. (1965) *The Theory of Business Enterprise*, New York: Augustus M. Kelley (originally published in 1904).

Veblen, T. (1969) *The Vested Interests and the Common Man*, New York: Capricorn Books (originally published in 1919).

Veblen, T. (1970) *The Theory of the Leisure Class*, London: Allen & Unwin (originally published in 1899).

Vincent, J. (1972) *The Formation of the British Liberal Party 1857–1868*, Harmondsworth: Penguin.

Vogel, E. (1979) *Japan as Number One: Lessons for America*, Cambridge: Harvard University Press.

Wallas, G. (1914) *The Great Society. A Psychological Analysis*, London: Macmillan.

Wallas, G. (1948) *Human Nature in Politics* with a foreword by A.L. Rowse, London: Constable (originally published in 1908).

Walzer, M. (1983) *Spheres of Justice. A Defense of Pluralism and Equality*, Oxford: Martin Robertson.

Walzer, M. (1984) 'Liberalism and the art of separation', *Political Theory* 12 (3): 315–30.

Webb, B. (1971) *My Apprenticeship. Volume One*, Harmondsworth: Penguin.

Wells, H.G. (1987) *The Future in America. A Search After Realities* London: Granville Publishing (originally published in 1906).

Wilde, O. (1899) *The Importance of Being Earnest: A Trivial Comedy for Serious People*, London: Methuen.

Williams, R. (1963) *Culture and Society 1780–1950*, Harmondsworth: Penguin in association with Chatto & Windus (originally published in 1958).

Williamson, C. (1960) *American Suffrage from Property to Democracy 1760–1860*, Princeton: Princeton University Press.

Wills, G. (1979) *Inventing America. Jefferson's Declaration of Independence*, New York: Vintage Books.

Wright, P. (1985) *On Living in an Old Country. The National Past in Contemporary Britain*, London: Verso.

Yankelovich, D. (1982) 'Reagan and the national psyche', *Psychology Today* 16 (1) 5–8.

Zylstra, B. (1968) *From Pluralism to Collectivism. The Development of Harold Laski's Political Thought*, Assen, Netherlands: Van Gorcum.

Name index

Addams, J. 83
Alford, R.R. 8
Amis, M. 3
Andrain, C.F. 8
Arblaster, A. 1, 5
Arnold, M. 45, 60, 116
Athos, A.G. 7

Beaumont, G. de 19, 23
Bell, D. 7, 9, 199
Bellah, R. 10, 197
Bentham, J. 19, 30, 33, 60, 62–3, 81, 96, 111, 153
Berger, P.L. 8
Bernstein, E. 164
Blackbourn, D. 6
Bloom, A. 1, 197
Bobbio, N. 8
Bosanquet, B. 111–12
Boutmy, E. 60
Bowles, H. 8
Bracknell, Lady 38
Brailsford, H.N. 80
Braudillard, J. 199
Bright, J. 44
Brittan, S. 11–12, 167, 169, 173–7
Brown, L. 7
Bryce, J. 11–12, 58–60, 67–76, 87, 92, 95, 99–101, 107–9, 114, 189–90, 193, 198; 'Preface' to Ostrogorski 68–9
Buddha 4
Bulmer, M. 121
Burawoy, M. 9
Burr, President A. 65

Burritt, E. 40
Bush, President G. 172

Cadbury, G. 193
Cade, J. 56
Caird, E. 60
Cannadine, D. 9
Carlyle, T. 30, 60, 62
Carnegie, A. 6, 11–13, 37–9, 41–8, 56, 64, 72, 75, 82–3, 87, 98–100, 102–3, 107, 157, 190, 193
Carnoy, M. 8
Chamberlain, J. 11, 13, 37–41, 48–57, 64, 90, 98–101, 103, 110, 117, 122, 136, 148, 152, 186, 190, 193, 199
Chamberlain, N. 56
Channing, W.E. 39
Châteaubriand 19
Clausewitz, C. von 121
Cleese, J. 3
Cleveland, President G. 65
Cloward, R.A. 11, 169, 172, 183, 190
Cobden, R. 95
Coleridge, S.T. 30, 60
Colls, R. 198
Comte, A. 30
Confucius 4
Cook, R. 202
Cooke, A.B. 49
Cooper, J.F. 19
Corrigan, P. 198
Craver, E. 133

218

Creswicke, L. 54
Crosland, C.A.R. 11–12, 151–2,
    162–9, 182, 186, 196, 202
Crosland, S. 164
Crozier, M. 8
Curry, E. 201
Curtis, J.L. 3

Dahl, R.A. 8
Dahrendorf, R. 10
Dawson, G. 52
Dedmon, E. 83
Dewey, J. 175
Dicey, A.V. 59–60, 108
Dickens, C. 62
Disraeli, B. 62
Dodd, P. 198
Dore, R.P. 8–9
Dorfman, J. 84
Dos Passos, J. 77–9
Dunn, J. 8

Durkheim, E. 115
Eley, G. 6
Ellis, A. 8
Engels, F. 125

Faher, F. 8
Finegold, K. 9
Fisher, H.A.L. 108
Foner, E. 9
Forsyth, M. 143
Freeman, E.A. 60
Freud, S. 13, 107, 110, 121, 131,
    133, 163, 165
Friedland, R. 8
Friedman, M. 1–3, 11, 169–73,
    187, 189
Friedman, R. 1, 169–73

Galbraith, J.K. 11–12, 151–61,
    162–3, 168–9, 182, 186, 189,
    196
Gershuny, J. 7
Gintis, H. 8
Gladstone, W.E.G. 12, 39, 49, 59,
    69
Goodell, G. 8
Gosnell, H. 121

Gould, K.M. 4
Grant, President U.S. 65
Green, J.R. 60
Green, T.H. 60, 111–12, 116

Habermas, J. 8
Hall, J.A. 8
Hart, V. 54
Hartz, L. 5, 198
Harvie, C. 60, 73
Haydl, J. 9
Hayek, F.A. 3, 11, 131–4, 144–50,
    165–7, 170, 173, 175, 186–9
Hegel, G.W.F. 111
Held, D. 8
Heller, A. 8
Hirsch, F. 7
Hirschman, A. 5
Hitler, A. 7, 118, 147
Hobbes, T. 174, 184
Hobhouse, L.T. 80, 93
Hobsbawm, E. 198
Hobson, J.A. 12, 77, 79–80,
    89–97, 9, 102, 108, 114, 117,
    188, 190, 195
Hoffman, J. 8
Holmes, O.W. 108
Holyoake, G. 53

Ikenberry, J. 9

Jackson, A. 20, 42, 65, 101, 187
Jackson, G. 3
James, W. 110
Jameson, F. 199
Jefferson, T. 5–6, 170
Jessop, B. 8
Jouvenel, B. de 175

Kant, I. 111
Kaplan, A. 121
Karl, B.D. 110
Katznelson, I. 9
Keane, J. 8
Kennedy, President J.F. 152
Kennedy, P. 1
Kergorlay, L. de 19
Keynes, J.M. 12, 80, 91, 111, 117,
    154, 159–60, 163, 166, 169,

176-7, 185, 188, 195
Kidd, B. 91
Klass, G.M. 9
Kumar, K. 7-8

Lasch, C. 199
Lash, S. 1, 199
Laski, H.J. 11-12, 108-22, 124,
  128-30, 144, 149, 162-3, 171,
  181, 185-7
Lasswell, H.D. 11, 13, 108-10,
  120-31, 185, 188, 195
Lenin, V.I. 12, 91
Lerner, M. 20
Lincoln, President A. 43, 65
Lindert, P.H. 9
Lippman, W. 78, 108
Lipset, S.M. 9
Louis XIV 136
Louis-Philippe 18
Lustig, R. 8

McCarthy, J. 58
McCloskey, R.G. 48
MacCormick, Mrs H. 83
MacDonald, R. 80, 116
Machiavelli 121
MacIntyre, A. 10
Macpherson, C.B. 8
Mahler, G. 133
Malthus, T. 30-1
Mann, M. 90
Marshall, A. 154
Marshall, G. 9
Marshall, T.H. 9
Marx, G. 78
Marx, K. 8, 13, 78, 107, 110, 121,
  125, 131, 134-5, 138, 157, 163,
  185
Massey, D.S. 9
Matthew, H.G.C. 6
Mayer, J.-P. 60
Merriam, C.E. 108-10, 128, 144,
  152; review of Hayek 131-2
Miliband, R. 2, 8, 11, 169, 180-5,
  190
Mill, J. 18-19, 55
Mill, J.S. 2, 11-12, 17-19, 21,
  27-38, 40, 42, 45, 47, 55-7,

60, 62-4, 68,76, 87, 94-6,
  98-9, 101-2, 111, 113-16, 122,
  158, 170, 176, 182, 189-90,
  193, 199; review of Tocqueville
  27-8
Miller, J.M. 4
Molotch, H. 201
Montesquieu, C. de 20
Moore, B. 9
Moore, G.E. 111
Moorhouse, H.F. 6
Morley, J. 60
Mulhall, S. 10
Mummery, A.F. 79

Nairn, T. 198
Nozick, R. 10, 175

O'Connor, J. 8
Oestricher, R. 9
Offe, C. 8
Olson, M. 1
Orloff, A.S. 9
Ostrogorski, M. 11-13, 58-69,
  75-6, 87, 89, 98-9, 102, 109,
  114, 143, 190, 193
Ouchi, W. 7
Owen, R. 31

Paine, T. 62, 107
Palmer, Mrs P. 83
Park, R.E. 108
Pascale, R.T. 7
Paul, E.F. 8
Pearson, C. 72-3
Peirce, C.S. 110
Piven, F.F. 169, 172, 176, 183,
  190
Plato 197
Pocock, J.G.A. 5
Przeworski, A. 8
Pullman, G. 87-8

Ralph, J. 56
Ranger, T. 198
Rawls, J. 10, 175
Reagan, President R. 1, 3, 153,
  172, 177, 179-80, 196-7
Reddy, W. 8

Rhodes, C. 91
Ricardo, D. 19, 30–1, 111
Riesman, D. 163, 185
Riley, J. 10
Robbins, L. 133
Rockefeller, E. 83
Roosevelt, President F.D. 117
Roper, J. 8–9
Roszak, T. 7
Rousseau, J.J. 107
Ruskin, J. 93

Sainte-Beuve 20
Samuel, H. 80
Samuelson, P.A. 133
Sandel, M. 10
Sayer, D. 198
Schumpeter, J.A. 11, 131–43, 144–5, 150, 163, 165, 170, 173–4, 188, 195, 200
Segal, G. 3
Seidman, S. 8
Shearer, D. 8
Skidelsky, R. 4, 111
Skocpol, T. 9
Smith, A. 1, 62, 81, 87, 93, 154, 167, 170
Smith, D. 8–9, 41, 56, 81
Smith, E.B. 65
Smith, P. 9
Spencer, H. 39–43, 46, 62, 77, 79, 81
Stalin, J. 7
Stead, W.T. 82
Strachey, J. 162
Sturge, J. 40

Taine, H. 60
Taylor, H. 17–18, 30

Thatcher, M. 1–2, 153, 167, 176, 184
Thompson, E.P. 9
Thorne, C. 1
Thrift, N. 198
Tocqueville, A. de 2, 5, 10–13, 17–30, 34–40, 42–3, 45, 60, 64–5, 67–8, 70, 72, 75, 87,95, 98, 100–1, 114, 116, 119, 122, 130, 165, 176, 187, 190, 193, 197, 199
Trevelyan, G.O. 60
Turner, B.S. 60

Urry, J. 199

Van Buren, President M. 65
Veblen, T. 5, 12, 177–89, 92–3, 96–9, 101–2, 108, 114, 117–19, 136, 158, 164, 188, 190, 195, 200–1
Vincent, J. 49
Vogel, E.F. 7

Wallas, G. 80, 108–9
Walzer, M. 10
Watt, J. 41
Webb, B. 41
Wellington, Duke of 21
Wesley, J. 46
Wilde, O. 38
William the Conqueror 21
Williams, P. 198
Williams, R. 198
Williamson, J.G. 9
Wilson, W. 78
Wordsworth, W. 19, 30–1, 60
Wright, P. 198

Yankelovich, D. 4

Subject index

absolutism 5, 20, 200
academics 79, 84, 110, 122, 173
advertising 3, 86–7, 93, 133, 154,
    160, 168, 173, 195; see also
    propaganda
aesthetics 81, 84, 111, 153, 200
AFDC see Aid to Families with
    Dependent Children
affluence, affluent society 12, 103,
    156, 165–6, 168, 182, 185, 189
Affluent Society, The 152–5; see
    also Galbraith, J.K.
Africa 91; see also North Africa;
    South Africa
agenda-setting 182
agitators 123
agriculture 29, 35, 42, 55, 142,
    154, 157; see also freeholders
Aid to Families with Dependent
    Children 179
Amalgamated Association of Iron
    and Steel Workers (USA) 48
American Civil War 6, 10, 44, 65,
    71, 107
American Commonwealth, The 58,
    70–2, 88; see also Bryce, J.
American Constitution 178
American Declaration of
    Independence 42, 170
American Democracy, The 119–20;
    see also Laski, H.
American Journal of Sociology 131
Americanisation 3, 198–9
anarchy, anarchism 24, 47, 175
Ancien Régime and Revolution, The

26; see also Tocqueville, A. de
architecture 200
aristocracy 21–2, 24, 26, 135–7,
    140, 199–200; English 5, 20–1,
    29, 33–5, 40, 42, 61–2, 95,
    107–8; French 17–18, 21
art 22, 56, 91, 199
Asia 91; see also South-East Asia
associations 24, 31, 67, 95, 115,
    197
atavism 199; see also emotion
Athens 200
Australia 11, 73, 91
Austria 133, 152; see also Austro-
    Hungarian Empire
Austro-Hungarian Empire 107, 132;
    see also Austria
authoritarianism 118, 142 175,
    183–4, 190, 201–2; see also
    hegemony; power
Autobiography 30; see also Mill,
    J.S.

balance of payments 167
Baltimore 20
banks, banking 4, 20, 79, 133–4,
    136; see also finance capital
Baptists 38
barbarian epoch, barbarian culture
    83–4
BBC see British Broadcasting
    Corporation
Belfast 58
Berkeley (California) 152
Bible 25

big business *see* corporations
Big Money, The 77-9; *see also* Dos Passos, J.
Bill of Rights 172
biology 41, 62
Birmingham 13, 21, 23, 38, 40, 44, 48-54, 56-7, 64-5, 90, 110, 193
Birmingham Liberal Association 49, 64, 103
Birmingham Political Union 40, 53, 62
Birmingham School Board 49-50
Birmingham University 56-7
Black Americans 39, 71, 178-80
Bloomsbury 111
Boers 90-1; *see also* South Africa
Bonn, University of 133
Boston 20, 108
Boston University 176
botany 51
Bourbon dynasty 18
bourgeoisie, bourgeois society 100, 136-8, 140, 142-3, 178, 200
Bournville (Birmingham) 193
Brandeis University 176
Break-Up of Britain, The 198; *see also* Nairn, T.
British Broadcasting Corporation 199
Bryce Committee 92
budget deficits 4, 173
bureaucracy, bureaucrats 5-7, 19, 34, 64, 68, 73-5, 77, 79, 98-101, 107, 114, 122-6, 132, 137, 139-41, 143, 146, 149, 152, 154-5, 160, 170, 172, 174, 179-80, 182, 189, 193, 195
bureaucratic symbiosis 160
business cycles 134, 138, 144, 156
Business Cycles 134-5; *see also* Schumpeter, J.A.
business enterprise 85-9, 119, 136-7, 187, 196; *see also* corporations; entrepreneurs
business people 52, 77, 81, 84, 87, 100, 119, 140, 155, 158-9, 163, 178, 185, 194, 195
business schools 158

Caesarism 114
California 4
California, University of 152
Calvinism 38-9, 152
Cambridge University 34, 111
Camden Town 92
Canada 4, 11, 20, 28, 73
capital 79, 82, 87, 92, 100, 117, 156-8, 161, 165, 177-8, 180, 185-6, 191, 195
Capitalism and Freedom 170; *see also* Friedman, M.
Capitalism, Socialism, Democracy 132, 138-41; *see also* Schumpeter, J.A.
Capitalist Democracy in Britain 176, 180; *see also* Miliband, R.
Carleton College 77
Carnegie Steel Company 48, 65; *see also* United States Steel Corporation
cash nexus 138
caucus 49, 53, 56, 65-6, 69
Central Nonconformist Committee 38
centralisation 32, 35-6, 100-1, 111, 113, 125-6, 133, 141, 145, 174, 179, 184, 188, 196
chance 148
charisma 195
Charity Organisation Society 79
Chartism 38
chauvinism 199; *see also* patriotism
Chicago 5-6, 11, 13, 47, 65, 77-8, 82-4, 108, 110, 133, 159, 200
Chicago Law School 173
Chicago University 78, 108-10, 132, 153, 170
Chicago World Fair *see* Columbia Exposition
China 1, 73
choice 131-2, 147, 155, 172
Christian Socialists 62
Christianity 5, 77, 85, 198; *see also* religion
Church of England 50, 54, 56, 59, 199
cinepatriotism 4; *see also* patriotism
citizens, citizenship 5, 9, 35, 42,

44–5, 52, 54, 65, 67, 71, 88,
92, 94, 101, 103, 112, 114–15,
124, 129–30, 154, 165, 171,
173, 177, 185, 188, 192, 197–8,
202; *see also* independent citizen
civic federations 67
civic gospel 52
civil rights 178
civilisation, civilising influences 11,
17–18, 28, 30–1, 41, 43, 82,
87, 89, 92, 95, 102, 116, 119,
126, 134–5, 140, 158, 187–8,
192, 196, 202
class 9, 18, 22, 28, 32–4, 50, 74,
99, 107, 118, 125–6, 134–5,
137–8, 164, 167–8, 170, 180,
185, 199
*Class and Space: The Nature of
Urban Society* 198; *see also*
Thrift, N.; Williams, P.
classics 59, 78
Clay Cross (UK) 181
Closing the American Mind, The
197; *see also* Bloom, A.
coalition government 176, 201
Cold War 8, 197
collective bargaining 161
collectivism 8, 80, 94, 108
colonies 18, 39, 84, 91–2
Columbia Exposition 82, 84 200
Columbia University 176
command system 171
commerce, commercialism 18, 29,
137, 189
common good 142, 197
Common Sense 5; *see also* Paine,
T.
common will 142–3
commonwealth 88, 93
communication 116
communism 31, 74, 115, 188
community, communal institutions
7, 24, 35, 46, 49, 51–2, 56, 62,
70, 81, 89, 94, 96, 99–101,
167, 181, 191, 197–8
comparative analysis 61, 71
compensatory model of capitalist
democracy 189–90, 192, 194,
197, 200–2

competition 9, 32, 41, 45–6, 81,
89, 134, 136, 140–1, 143, 146,
159, 164–5, 179, 200
Complete Suffrage Union 40
conciliation boards 95
conformism 163
Conservative Enemy, The 167; *see
also* Crosland, C.A.R.
conservativism 2–3, 39, 43, 50, 56,
90, 98, 116, 132, 138, 153,
167, 180, 198
conservatory model of capitalist
democracy 2, 192, 194, 201–3
*Considerations on Representative
Government* 32–3, 36; *see also*
Mill, J.S.
conspicuous consumption 85, 119,
164, 200
Constitution of Liberty 133–4, 144,
148–9, 187; *see also* Hayek,
F.A.
Constitutional Democratic Party
(Russia) 58
consumerism *see* consumption
consumption 92–3, 95, 131, 139,
155, 159, 161, 165–8, 175,
186–7, 189, 196, 199, 201; *see
also* conspicuous consumption
containment 180–3
contentment *see* happiness
contracts 140, 146, 175
contradiction 118, 120
convenient social virtue 159
co-operative movement 30–1, 101
Corn Laws 29, 62
Corporation Street (Birmingham) 51
corporations 3, 66, 77, 82, 87–9,
94, 96, 107, 131, 146, 155–7,
160, 166, 178–80, 184, 186–9,
191, 195–6; *see also* business
enterprise; mature corporation;
multinational companies
corruption 24, 64–5, 74, 102, 110,
115
country town 82
craftsmanship 85
creative destruction 139
credit 4, 87, 116, 134–5
crime 51

Crisis and the Constitution, The
116; *see also* Laski, H.
critical spirit 141
critical theory 8
culture, 3, 9, 29, 35, 54, 60, 67–8,
81, 84, 87–9, 119, 131, 136,
142, 165, 171–2, 184, 186,
197–9, 200
Culture and Society 198; *see also*
Williams, R.
Cumberland 31
Czechoslovakia 132

Daily Herald 108
death duties 46, 165
debt 155, 159
decision-making processes 127, 174
defence 160, 171
deference 125–7
delegitimisation 2, 192–3, 196, 199
Democracy After the War 95; *see*
also Hobson, J.A.
Democracy in America 17, 20–1,
25–6, 46, 60, 197; *see also*
Tocqueville, A. de
Democracy in Crisis 116; *see also*
Laski, H.
Democracy and the Organisation of
Political Parties 58, 60–9; *see*
also Ostrogorski, M.
Democratic party 196
democratic personality 121
Denbigh 54
dependence effect 154
dependency culture 4
depression 10, 89, 93, 126, 133,
144, 146, 171; *see also*
recession
Derby 40, 79
Derby Grammar School 79
despotism 5–6, 23–5, 90, 92, 99,
114, 148, 175, 187
desubordination 182–3
Dial 78, 82
Dissent *see* Nonconformity
downward instability 160
Duma (Russia) 58
Dunfermline 37
dynastic principle 89

East India Company 18
École Libre des Sciences Politiques
60
ecology, ecological factors 1–2,
7–9, 152, 160–1, 179, 192,
201–3; *see also* pollution
economic growth 2, 6–10, 31, 35,
139–40, 145, 151, 154, 159,
162–3, 165–9, 174, 182, 185,
189–90, 192, 195–6, 200–2
Economic Planning Agency (Japan)
7
economics, economists 77–8, 93,
119, 128, 132–4, 138, 152, 154,
159–62, 169, 188, 195; *see also*
political economy
Economics and the Public Purpose
158–61; *see also* Galbraith, J.K.
Economist, The 4, 7
Edinburgh Review 27
education 20, 22, 27, 29, 30, 32,
34–5, 38, 42, 44, 47, 51–3, 55,
63, 68–70, 74, 81, 92, 94,
99–100, 102–3, 108, 112–13,
116, 119, 124, 149, 152, 154,
158, 160–1, 164–5, 178, 182,
189, 191, 197
Education Act (1970) 38, 50
efficiency 9, 64, 88, 110, 154, 162,
166, 170, 184
eggs 201
Egypt 136, 200
elaboration 2, 192–3, 195–6
elections, electorate 6–7, 10, 21,
24, 34, 44, 54, 61, 63–5, 70,
96, 117, 142, 153–4, 160, 167,
170, 173–4, 178–81, 187–9, 195
elective dictatorship 176
elites 125–7, 130, 195
elitist model of capitalist democracy
188, 191, 194–5
emancipation 62, 85, 119, 158, 160
emotion 18–19, 63, 91, 141, 200;
see also atavism
employment 111, 160, 163, 166,
186; *see also* unemployment
enclosures 55
End of Organized Capitalism, The
1; *see also* Lash, S.; Urry, J.

engineers, engineering 84, 96, 99
English Civil War 55
Englishness 70, 72, 99, 198–9
Englishness, Politics and Culture 1880–1920 198; *see also* Colls, R.; Dodd, P.
entail 42, 44
enterprise 3, 145, 154; *see also* entrepreneurs
entrepreneurs 37, 46, 87, 102, 134, 139–40, 145, 155, 159, 186, 188, 196; *see also* business enterprise; corporations; industry
environment *see* ecology
Environmental Protection Agency (USA) 179
equality 9, 22–9, 31, 35, 42–5, 61, 65, 68, 75–6, 81, 95, 101, 113, 116–17, 149, 151, 155, 160–5, 167–70, 175, 180, 184–5, 189–90, 193
ethical imperialism 139
ethics *see* morality
ethnicity 9, 65, 83, 134, 198; *see also* race
Evangelical movement 62
evolution 39, 43, 46, 81, 95–6, 118, 138, 144–5, 148
exceptionalism 9
exchange rate 167
Exclusive Brethren 152
Exeter 79
experience 110, 112, 124, 128–9, 139, 144, 152, 184, 187
experts 95, 112, 114, 140, 146–7, 155–6, 179, 189, 192
exploitation 102, 159, 163, 183
extensive analysis 125
external orientation 125

Fabianism 117, 172, 182
factories *see* industry
facts 70, 192–3, 195–6
family 137, 141, 160, 164
fascism 117, 125, 139, 147, 188
fatalism of the multitude 67
Faversham 79
Federal Reserve Board 171

federalism 24, 43, 71, 113, 161, 178–9
females, position of 83–4
feminism 30, 85
feudalism 5–6, 21, 44, 66, 83, 137, 140–1, 174, 178
finance capital 91, 95, 118, 135, 140; *see also* banks
Fish Called Wanda, A 3
Food Administration (USA) 78
football hooliganism 199
France 17–20, 25–6, 73, 91, 152, 200; *see also* French Revolution
franchises 68, 96
Free to Choose 169–72; *see also* Friedman, M.; Friedman, R.
free enterprise 152, 171–2
free market *see* free enterprise
free trade *see* free enterprise
freedom 3, 6, 50, 66, 70, 94, 96, 99, 113, 116, 132, 139, 143, 145, 147–8, 169–70, 178, 183, 192, 196–7, 202; *see also* liberty
freeholders 6, 25, 31, 101; *see also* agriculture
Frieburg 133
frontier 6–7, 10, 20, 23, 25, 66, 73
Fulham 108
function, functional theory 112, 114, 125, 137
Future of Socialism, The 152, 162, 164; *see also* Crosland, C.A.R.
General Motors 156
General Strike (1926) 108
general will 112
geology 59
Germany 6–7, 85, 91, 107, 111, 132, 145–7, 152, 171; *see also* Third Reich
Glasgow University 59
glasnost 1, 7, 197
Gorbachev, Mikhail 7
gospel of wealth 45–7, 52
Gospel of Wealth, The 42–5; *see also* Carnegie, A.
government 10, 12, 22, 24, 26, 28, 33–5, 48, 52, 88–90, 92, 94, 100–2, 110, 113, 116, 122–3, 125, 129, 132, 138, 142, 146,

148, 152–4, 157–8, 160–2,
169–73, 176, 178–9, 181–2,
185, 187, 189, 192, 195–6, 201
Grammar of Politics, The 112–15,
122, 187; *see also* Laski, H.
Graz, University of 133
*Great Arch. English Formation as
Cultural Revolution, The* 198;
see also Corrigan, P.; Sayer, D.
Great Society, The 101; *see also*
Wallas, G.
green parties 201–3; *see also*
ecology
greenhouse effect 201
Grimsby constituency (UK) 152
Grodno 58
growth *see* economic growth

Habits of the Heart 197; *see also*
Bellah, R.
Halstead Street (Chicago) 83
handicraft era 81
happiness 22, 42, 80, 165, 189, 192
Harvard University 24, 108, 133,
152
Hawaii 69
Haymarket (Chicago) 47, 82
hegemonic model of capitalist
democracy 100, 102, 190–1,
194–5
hegemony 9, 100–1, 182, 188; *see
also* authoritarianism; power
Higher Learning in America, The
158; *see also* Veblen, T.
historical sociology 134, 144
history 30, 59–60, 199
Homestead Steel Works 39, 47–8
House of Commons 21, 27, 33, 59,
152, 180; *see also* parliamentary
system
House of Lords 48, 113, 182, 186;
see also parliamentary system
Hull House (Chicago) 83
human nature 75, 81, 107, 109–10
Human Nature and Politics 109; *see
also* Wallas, G.
Hurst Street Chapel (Birmingham) 51

idealism 111–12

ideology 107, 151, 159–60, 162,
166, 173, 181, 183–4, 186, 188,
193, 196, 198–9
If Christ Came to Chicago! 82; *see
also* Stead, W.T.
'illth' 93
*Imperial Germany and the Industrial
Revolution* 85; *see also*
Veblen, T.
imperialism 6, 49, 89–90, 92, 108,
114, 120, 126, 134, 136–8
*Imperialism: The Highest Stage of
Capitalism* 91; *see also* Lenin,
V.I.
Imperialism and Social Classes
134–8; *see also* Schumpeter,
J.A.
Imperialism: A Study 91–2; *see also*
Hobson, J.A.
'improperty' 95
income 125, 127, 130–1, 139,
162–4, 167, 169, 171, 175, 196
independent citizen 99, 114, 193;
see also citizenship
India 73, 152
India House 19
individualism 3, 6–7, 17–18, 22,
24, 27, 33, 35, 38, 45, 60,
62–3, 68, 94, 111, 116, 126,
130–1, 136–7, 140, 145, 155,
159, 165, 170, 174–5, 184,
186–7, 190–2, 196–7, 199–200,
203
industrial system 155, 157–8
industrialism *see* industry
industrialists *see* industry
industry 5–7, 9–12, 17, 23, 26, 31,
35, 37–8, 42, 45, 50, 57–8, 62,
87, 98–101, 136, 144, 158,
164–5, 186, 193
inequality *see* equality
inflation 11, 134, 139, 155, 160–1,
167, 170, 172, 174, 176–7, 196,
200
inheritance 25, 31, 35, 80, 101,
114, 165
innovation 134–5, 137, 140, 154,
160, 166, 170, 186, 198, 202
intensive analysis 125

interest rates 111, 141
international relations 119, 121,
    126, 140, 147, 161, 172, 197,
    202–3
Invention of Tradition, The 198; *see
    also* Hobsbawm, E.; Ranger, T.
investment 79, 92, 134, 140,
    155–6, 159–60, 166, 186, 202
invisible hand 163, 167
invisible political hand 172
Ireland, Irish 18, 66
Irish Home Rule 39, 56
irrationality 110, 122, 129, 149; *see
    also* reason
Italy 145, 152

Japan 1, 4, 7–9, 73, 171, 177
jingoism 91
journalism *see* press
jury 25
just wage 174
justice 31, 113, 147, 196, 202; *see
    also* law

Kilauea 69
kingship 5
knowledge 32, 80, 145–6, 148,
    189, 192

labour 5, 10, 30–1, 38, 47–8, 53,
    79, 81–2, 88, 94–5, 116,
    119–20, 154–8, 161, 163,
    165–7, 171–2, 174, 177–82,
    184–5, 195; *see also* wages
Labour government (1929) 108, 116
Labour government (1945) 108, 119,
    162, 181
Labour government (1964) 152
Labour government (1974) 152
Labour party 12, 108, 114, 118,
    151, 162, 166, 181, 184, 196
laissez-faire 107, 118–19, 145, 166,
    177, 179
land *see* property
Latin America 70, 99
law 5, 9, 20, 22, 25, 29, 32–3, 43,
    59, 73, 80, 94, 98, 101, 108,
    114, 145–9, 171, 173, 175, 182,
    190, 192–3, 196, 198; *see also*

justice
Law, Legislation and Liberty 144;
    see also Hayek, F.A.
leadership, 99–102, 127–8, 135,
    137–9, 143, 180–1, 191, 195
League of Nations 92
league system 67
Leeds University 176
leisure 131, 158
leisure class 29–30, 84, 101, 141,
    149, 186
liberalism 5, 8, 10, 13, 18, 20, 39,
    44, 48–51, 53, 55–6, 64, 69,
    73, 75, 79, 94–5, 99, 101, 103,
    107–8, 116–17, 145–7, 153–4,
    167, 172, 180, 198–9
liberty 5, 23, 25–7, 63, 65, 67, 70,
    74–6, 82, 94, 109, 111–13, 116,
    129, 131, 134, 158, 165–6, 175,
    187, 198, 202; *see also* freedom
Liberty in the Modern State 115–16,
    187; *see also* Laski, H.
Liverpool 21
Local Community Research
    Committee (Chicago) 110
locality 9, 23–4, 29, 35, 43, 49,
    52, 102, 110, 113, 142, 161,
    179, 181; *see also* patriotism
London 18, 21, 40, 113, 164
London County Council 108
London Extension Board 79
London School of Economics and
    Political Science 108, 128, 133,
    176, 181, 187
Lonely Crowd, The 163; *see also*
    Riesman, D.
lower middle class 53, 81, 118,
    140, 147

McCormick works (Chicago) 82
machine politics 65–6, 109, 143,
    178; *see also* political parties
machines see technology
majorities 172, 176, 183
majority, tyranny of 25, 28–9, 32,
    67, 71
management 7, 87, 155, 157, 165–6
Manchester 5, 21, 26, 50
Manchester Guardian 90

Manchester School 80, 111; *see* political economy
manipulative political science 110, 125
manipulatory model of capitalist democracy 2, 100–2, 188, 191, 193–5
Manitowoc County 78
manpower planning 157
manufactured will 143
market 32, 92–4, 96, 100, 132, 135, 139, 143–4, 146–7, 153, 155–61, 166, 170–1, 173, 177, 179, 187, 190–2, 202
market system 159–60, 196
marxism 8, 111, 117, 162–3, 176, 185
mass 125–7, 185
mass media 7, 119, 126, 163, 181
Massachussetts 24
materialism 22, 131, 149, 155, 199–201
mature corporation 157; *see also* corporations
mechanics' institutes 12
mediatory model of capitalist democracy 100, 102, 191, 193–4
Medicaid 175
meritocracy 149
Methodists 62
middle class 17, 25, 28–9, 32, 35, 37, 60 64, 66, 116, 119, 152, 168, 189, 199
middle-class examinations 34
migration 10, 38–9, 42, 44, 66, 71, 126, 132
military 1, 118, 182
millenarianism 201
minimalist model of capitalist democracy 189, 192, 194, 196–7, 199–203
minorities 63, 100, 119, 147, 171–2, 176, 183, 188, 190–2, 195
minority clause 63–4
Missouri, University of 78
mode of production 135–6, 141
Modern Democracies 58, 70, 72–9, 198; *see also* Bryce, J.

monarchy 24–5, 33, 42, 44, 48, 50, 182
monetary policies 155, 161, 170, 172–3, 179
money 74, 134–5
Money 3; *see also* Amis, M.
monism 144
monopoly 66, 79, 89, 137, 140, 145, 171
moral economy 177, 179
morality 10, 25, 28, 30, 39–41, 52, 60, 63, 67, 69–70, 74, 77, 81, 87–8, 90–4, 96, 99, 101, 103, 111, 115, 140, 143, 146–8, 151, 173–4, 197, 200, 203
Moravia 132–3
multinational companies 160, 178; *see also* corporations
municipal socialism 52, 90, 101, 181
municipalities 51, 62, 64, 100–1, 178, 182, 184, 199

narcissism 123, 199–200
narrative 199
Nation 80, 114
nation, nationality 17, 107, 126, 196
national character 70, 100, 197–9
national culture 197–9
National Defense Advisory Committee (USA) 152
National Education League (UK) 38, 49
National Executive Committee (Labour party) 108
National Liberal Federation (UK) 49, 53, 64
National Life and Character: A Forecast 72–3; *see also* Pearson, C.
national socialism 147
National Tax Limitation Committee 172
National Tax Payers Union 172
nationalisation 51, 151, 162, 166
natural rights 55, 81, 84, 88, 165
nature 201
Near East 59

neighbourliness 25, 116
neolithic age 84
new class 155
New Class War, The 176–80; *see also* Piven, F.F.; Cloward, R.A.
New Deal 10, 117, 143, 154, 171–2, 178
New England 20, 26, 100
New England township 24, 28, 39, 66, 100, 114, 168
New Industrial State, The 155–8; *see also* Galbraith, J.K.
New Jersey 80
New Liberals 80
New Orleans 20
new political settlement 176
New School for Social Research (New York) 78
New York 6, 19–20, 56, 78
New Zealand 11, 73
Nikko 4
Nineteenth Century 12
Nobel prize 133
nobility *see* aristocracy
Nomura 4
Nonconformity 26, 38–41, 49–50, 54, 75
Normandy 21
North Africa 152; *see also* Africa; South Africa
Norway 78
nuclear energy 160
Nuffield College (Oxford) 173

Office of Price Administration (US) 152
Ohio 20, 23
oligopoly 140, 145
On Liberty 17, 32–3; *see also* Mill, J.S.
On Living in an Old Country 198; *see also* Wright, P.
Ontario 151
Ontario Agricultural College 152
opportunity 7, 47, 113, 129, 134–5, 140–1, 159, 170
optimism 1, 68–9, 75, 109, 133, 169, 172, 176; *see also* pessimism

organic unity 93, 96
organisational capacity 195
overheating 202
overload 183, 201–3
overproduction 88, 134
Oxford Movement 62
Oxford Union 152
Oxford University 21, 34, 59, 72, 109, 152, 173
ozone layer 201

Paris 58
parliamentary reform bill (1832) 21, 40, 64
parliamentary reform bill (1867) 63–4, 180
parliamentary reform bill (1884) 54
Parliamentary Socialism 180–3; *see also* Miliband, R.
parliamentary system 117, 142, 175–6, 180–1; *see also* House of Commons; House of Lords
parochial institutions 35
parochialism 125, 167, 199
participation 99, 111, 181
participatory model of capitalist democracy 2, 100–2, 188, 191, 193–4
patents 146
paternalism 30, 82, 102, 193, 198
paternalistic model of capitalist democracy 100, 102, 191, 193–4
patriotism 23–4, 65–6, 74, 88, 101; *see also* chauvinism; cinepatriotism
patronage 50, 178
pecuniary interest 81, 85–6, 89, 96, 98, 190
people, the 12, 24, 26, 37, 44, 49, 51–4, 60, 70, 74, 77, 96, 98–102, 122–3, 129, 141–2, 155, 169, 178, 181, 184–6, 188–90, 195–7; *see also* the poor
people's colleges 12
perception 110
perestroika 2, 7, 197
performance 53–4, 65, 83, 112, 119, 129, 137–9, 149, 173, 181, 185–6, 196

Persia 136
personality 110, 112–13, 120–1,
   123, 125, 129–30, 140, 160; *see
   also* democratic personality
pessimism 1, 75, 96, 172, 176; *see
   also* optimism
petty bourgeoisie *see* lower middle
   class
Philosophical Radicals 62
*Philosophical Theory of the State,
   The* 111; *see also* Bosanquet, B.
philosophy 41, 60–1
Physiology of Industry, The 79; *see
   also* Hobson J.A.; Mummery,
   A.F.
Pinkerton men 48
Pittsburg 38, 48
planning 100, 110, 131–2, 145–7,
   149, 156–8, 161, 166, 187–8
planning system 159–61
plebiscites *see* referendum
plutocracy 66, 87, 103, 170, 200;
   see also industry
poetry 19
Poland 21
police 26
policy sciences 121–2, 126
political economy 17, 27, 30, 63,
   79, 81, 93, 111, 114, 197; *see
   also* economics
political parties 49, 53, 58, 61–9,
   71, 75, 88, 99, 101–3, 113–14,
   119–20, 125, 130, 142, 173–4,
   180, 188, 190–1, 201–3; *see
   also* machine politics
political science 59, 108, 110, 128,
   131, 149, 188, 195; contemplative 110; manipulative 110, 125
political trade cycle 174
*Politics: Who Gets What, When and
   How* 121, 125; *see also*
   Lasswell, H.
pollution 146, 201; *see also* ecology
pools *see* trusts
Poor People's Movements 177; *see
   also* Piven F.F.; Cloward, R.A.
poor relief 32, 34, 62
poor, the 23, 51, 72, 134–9, 155,
   178–9, 184, 190, 202; *see also*

the people
Poplar (UK) 181
population 31–2, 35, 91
positivism 138
post-industrialism 197
post-modernism 197, 199–200
power 110, 113, 126, 138, 145–6,
   163–4, 188; *see also*
   authoritarianism; hegemony
Power and Personality 120, 122,
   126–7; *see also* Lasswell, H.
Power and Society 121; *see also*
   Lasswell, H.; Kaplan, A.
pragmatism 12, 110, 121
predatory instinct 84, 98, 136
prejudice 122
preliminary pollings 68
Presbyterians 38–9, 58, 75
press 24–5, 40–1, 48, 53, 55, 67,
   79, 91, 108, 122, 173
pressure groups 174, 188, 191
price system 93, 125, 134, 139,
   145–6, 155–6, 160–1, 166, 171–4
primogeniture 42, 44
Prince of Wales 48
Principia Ethica 111; *see also*
   Moore, G.E.
Principles of Political Economy 27,
   30–2; *see also* Mill, J.S.
prisons 19–20, 62, 65
private sphere 12, 24, 31, 43, 49,
   52, 66, 68, 83, 94, 98, 100,
   102–3, 110, 117, 124, 128–9,
   136–7, 140–2, 145–6, 149, 151,
   161, 164–5, 168, 171, 174, 177,
   185–6, 190–2, 197, 203
productivity 134
Professional Ethics and Civic Morals
   115; *see also* Durkheim, E.
professions 35, 40, 50, 52, 81, 98,
   114, 119, 122, 129, 134–6, 146,
   155, 161, 180, 188, 193, 195
profit 7, 9, 31, 77, 79, 89, 92–3,
   117, 134, 157, 159, 166–7, 171
progress 46, 131, 145, 170
proletariat 24, 137–8; *see also* the
   working class
Prolegomena to Ethics 111; *see also*
   Green, T.H.

propaganda 7, 74, 101, 123, 136,
186, 189, 195, 202; *see also*
advertising
*Propaganda Techniques in World
War I* 121; *see also* Lasswell, H.
property 5, 11–12, 18, 23–4, 31,
35, 39, 43, 45, 49, 51–2, 54–5,
77, 81, 83–4, 88–90, 99, 101,
112–13, 115, 122, 129, 138,
140–2, 146, 175, 177–8, 182,
185–6, 190–2, 200, 203
proportional representation 34, 63,
68
protectionism 49
psychoanalysis 121
psychology 41, 81, 109, 117, 120,
126, 185, 189, 191
psychopathology 123–4
Psychopathology and Politics
121–4; *see also* Lasswell, H.
public cognizance 160
public interest 31, 33, 68, 102,
112, 123, 159–61, 184
public opinion 17, 24, 27–9, 33,
39–41, 43, 50, 62, 65–7, 69,
71, 74, 92, 99, 101, 114, 122,
142–3, 148, 163, 172, 175, 184
public ownership *see* nationalisation
public sphere 12, 24, 31–3, 39, 43,
46, 49, 51–3, 66, 82–3, 90,
93–4, 98, 100–2, 110, 118,
128–9, 141–2, 151–2, 155,
160–1, 164, 166–8, 174, 181,
187, 190, 192–3, 196–7
public spirit 28, 35, 64, 99
Pullman (Chicago) 82, 102
Puritanism 55, 98, 111, 151, 165,
168

Quakers *see* Society of Friends

race 9–10, 180, 182; *see also*
ethnicity
radicalism 30, 37, 40, 48–9, 51,
55, 60, 151, 167, 176, 182, 184
railroads 40, 56, 62, 72, 83
railways *see* railroads
Rationale of Judicial Evidence 19;
see also Bentham, J.

rationality *see* reason
rationing 125
Readers' Digest 132
realism 112, 132, 195
reason 18, 30, 63, 81, 86, 93,
95–6, 99, 102, 107, 109, 112,
116, 122, 124, 127–9, 136, 140,
142, 144, 147, 174, 185; *see
also* irrationality
recession 134, 200–1; *see also*
depression
redistribution 114, 163, 166, 169,
175
referenda 73, 95, 99, 128
*Reflections on the Revolution in Our
Time* 118–19; *see also* Laski, H.
reform 21, 50–1, 62, 67, 90, 93,
102, 151, 158, 160–1, 182, 198
Regulating the Poor 177; *see also*
Piven, F.F.; Cloward, R.A.
regulatory model of capitalist
democracy 2, 189–91, 194–6
relativism 197
relegitimisation 2, 190, 192–3, 195
religion 5, 9, 20, 25, 33, 39, 42,
52, 62, 70, 81, 84, 92, 122,
180, 182, 201; *see also* Baptists;
Calvinism; Christianity; Church
of England; Evangelical
movement; Exclusive Brethren;
Methodists; Presbyterians;
Puritanism; Society of Friends;
Swedenborgians; Thirty-Nine
Articles; Unitarianism
Republic, The 159; *see also* Plato
republicanism 42, 48, 54, 98, 133
research and development 156
restrictive practices 146
retail trade 82
revisionism 198
revolution 74, 99, 101, 109, 115,
117–18, 125–6, 135, 163, 167,
184, 198; American (1776) 5,
11, 25, 62; English (1688) 20;
French (1789) 18, 20, 62, 107;
French (1830) 27; Russian (1917)
6, 12, 73, 78, 107, 118, 125
Rise and Decline of Nations, The 1;
see also Olson, M.

Rise and Decline of Western Liberalism, The 1; *see also* Arblaster, A.
Rise of European Liberalism, The 116–18; *see also* Laski, H.
Rise and Fall of the Great Powers, The 1; *see also* Kennedy, P.
Road to Serfdom, The 7, 131–3, 144–8, 153; *see also* Hayek, F.A.
Roman Empire 22, 34, 200
Romantic movement 31, 62
royal commissions 114
Russia 1–2, 7–8, 121, 133, 145, 155, 171, 185; *see also* Russian Revolution

sabotage 86
safety 125, 127
St Louis *Post-Dispatch* 48
St Petersburg 58
Saint-Simonians 30
Salisbury (UK) 21
salmonella 201
Salzburg 133
savings 156, 160; *see also* thrift
Say's Law 94, 111
science 21–2, 60, 62, 81, 84, 89, 91, 96, 100, 109, 121–2, 124, 129, 133, 145, 152, 158, 189
Scotch-Canadians 151
Scotland 17, 48, 58
security 163, 189, 192, 203
self-criticism 197
self-improvement 47
selfishness 199
self-observatories 120
self-realisation 113
Sensory Order, The 144; *see also* Hayek, F.A.
serfdom 7, 184
service class 147
'Six Hundred', the (Birmingham) 64
Sixty Years of an Agitator's Life 53; *see also* Holyoake, G.
slavery 10, 26, 44, 62, 126
social contract 197
social control 131
Social Darwinism 91

social democracy 131, 151, 167
social engineering 131, 145, 162
social intimidation 67–8
social observatories 128
Social Science Research Committee (USA) 110
social sciences 114, 131, 138, 166, 185; *see also* sociology
social security 171, 177–8, 185
social service state 117; *see also* welfare state
social services 172, 176
Social Statics 40; *see also* Spencer, H.
socialism 6, 32, 56, 66, 88, 90, 95, 116–20, 126, 132–4, 138–9, 141–7, 149, 151, 153, 161–5, 167, 171–2, 181–2, 184, 187–9, 202
Socialism Now 167; *see also* Crosland, C.A.R.
Society of Friends 193
sociology 41, 138
South Africa 90–1; *see also* Africa; North Africa
South Gloucestershire constituency (UK) 152
South-East Asia 1, 197, 203; *see also* Asia
South, the (US) 10, 107, 171
sovereignty 82, 109, 113
Soviet Union *see* Russia
spoils system 49, 65
stable environment 192, 196, 202–3
Stanford University 78
state 6, 11–12, 24, 43, 77, 94, 96, 99, 107, 109–14, 116, 118, 122, 124, 129, 131, 137, 142–3, 147–9, 153–5, 157–61, 177, 179, 181–3, 186, 188–90, 192, 195, 198
State in Theory and Practice, The 116–18; *see also* Laski, H.
State in Capitalist Society, The 180; *see also* Miliband, R.
statistics 110, 133
steam engine 41
steel industry 38
stereotypes 116
stock market 200

stockyards (Chicago) 83
strikes 47–8, 82, 143, 164, 167
subjectivity 128–9
sub-parliaments 28
suburbs 66
surplus value 137
Swedenborgians 39
Switzerland 73
syndicalism 96, 114
System of Logic 28; *see also* Mill, J.S.

taxation 4, 34, 95, 111, 117, 139, 142, 149, 153, 155, 161, 165–8, 170, 172, 178–9, 184–5, 196, 200
Taylorism 135
technocrats 186
technology 45, 62, 73, 79, 84–7, 89, 99, 118, 135, 140, 146, 154, 156–7, 166, 170
technostructure 155, 157–61
temperance 51
tension level 123, 125, 127, 189–90, 192, 195, 197
territorial principle 114, 125
Thatcherism 176
theatre 200
Theory of Business Enterprise, The 82; *see also* Veblen, T.
Theory of Economic Development, 134; *see also* Schumpeter, J.A.
Theory of the Leisure Class, The 82–5, 93; *see also* Veblen, T.
therapy 197
Third Reich 126; *see also* Germany
Thirty-Nine Articles 59
thrift 79, 88; *see also* saving
totalitarianism 166
Touch of Class, A 152
Towards International Government 92; *see also* Hobson, J.A.
Tower Hamlets (UK) 59
towns *see* urbanisation
trade unions *see* labour
transformation 2, 192–3, 195–6
Transvaal 91
Treasury 12
Trinity College (Oxford) 152

Triumphant Democracy 45–7; *see also* Carnegie, A.
trust 25, 54, 178, 184
trusts 66, 89, 92, 136
tyranny *see* despotism

Ulster 182
Unauthorised programme 55
underconsumption 88–9, 91
unemployment 8, 116, 154–5, 170, 173–4, 177–80, 182, 196; *see also* employment
Unitarianism 38–9
United Nations 202
United States Congress 160, 172
United States Steel Corporation 87; *see also* Carnegie Steel Company
universities 32, 79, 84, 99, 101, 156, 197, 199
urban renewal 172
urban riots 182, 196
urbanisation 5–6, 9–10, 26, 29, 39, 42–3, 62, 66
USSR *see* Russia
utilitarianism 19, 5, 62–3, 68, 81, 111
utopianism 31

values 4, 192–3, 195–6
vendibility 87
vested interests 192
Vienna 13, 121, 132–3; University of 132–3
violence 20, 40, 48, 74, 82, 109, 125, 132
volcanoes 56, 69

wage-price spiral 155
wages 95, 155, 157, 160–1, 165–6, 172, 174, 177; *see also* labour
Walks in the Black Country and its Green Border-land 40; *see also* Burritt, E.
war 5, 89, 122, 125–6, 129–30, 136, 139, 185; Boer 90–1; Falklands 199; Spanish-American 89; First World 2, 6, 11–12, 73, 78, 81, 92, 96, 100, 107, 117, 122, 132, 138, 185, 193; Second

World 1, 10, 118, 121–2,
152–3; *see also* Cold War
Washington 2, 69, 164, 172
Washington Monument 71
Wealth of Nations, The 5, 170; *see
also* Smith, A.
welfare state 149, 163–4, 171, 178;
see also social service state
Westmorland 31
will-power 167
Wolverhampton Express 41

working class 17, 27, 30, 33, 35,
37, 45, 56, 71, 99–100, 118,
144, 147, 157, 165, 167, 177,
179–86, 188, 191; *see also*
proletariat
*World Politics and Personal
Insecurity* 125–6; *see also*
Lasswell, H.

Yale University 108
Yamaicha 4
Young England